THE REVOLUTIONARY WAR

Recent Titles in
The Greenwood Press "Daily Life Through History" Series

Nature and the Environment in Pre-Columbian American Life
Stacy Kowtko

Science and Technology in Medieval European Life
Jeffrey R. Wigelsworth

Civilians in Wartime Africa: From Slavery Days to the Rwandan Genocide
John Laband, editor

Christians in Ancient Rome
James W. Ermatinger

The Army in Transformation, 1790–1860
James M. McCaffrey

The Korean War
Paul M. Edwards

World War I
Jennifer D. Keene

Civilians in Wartime Early America: From the Colonial Era to the Civil War
David S. Heidler and Jeanne T. Heidler, editors

Civilians in Wartime Modern America: From the Indian Wars to the Vietnam War
David S. Heidler and Jeanne T. Heidler, editors

Civilians in Wartime Asia: From the Taiping Rebellion to the Vietnam War
Stewart Lone, editor

The French Revolution
James M. Anderson

Daily Life in Stuart England
Jeffrey Forgeng

THE REVOLUTIONARY WAR

Charles P. Neimeyer

The Greenwood Press "Daily Life Through History" Series

American Soldiers' Lives
David S. Heidler and Jeanne T. Heidler, Series Editors

GREENWOOD PRESS
Westport, Connecticut • London

Library of Congress Cataloging-in-Publication Data

Neimeyer, Charles Patrick, 1954–
  The Revolutionary War / Charles P. Neimeyer.
     p. cm.—(Greenwood Press "daily life through history" series, ISSN 1080-4749) (American soldiers' lives)
Includes bibliographical references and index.
  ISBN 0-313-33228-2 (alk. paper)
  1. United States. Continental Army—Military life. 2. United States—History—Revolution, 1775–1783—Social aspects. 3. Soldiers—United States—Social conditions—18th century.
I. Title.
  E259.N455   2007
  973.3'4—dc22   2006038686

British Library Cataloguing in Publication Data is available.

Library of Congress Catalog Card Number: 2006038686
ISBN-10: 0-313-33228-2
ISBN-13: 978-0-313-33228-9
ISSN: 1080-4749

First published in 2007

Greenwood Press, 88 Post Road West, Westport, CT 06881
An imprint of Greenwood Publishing Group, Inc.
www.greenwood.com

Printed in the United States of America

The paper used in this book complies with the
Permanent Paper Standard issued by the National
Information Standards Organization (Z39.48-1984).

10 9 8 7 6 5 4 3 2 1

To the Neimeyers—

Charles John, Patricia Joann, Terry Francis, Cheryl Ann, Janet Lousie, Kelli Virginia, Patrick Roger, and Christopher Ryan—and to Jake.

CONTENTS

SERIES FOREWORD

More than once during the military campaigns undertaken by American armies, leaders in both civilian and martial roles have been prompted to ask in admiration, "Where do such people come from?" The question, of course, was both rhetorical and in earnest: the one because they knew that such people hailed from the coasts and the heartland, from small hamlets and sprawling cities, from expansive prairies and breezy lakeshores. They were as varied as the land they represented, as complex as the diversity of their faiths and ethnic identities, all nonetheless defined by the overarching identity of "American," made more emphatic by their transformation into "American soldiers."

They knew and we know where they came from. On the other hand, the question for anyone who knows the tedium, indignity, discomfort, and peril of military service in wartime is more aptly framed, "Why did they come at all?"

In the volumes of this series, accomplished scholars of the American military answer that question, and more. By depicting the daily routines of soldiers at war, they reveal the gritty heroism of those who conquered the drudgery of routine and courageously faced the terrors of combat. With impeccable research and a deep understanding of the people who move through these grandly conceived stories—for war, as Tolstoy has shown us, is the most grandly conceived and complex story of all—these books take us to the heart of great armies engaged in enormous undertakings. Bad food, disease, haphazardly treated wounds, and chronic longing for loved ones form part of these stories, for those are the universal afflictions of soldiers. Punctuating long stretches of loneliness and monotony were interludes of horrific violence that scarred every soldier, even those who escaped physical injury. And insidious wounds could fester because of ugly customs and ingrained prejudices: for too long a span, soldiers who happened to be minorities suffered galling injustices at the hands of those they served, often giving for cause and comrades what Lincoln called "the last full measure of devotion," despite unfair indignities and undeserved ignominy. And sadly, it is true that protracted or unpopular wars could send veterans returning to a country indifferent about their sacrifices, sometimes hostile to the cause for which they fought, and begrudging even marginal compensation to their spouses and orphans. But quiet courage, wry humor, tangible camaraderie, and implacable pride are parts of these stories as well, ably conveyed by these gifted writers who have managed to turn the pages that follow into vivid snapshots of accomplishment, sacrifice, and triumph.

Until recently the American soldier has usually been a citizen called to duty in times of extraordinary crisis. The volunteer army of this latest generation, though, has created a remarkable hybrid in the current American soldier, a professional who never-theless upholds the traditions of American citizens who happen to be in uniform to do a tough job. It is a noble tradition that ennobles all who have honored it. And more often than not, they who have served have managed small miracles of fortitude and resolve.

Walter Lord's *Incredible Victory* recounts the story of Mike Brazier, the rear-seat man on a torpedo plane from the carrier *Yorktown* in the Battle of Midway. He and pilot Wilhelm Esders were among that stoic cadre of fliers who attacked Japanese carriers, knowing that their fuel was insufficient for the distance to and from their targets. Having made their run under heavy enemy fire, Esders finally had to ditch the spent and damaged plane miles short of the *Yorktown* in the rolling Pacific. He then discovered that Brazier had been shot to pieces. Despite his grave wounds, Brazier had managed to change the coils in the radio to help guide the plane back toward the *Yorktown.* In the life raft as he died, Mike Brazier never complained. He talked of his family and how hard it had been to leave them, but he did not complain. Instead he apologized that he could not be of more help.

In the great, roiling cauldron of the Second World War, here was the archetype of the American soldier: uncomplaining while dying far from home in the middle of nowhere, worried at the last that he had not done his part.

Where do such people come from?

We invite you to read on, and find out.

David S. Heidler and Jeanne T. Heidler
Series Editors

PREFACE

If there was ever a "G.I. Joe" of the American Revolution, it certainly had to be Connecticut soldier Joseph Plumb Martin. He was only fifteen years old when he first enlisted as one of the new "six months levies" for the New York campaign of 1776. Yet during the course of the war, he was to enlist three times. Martin became a soldier not out of any particular sense of patriotism. Rather, like many young men and women who join the armed forces today, he did so mainly for adventure and because his prospects as a laborer on his grandparents' farm did not much appeal to him. Hence, in his words, he became a soldier "in name at least, if not in practice."

This book is about the everyday life of Revolutionary War soldiers like Martin. Although the chapters of this book are arranged chronologically and I have tried to cover in general detail the larger battles and campaigns of the Continental army during the war, it is really not about those per se. Too often, historians of the Revolution focus on the *activity* of the army without noticing what was taking place *inside* the army. Thus, the intent of the entire book is to shed some light on the lives of men and women in the ranks, in the army camps, and on the march.

There can be no doubt that, as Revolutionary era historian John Shy once noted, "the bedrock facts of the American Revolutionary struggle, especially after the euphoric first year, are not pretty."[1] Throughout the war, soldiers were subject to periods of intense privation—much of it due to the sheer incompetence of congressional and army officials. Most of these officials were not purposely bad at their jobs; more often, they simply had little or no experience in raising or maintaining a standing army even in peacetime, much less on the fly in the middle of a war.

The stories told by Continental soldiers in their diaries and journals are largely ones of suffering and deprivation. Throughout the long eight years of war, there are occasions where out of sheer desperation men boiled their shoes for food or, as Martin did at Morristown, New Jersey, after having nothing to eat for some time, gobbled down a contaminated ox's liver only to heave it back up the next morning. The diaries and journals of Revolutionary-era veterans are replete with such recollections. One recent monograph *argued that* the image of the long put-upon Continental soldier who bled and died in the cause of liberty made an "evocative and powerful" postwar political tool. Hence it was useful to emphasize the suffering aspect of service more than anything else. This image became so ingrained and so powerful that it had a tendency to eclipse any positives that might have come out of the Revolutionary experience. And indeed the men on occasion did suffer greatly, but their life, as we shall discover, was not one of continual starvation and pain. Rather, army life then, as now, was often a case of "hurry up and wait." Men would sometimes get plenty to eat and at other times nothing at all for days. Some men never had a problem with getting shoes, and others went barefoot even in winter. In sum, the iconographic image of the suffering soldier gives us only a partial window on what it was like to be in the ranks. Their experience was certainly more nuanced than the image of a rag-clad Continental standing guard at Valley Forge, Pennsylvania.

The problem with studying the men and women who served during the American Revolution is that their history is so thoroughly encrusted with iconography. The story of Molly Pitcher is a classic example of this problem. Margaret Corbin (also known as Captain Molly) and Mary Ludwig Hays (also known as Molly Pitcher) were in fact real women serving with the army in a camp follower capacity. Many contemporary observers of the army scene vividly recall in a number of accounts both women man-ning cannons when their husbands were allegedly shot down near their post. Yet the story of Molly Pitcher was unheard of until the 1876 Centennial celebrations of that year. Hence, although the legend of Molly Pitcher is likely a compendium of a number of women, this single, oft-repeated historical event serves to diminish the real service of thousands of other women who fought and served in the army, either masquerading as male soldiers or more often as the logistical and support backbone for army opera-tions in camp and on the march. Another example is that of African American soldier Pompey Lamb. Lamb was credited by nineteenth-century historian Benjamin Lossing in 1855 with guiding Anthony Wayne and his assault troops at Stony Point, New York. It was here that Wayne and his men, using only the bayonet, captured more than six hun-dred British soldiers in a daring night assault. Again, modern research evidence has revealed that Lamb did in fact serve in the Orange County, New York, militia, and some-one by that name had enlisted in 1780 in the 2nd New York Regiment. But all contem-porary accounts of the battle (both British and American) fail to mention Lamb at all. Yet we see the story again and again. As in the case of Molly Pitcher, this likely fabri-cation surrounding Lamb obscures the fact that Lieutenant Colonel Fleury was the first man over the parapet or that Pennsylvania Lieutenant George Knox led the first storm-ing party into the fort. The Lamb fabrication is just the sort of nineteenth-century whimsy that makes documenting the service of the men and women of the army so difficult and does not even properly credit the *actual* service of Lamb as well as the hundreds of other African Americans who valiantly served alongside men like Martin.[2]

The central question of who served and why is still very alive as a topic of debate among today's Revolutionary era historians. Questions of what was service really like, stripped of all the iconography and hyperbole, for the average "G.I. Joe" (and "Jane") in the ranks remain. Yet men served and more than a few, like Martin, reenlisted, know-ing full well that they would continue to be subjected to such poor treatment. They must have concluded that although life in the army was bad, life after the war, regardless of who ultimately prevailed, was not going to ever be the same again. Moreover, most of the men called themselves "volunteers." And therefore they believed that the state owed them something for agreeing to give up their civil rights, if only for a little while. They firmly recognized the value of a contract and saw their enlistment papers in just that light. They also, almost instinctively, recognized that service itself was of some value, and that, probably more than anything else, was why men like Martin reenlisted and remained with the army until the very end of the war.

Nonetheless, it is clear that the soldiers were not fatalistic fools. As I noted in my earlier work on the army, "soldiers whose sole possession was often only their own body reacted strongly to governmental attempts to commandeer them." Americans went off to war knowing that they were supposed to be paid for their services usually for a specific amount of time; they were to be fed a standard and ample ration, given an annual suit of clothes, and usually combined into units that consisted of their relatives and friends. This "moral economy" was tremendously important to the men, and when the government reneged on its part of the bargain, the soldiers tended to become angry and, on several notable occasions, mutinous. Martin was certainly no exception to this rule, "growling," as he stated, "like a soreheaded dog" when he returned to the Morristown encampment and had received no food. Martin freely admits that he was an active participant in the great Connecticut line mutiny of 1780, yet at the end of the war when he has a chance to go home, he takes the place of a man who had six months left to serve on his enlistment contract. The contractual agreement between the soldier and the state was what set them apart from unfree labor, a concept that every eighteenth-century American was very familiar with, and Martin was always very careful to note the exact amount of time he had agreed to serve.

Most of the extant diaries and journals of Revolutionary veterans must be read very carefully. Many had been written long after the war had ended, and indeed some of them had already incorporated snippets of the postwar iconography that had begun to take hold of American historical memory even before the veterans themselves passed into history. Yet most extant diaries reveal little about patriotism or what motivated them to fight. These were plain-spoken men, and they were more concerned about what they were being given to eat or where to get firewood or clean water or better rations than anything else. They could wax eloquently about suffering and service after the war, but when they were actually in the ranks their daily ration mattered more. In sum, most Revolutionary War enlisted men were more often less concerned about ideology than with survival. Often survival meant not running afoul of one's own officers and the harsh Articles of War. Military justice, diets, camp regulations, clothing and equipment, drill, and guard duty took up significant amounts of an enlisted man's time on a day-to-day basis.

American Soldiers' Lives: The Revolutionary War is divided into seven chapters and includes a separate chronology of the events of the Revolutionary War, from 1775 to 1783. It ends with a selected, topically arranged bibliography of important sources and a comprehensive index.

The first chapter is an analysis of the Army of Observation and the first American attempt to seize Canada. The army that greeted George Washington in early July must have been quite a shock to him. Ill-disciplined mobs of soldiers roamed about freely, firing their muskets at passing geese or just for the sheer thrill of hearing the weapon go off. Washington was determined to work with what he had, but he always kept in mind his desire to create a "respectable army." This was to be an army of virtuous, republican minded, long-termed soldiers, disciplined by an ironclad and effective set of Articles of War. The fact that Washington never quite achieved such an army is beside the point. He never gave up on trying to professionalize the Continental army. Moreover, Washington's "new model army" of long-termed soldiers was much more eclectic than has heretofore been acknowledged. This especially applied to those soldiers who hailed from the middle states. For example, a historical analysis of Maryland General William Smallwood's recruits in 1782 revealed that the majority of Smallwood's men were foreign born and many were not even from the state of Maryland. Late in the war, the army was taking men as they got them. At the beginning, however, the composition of the army was much more homogenous, with men living in the towns that recruited them and hailing from the states that sent them off to war. But over time, this paradigm considerably changed.

Chapter 2 is the story of the transition between the Army of Observation and the new army raised following the Canadian debacle of 1775–1776. This new army was not exactly the long-termed force that Washington so strongly desired, but at least it was one that actually represented "the continent," with companies of riflemen from Virginia, Maryland, and Pennsylvania joining "Continental" regiments raised in New England and the middle states and sent off to defend New York City. Here for the first time the army is forced to confront the ravages of smallpox. This great killer of mankind played a significant role in the American failure in Canada, where hundreds of disease-ridden soldiers, most of whom had never been more than twenty miles away from their homes, now found themselves dying by the dozens in makeshift hospitals in Canada and upstate New York. The army was driven in defeat from New York and across the state of New Jersey, and these were indeed "times that tried men's souls." That Washington and his army were able to pull off a miracle victory just in time to turn things around for the American cause has been well documented. What is not as well known is that the soldiers themselves nearly cost him the element of surprise well before their attack even started.

Chapter 3 outlines the creation of Washington's new model army. This army took men as they came and were not beyond inducing immigrants, enemy prisoners of war (POWs), and just about any man who was healthy enough (and perhaps gullible enough) to become a soldier for "three years or the duration of the war." For the first time since 1775, the army recruited a significant number of African American soldiers. These men served side by side with other soldiers and were liberally scattered throughout nearly every army brigade (with the notable exceptions of the states of Georgia and South Carolina). While there were experiments in trying to form all–African American regiments such as the one partially created in the 1st Rhode Island regiment in 1778, most African Americans served as Continental infantry or artillerymen and for longer terms than many of their fellow soldiers. By this time, the army was in dire need of a policy on how to handle POWs. After two years of fighting, both sides had captured a large number of men, yet the concept of fair and equitable treatment of each side's captives was still in a relatively nascent stage. As a result, most were severely mistreated, and British prison hulks near Brooklyn, New York, such as the infamous *Jersey,* became renowned as places of hellish pain and death. Finally, again, owing to significant campaigning and fighting on the part of the army, hundreds of men needed medical and hospital care on a daily basis. However, medical science and practice during this time was rudimentary at best and many men stood a better chance of survival if they avoided the hospitals at all costs.

Chapter 4 focuses on the role that women played in the manning and functioning of the Continental army in camp and on the march. Revolutionary-era historians have referred to the American army camps as "Continental communities," and indeed they were just that. Women performed a variety of logistical and support functions that the army could do little without. Moreover, a few women even went so far as to masquerade as men, such as Deborah Sampson, in order to participate in the war. Many historians now believe that the single Sampson case may be just the tip of the iceberg and perhaps dozens of women similarly served and simply got away with their "masquerade." This chapter also provides an analysis of the campaigns around Philadelphia and the legendary winter the army spent at Valley Forge. New evidence reveals that although the army did indeed truly suffer greatly there, it was not as bad as the later winter encampment at Morristown. In reality, the army never did very well when it was placed in any winter encampment from 1777 to 1781. The commissary and quartermaster departments, never very effective, started to unravel during the army's winter at Valley Forge, and these failures as well as those of the Congress and the states to adequately support the army were the main culprits behind all the suffering endured by the soldiery.

Chapter 5 shows what it was actually like to be a Continental soldier in the ranks. Whether at Peekskill, New York; Valley Forge; or Morristown; most of these army camps were operated with similar regularity. The soldiers themselves lived in log huts in the winter and were "under canvas" in the warmer months or simply slept out in the open. They worried about how to supplement their rations, whether they would get paid, and relieved the monotony of camp life through a variety of games and activities. They drank excessively (if they could find liquor), gambled, and swore tremendously to Washington's great consternation. They lived a very rugged life. They stood guard duty, were inspected and drilled by the likes of the Prussian drillmaster, Major General Friedrich Wilhelm von Steuben, and, if literate (not all that many were), wrote letters home to their family and friends. Uniforms, weapons, and rations were constantly on the minds of the men, and they were an integral part of what it was like to be a soldier then. Finally, at least some of the men demonstrated a piety in camp that might astound a modern reader. For many in the ranks (especially those from New England), religious services were a very important part of army camp life, and Washington actively encouraged his men to participate in them.

Chapters 6 and 7 focus on the official establishment of the French alliance and on the fighting in the South, respectively. That the French could now openly and actively support the war was a matter of no small consequence. Their entrance into the conflict transformed the stakes that were involved. No longer was the fight along the periphery of the British empire. Rather, the introduction of the French made the war a more European and thus more worldwide conflict. It was during this time at Morristown that the army spent its most difficult winter in its existence. Hundreds of soldiers perished because of poor diet and the extreme cold. For the first time in contemporary memory, the waters in and around New York City froze solid, so that it enabled both sides to engage in vicious raids and a high level of partisan activity. This sort of fighting presaged what the army would experience in the final three years of the war in the southern theater. It was here that the war devolved into what became nearly an all-out civil war.

Yet after all was said and done, the Americans had pulled it off. They won their independence from the British. And even Martin himself suspected that it was not American tactical brilliance or British ineptness that had brought them the victory; rather it was the soldier in the ranks, who suffered and starved along with his comrades. Because of the sheer perseverance of the soldiers in the ranks, they had ultimately won the day. In the end, Martin commented that "fighting the enemy is the great scarecrow to people unacquainted with the duties of an army…. I was never killed in the army; I never was wounded but once; I never was a prisoner of the enemy; but I have seen many that have undergone all these…but reader, believe me, for I tell a solemn truth, that I have felt more anxiety, undergone more fatigue and hardships, suffered more in every way, in performing one of those tedious marches than I ever did in fighting the hottest battle I was ever engaged in." Martin fully believed that "the laborer is worthy of his meat."[3] Without men like Martin, there could not have been great generals like George Washington or Nathanael Greene. This, therefore, is a book about the soldiers and what it was like during the American Revolution.

NOTES

1. John Shy, *A People Numerous & Armed: Reflections on the Military Struggle for American Independence*, rev. ed. (Ann Arbor, MI: University of Michigan Press, 1990), 23.

2. Don Loprieno, "Pompey Lamb Revisited: Black Soldiers in the American Revolution," Stony Point Battlefield State Historic Site, http://www2.lhric.org/spbattle/Pomp.html (accessed June 26, 2006).

3. James Kirby Martin, ed., *Ordinary Courage: The Revolutionary War Adventures of Joseph Plumb Martin*. 2nd ed. (St. James, NY: Brandywine Press, 1999), 165.

ACKNOWLEDGMENT

The more I read Joseph Plumb Martin's post–Revolutionary War journal, the more I am convinced that we still make soldiers like we used to. Private Martin was clearly a typical "G.I." of his era and certainly worthy of those of the "greatest generation" of World War II fame and in many ways resembles those currently in service in defense of our country overseas. This book is dedicated to intrepid soldiers like Joseph Martin of Connecticut and to those Revolutionary heroes who died in squalor aboard the infamous prison ship *Jersey* and were known but to God. But I wish to especially commend this book to those men and women presently serving today defending our nation against the evil of terrorism. We still make them like we used to.

I am especially indebted to my outstanding assistant Ellyn Koski for helping me in the preparation of this book. Her illustration suggestions and proofreading skills were highly valued by me, and even her daughter Theresa pitched in on occasion. I am also thankful for the help of Ms. Johanna Jean of Regent University, who always had a kind word of encouragement for me as I struggled to produce this work, and also thankful to Dr. Barry Ryan, who gave me the time to get his research completed. And finally, I must acknowledge the help and support of my wonderful wife, Janet Louise Neimeyer. She was always there as a word of support and helped with proofing my bibliography.

I also especially thank Dr. James Kirby Martin of the University of Houston. Jim Martin took time from his extremely busy schedule to provide me with some sound scholarly advice and suggestions for the book. I am proud to say that his work in the field of the American Revolution has been an inspiration for me since my graduate school days at Georgetown. And finally, I thank my editors at Greenwood Press, Anne Thompson and David Heidler, and Bharath Parthasarathy at Textech, who patiently endured the various changes that any book production must have. Everyone at Greenwood has been very supportive throughout the project.

TIMELINE

1775

April 19, 1775	The Battle of Lexington and Concord—British General Thomas Gage orders a predawn raid on colonial military stores alleged to be hidden in and around Concord, Massachusetts. The British kill eight militiamen at Lexington Green, where "the shot heard round the world" was fired in the opening moments of the Revolution.
May 10, 1775	Fort Ticonderoga, New York—Ethan Allen and his Green Mountain Boys and Benedict Arnold seize Fort Ticonderoga without the loss of a man on either side.
June 15, 1775	Washington Takes Command—George Washington of Virginia is appointed by Congress as commander in chief of the Army of Observation and arrives at Cambridge, Massachusetts, on July 2, 1775.
June 17, 1775	The Battle of Bunker Hill—The British successfully drive off the colonial militia defending Breed's Hill (erroneously called Bunkers Hill), Massachusetts, after three bloody assaults. Patriot leader Dr. Joseph Warren is killed during the fighting.
October/November 1775	Benedict Arnold's Wilderness March—During these two months, Benedict Arnold leads a group of approximately seven hundred men on an epic journey through the northern Maine wilderness on his way to Québec with the hope of gaining Canada for the American cause.

December 31, 1775   Failure at Québec—The combined forces of Benedict Arnold and Major General Richard Montgomery attempt to take Québec by storm and fail. Montgomery is killed and Arnold severely wounded.

1776

January 1776   The British Fail at Charleston—Sir Peter Parker's British fleet attempts to seize the port of Charleston, South Carolina. The American fortifications at Forts Sullivan and Moultrie hold out and the British are forced to retire.

January 1776   *Common Sense*—Thomas Paine writes the pamphlet *Common Sense*. Immediately, Congress orders thousands of copies of the pamphlet to be distributed to all the colonies. In it, Paine lays out the case for American independence.

June 28, 1776   Boston is Evacuated—The British evacuate Boston after George Washington fortifies strategic Dorchester Heights with artillery.

June/July 1776   The British Arrive in Force—British General William Howe shows up off New York City with a massive invasion force of nearly thirty thousand soldiers.

July 4, 1776   Independence—Congress passes a Resolution of Independence on July 2, 1776. It becomes official two days later on July 4, 1776.

August 27–29, 1776   The Battle of Long Island—General William Howe with approximately fifteen thousand troops (including newly arrived Hessians from Germany) defeats elements of George Washington's Continental army. The Americans retreat to Brooklyn Heights, and on the evening of August 29, Washington orders John Glover's Marblehead fishermen to assist in bringing off the army from Long Island over to Manhattan. The retreat was nothing short of miraculous.

September 16, 1776   The Battle of Harlem Heights—Outflanked once again on Manhattan, George Washington's army is forced to fight a rearguard action at Harlem Heights and temporarily repulses the British attackers. Nevertheless, Washington is forced to continue to retreat into Westchester County, New York.

September 20, 1776   The Great New York Fire—As the Continental army retreats northward up Manhattan Island, a massive fire breaks out in New York City and consumes over one-fourth of the entire town. The British suspect it was set by American incendiaries.

September 22, 1776

Nathan Hale—Volunteer spy Nathan Hale is caught by British troops in New York City and is executed without a trial.

October 11, 1776

The Battle of Valcour Island, New York—Benedict Arnold's fleet of gunboats are attacked and destroyed by British Governor General Guy Carleton after a seven-hour battle on Lake Champlain.

October 28, 1776

The Battle of White Plains—George Washington's Continental army is attacked and defeated with heavy losses at White Plains, New York. Washington continues his retreat westward.

November 1776

The Loss of Forts Washington and Lee—Against his better judgment, George Washington tries to hold on to two Hudson River forts: Washington and Lee. Fort Washington, on the east bank, is taken by the British in November with the loss of nearly three thousand troops and thousands of muskets and numerous cannons. Four days later, the British cross to the west bank and take Fort Lee without firing a shot. The loss of the forts dooms New York, and Washington retreats southward across New Jersey toward the Delaware River and crosses over on December 11.

December 6, 1776

Newport, Rhode Island—A six-thousand-man British landing force seizes Newport, Rhode Island, without the loss of a soldier.

December 25–26, 1776

The Battle of Trenton, New Jersey—With his soldiers' enlistments about to expire, George Washington, in a daring night crossing of the ice-choked Delaware River, delivers a surprise attack against a thousand-man Hessian detachment under Colonel Johann Gottlieb Rall and captures most of them in a dawn assault. The victory provides a much needed boost to patriot morale.

1777

January 3, 1777

The Battle of Princeton, New Jersey—George Washington follows up his electrifying victory at Trenton with a second victory over the British at Princeton in just over a week. The British are forced to retreat all the way to New Brunswick, New Jersey,

	and Washington goes into winter quarters near Morristown, New Jersey.
June 14, 1777	The Flag—The official flag of the United States is established by Congress to consist of alternating 13 white and red stripes with a blue field of 13 white stars.
July 6, 1777	Ticonderoga, New York—Invading troops from Canada led by General John "Gentleman Johnny" Burgoyne seizes Fort Ticonderoga and is now threatening to take Albany, New York.
July 27, 1777	The Marquis de Lafayette—A nineteen-year-old French volunteer, the Marquis de Lafayette, arrives from France and quickly proves his valor and worth to George Washington and the American cause.
August 16, 1777	The Battle of Bennington, Vermont—New Hampshire militia under General John Stark severely mauls a six-hundred-man Hessian detachment.
August 25, 1777	The Philadelphia Campaign Opens—British General William Howe lands his army at Head of Elk, Maryland, on his way to attacking the American capital of Philadelphia.
September 11, 1777	The Battle of Brandywine—British General Howe attacks George Washington's force at Chadds Ford, Pennsylvania, along Brandywine Creek and once again defeats the Continental army. Washington is forced to retreat toward Philadelphia.
September 21, 1777	The Paoli Massacre, Pennsylvania—In the early morning hours of September 21, 1777, Anthony Wayne's Pennsylvania brigade is surprised by General Charles "no flint" Grey. According to eyewitnesses, the British bayoneted a number of surrendered Americans and refused to grant them quarter.
October 7, 1777	The Battle of Saratoga, New York—After several earlier engagements at Freeman's farm, British General John Burgoyne is defeated by American forces led by Major General Horatio Gates.
October 17, 1777	Surrender—John Burgoyne formally surrenders his army to Horatio Gates. This event is clearly one of the most important turning points in the war. News of the American victory is wildly celebrated in the states,

and Benjamin Franklin moves quickly at the Court of Versailles to formalize a Franco-American alliance.

December 17, 1777 — Valley Forge—The Continental army arrives at its winter cantonment at Valley Forge, Pennsylvania. It is a time of suffering and privation for the soldiers.

1778–1779

February 6, 1778 — The Franco-American Alliance—A formal treaty of alliance is signed between the United States and France. With the stroke of a pen, the war is transformed into a worldwide struggle.

February 23, 1778 — Baron von Steuben—Prussian officer "Baron" Friedrich Wilhelm von Steuben arrives at Valley Forge and is assigned duties with the army as "acting" inspector general. Von Steuben immediately embarks on a vigorous program of army-wide inspections and drill.

June 18, 1778 — Philadelphia Regained—British General William Howe is replaced by Henry Clinton, who makes the decision to return his army via an overland march to New York City. American forces immediately reoccupy the city.

June 28, 1778 — The Battle of Monmouth Court House, New Jersey—Hoping to catch Clinton before he gains the safety of his New York City defenses, George Washington fights a battle near Monmouth Court House in nearly one-hundred-degree heat. During the battle, Washington criticized the action of his erratic second in command, Major General Charles Lee, causing Lee to eventually leave the army for the rest of the war.

August 1778 — The Battle of Newport, Rhode Island—In the first attempt at Franco-American combined operations, American forces under Major General John Sullivan and French forces under Admiral d'Estaing fail to dislodge the British grip on Newport and are forced to retreat after a severe summer storm dismasts most of the French fleet.

December 1778–January 1779 — Savannah and Augusta, Georgia—Beginning a new "southern strategy" campaign, the British capture Savannah on December 29, 1778, and Augusta, Georgia, a month later.

September 23, 1779	*Bon Homme Richard*—Commanding the Continental frigate *Bon Homme Richard,* Captain John Paul Jones defeats the HMS *Serapis.* In response to a British demand to surrender, Jones was heard to shout, "I have not yet begun to fight." Jones' fighting spirit establishes a tradition for the fledgling U.S. navy.
October 17, 1779	Morristown—George Washington establishes his army at Morristown, New Jersey. The winter at Morristown will rival that of Valley Forge and in some ways surpass it in the amount of suffering and privation endured by the soldiers.

1780

May 12, 1780	Charleston, South Carolina—The British smash their way past Fort Moultrie and capture the town of Charleston, South Carolina. The number of Americans captured is over 5400 men. British losses are less than 250.
July 11, 1780	Rochambeau Arrives—Six thousand French soldiers under French General Rochambeau arrive at Newport, Rhode Island.
August 16, 1780	The Battle of Camden, South Carolina—American forces under Major General Horatio Gates are nearly annihilated by the British under General Charles Cornwallis.
September 1780	Arnold and Andre—Major John Andre is captured near Tarrytown, New York, and evidence is found on his person that Benedict Arnold had been secretly collaborating with British General Henry Clinton to surrender the American garrison at West Point. While Andre is hanged as a spy, Arnold makes his escape to the HMS *Vulture* on the Hudson River.
October 7, 1780	King's Mountain, South Carolina—American militia catches a force of one thousand loyalists led by British Major Patrick Ferguson and virtually annihilates them at King's Mountain. Allegedly, the Americans refused to grant quarter for loyalists trying to surrender.
October 14, 1780	Greene Takes Command—American Major General Nathanael Greene arrives to take command of the

southern army and rally what is left after the debacle of Camden, South Carolina.

1781

January 1781

Mutiny in the Ranks—Mutiny breaks out over a
dispute in the soldiers' terms of enlistment in the
Pennsylvania and, later, New Jersey lines. The
Pennsylvania line complaint is resolved through
negotiations. However, the New Jersey mutiny ringleaders are executed.

January 17, 1781

The Battle of Hannah's Cowpens, South Carolina—
American General Daniel Morgan leads a combined
force of militia and regular troops to defeat Colonel
Banastre Tarleton.

March 15, 1781

The Battle of Guilford Court House, North
Carolina—American forces under Nathanael
Greene inflict heavy losses on Charles Cornwallis'
British army at Guilford Court House. Although he
retains the field, Cornwallis decides to abandon the
Carolinas and move toward Virginia.

September 1781

The Battle of the Capes—French naval forces under
Admiral Count de Grasse defeats the British
squadron guarding the Chesapeake Bay.

September 28, 1781

The Siege of Yorktown, Virginia—Bringing his
Continental army and the troops under Rochambeau
southward, George Washington invests Charles
Cornwallis' army at a place called Yorktown and
begins siege operations against Cornwallis.

October 17–19, 1781

The Battle of Yorktown—After resisting for as long
as he could, Charles Cornwallis is forced to surrender to George Washington and Rochambeau. As the
British troops march out to lay down their arms, a
military band plays the tune "The World Turned
Upside Down." With the second loss of a British
field army in North America, there is now a strong
movement in Parliament to end the hostilities.

1782

March 20, 1782

Lord North—British Prime Minister Lord North,
one of the most active proponents for a vigorous

prosecution of the war in America, resigns. His successor, Lord Rockingham, immediately begins negotiations to end the hostilities.

1783

February 4, 1783	Hostilities End—On this date, the United Kingdom declares an official end to hostilities against America.
March 10, 1783	Newburgh Conspiracy—Disgruntled American army officers circulate a petition that threatens to defy the new national government. George Washington is able to defuse the situation and talks the officers out of their proposed scheme.
September 3, 1783	The Treaty of Paris—A formal treaty is signed by Great Britain and the United States that officially brings the war to an end. America has won its independence.
November 2, 1783	George Washington—George Washington delivers his farewell address to the army and begins his journey home to Virginia.
November 25, 1783	The Last of the British—The last British troops in America pull out of New York harbor. The British still retain possession over several disputed western outposts.

1 CITIZEN-SOLDIERS: THE ARMY OF OBSERVATION

As every American schoolchild quickly learns, it was during the early-morning hours of April 19, 1775, that British "redcoats" attempted to seize the provincial military stores then known to be hidden away by patriots in the peaceful hamlet of Concord, Massachusetts. And as the story goes, thanks to the diligence of alarm riders like Paul Revere and William Dawes, the ever vigilant colonial militia "turned out" in swarms and ultimately sent the British reeling back into the port of Boston.

And the truth be told, the New England militia performed magnificently that day. Moreover, within a week of the fighting on Lexington Green, it was estimated that nearly sixteen thousand men, from various New England colonies, were milling about the outskirts of Boston. Their sheer numbers managed to keep the approximately three to four thousand redcoats securely penned up inside the city itself until the militia "army" could get themselves properly organized. Eventually known as the New England Army of Observation, this patriot military force surrounding the British inside Boston was something of a unique entity in 1775. However, this number quickly dwindled as farmers, day laborers, and merchants dropped out of their units in ones and twos in order to take care of their affairs at home. At other times, whole companies left the army to return to their lives in the surrounding countryside.[1]

The Army of Observation was exceptional because it was nearly entirely comprised of militia formations. These first American soldiers esteemed themselves as "volunteers," and, as one earlier Virginia militiaman had wryly commented, the militia were "soldiers when they chose to be."[2]

> Politically and economically, the system fit the early needs of the colonies because the militia reflected the predominant social order (with officers drawn from local elites) and because the burden although widespread was minimal.[3]

Moreover, it was believed, an active militia was the most reliable force to have on hand. This was due to the Whiggish sentiments of the New England colonial elite who feared regular forces as potential tools of oppression. Indeed, one of the main

The Battle of Bunker Hill. (*Courtesy of the Library of Congress*)

disagreements they had with their military governor, General Thomas Gage, was over the quartering of regular troops within their midst. Further, there may also have been clear-cut economic reasons for the colonies to not want to maintain regular forces for self-defense. Regular troops were very expensive, and their loyalty was assumed to belong to whoever paid them.

Hence, the fear was that unless the colony provided troops on demand for emergencies, regular troops, loyal to the royal governor who maintained them, might use such forces to suppress civil liberties. Thus, colonial hostility toward standing armies became part and parcel of Revolutionary War iconography.

And for the most part, New England was politically and geographically well suited for a citizen-army. The independence of town life, the closeness of towns to each other, and a relatively excellent road network that connected most of the larger towns meant that each town government could organize and equip militia companies as they saw fit. For example, by the early spring of 1775, the prosperous town of Sudbury, Massachusetts, could afford to have approximately 350 men on its militia roles. These men were grouped into five separate companies. The Provincial Congress recommended that each New England town train and equip at least one-fourth of its total militia force as "minute companies," and Sudbury formed two of them—one each for the east and the west sides of the town. However, smaller towns such as Medford, Massachusetts, only enlisted twenty-five men into their minute company. Concord's first attempt at forming minute companies during the cold winter months of January 1775 was largely unsuccessful. Initially totaling a paltry sixty men, the town of Concord was only willing to pay its men "one shilling 8 pence for drilling two half days a week." Day laborers, on the other hand, could usually command 2 shillings a day.[4]

But what we do find in the spring of 1775 is that a large number of adult males in New England performing some form of military service. For example, an analysis of the town of muster rolls for the Lexington militia showed that a large percentage of its adult male population, capable of bearing arms, were present for duty in April 1775. Lexington listed 141 men on its muster rolls. "The total number of male polls" in 1775 was 208. Thus, an astounding 68 percent of the adult male population of this particular town found themselves under arms during the first few months of the war. Although this figure excluded the very indigent, Lexington in 1775 was a relatively prosperous town and it can be reasonably assumed that militia participation at least in this section of New England was fairly widespread.[5]

And the New England militia was certainly not as youthful as one might assume. The typical age of a New England militiaman was considerably older than the average age of later Continental soldiers (who were generally twenty-one years of age). In Concord, the age of their militiamen was around twenty-nine years. In Sudbury it was thirty. In Lexington, the average was thirty-two. Moreover, the "minutemen in many towns appear to have been younger" than those in standard (or non-minute) militia companies. What this meant was that although the standard militiaman of April 1775 was likely to be firmly rooted to his particular community, the requirements of more rigorous duty and readiness with minute companies attracted a younger cohort of men.[6]

Historian John Shy, whose pathbreaking work on the colonial militia paved the way for further study on this important colonial military institution, noted that the "clustering of manpower and the cohesive atmosphere in the town community gave New England greater military strength." However, because towns and geographic linkages were more scattered in the Chesapeake and southern colonies, the militia establishments there were relatively weak. Comparing the New England response with that of Virginia during dual Indian wars that occurred in each region in 1676, Shy noted that the New England militia forces performed much better than their southern counterparts. The colonies of Georgia and Virginia clearly favored small bands of full-time rangers over those of the militia. The Virginia system relied on "a short term general militia" and called out men only sporadically with little or no training or equipment. Instead of actual defense, these particular colonial militias largely performed ceremonial and law enforcement roles in

Minutemen being fired upon by British troops at the Battle of Lexington. (*Courtesy of the Library of Congress*)

catching runaway slaves or putting down nascent slave revolts. Thus, "patterns of settlement" and geography greatly matter for the early effectiveness of American military institutions such as the colonial militia.[7]

New England and, indeed, the rest of colonial America all had long-standing laws that required most men between the ages of seventeen and sixty to perform some sort of military service. This meant that, in theory, most able-bodied males were required to perform service in the militia. However, over time, and owing to the lessening threat from eastern woodland tribes, the requirement to serve in the militia was modified by most colonies, and several classes of citizens such as millers, judges, clergymen, and others deemed necessary for the economic and political functioning of the towns were exempted from drill. However, in New England, where the military threat in 1775 was much more tangible, few missed drill. The Alarm Lists in the Massachusetts Archives mention "473 companies." Of these, "217 [were] minute men units." In John Nixon's Sudbury minute company, only a single militiaman, Hosea Brigham, missed more than once. Fines may have served to keep attendance up, and only six men out of sixty of Nixon's men missed a single drill. One militiaman noted that "the young Men in the Winter months made a Practis of calling on their officers Evenings and going through the Manual Exercise in Barn Flours. I had exercised many a Night With my Mittens on. . . ."[8]

The common New England militiaman was a military bargain. Most towns, but not always, expected militiamen to supply their own arms, and these weapons came in a wide variety from smoothbore muskets to ancient fowling pieces and a few rifles. Further, there was no need for the towns to provide much in the way of clothing because most militiamen wore the clothes that they had on their backs. "Few had cartridge boxes or bayonets. Their precious few bullets were carefully wrapped in handkerchiefs and carried in pockets or under hats." They carried their gunpowder in powder horns or made loose paper cartridges and kept these in their pockets as well. This worked as long as it did not rain. A few carried swords, hunting knives, or tomahawks. Most carried along some form of rations that they had been able to purloin from home. Usually, it was a few pieces of jerked meat or course bread. After a few days on active duty, either many militiamen expected to return home or the towns were required to feed and house them at public expense. The longer they remained in the service of the province, the more expensive it was for the towns to keep them in the field.[9]

Many of these local militia companies were extraordinarily linked by kinship. Captain John Parker commanded the Lexington militia on April 19, 1775. More than one-quarter of his men "were related to him by blood or marriage." Of the fifty-two men listed in one of Concord's minute companies, nineteen (or 37 percent) were directly related to just four families.[10] The "east company" of militia from Easton, Massachusetts, sent forty-seven men toward Boston on April 19, 1775. Of this group, eleven (or nearly 23 percent) were members of just two families (the Randalls with six and the Drakes with five). And the tradition of the militia, especially in New England, was to elect their officers. Although this did not guarantee that the "best men" would become officers, these leadership positions usually fell to respected and established members of individual communities, preferably someone like Parker who had previous military experience during the Seven Years War. Occasionally, "militia companies even adopted 'documents' or covenants—stating their principles and concerns, their rules of behavior, and their limits or restrictions upon their officers' authority."[11]

In the south, however, the standard militia company's military performance was as varied as their units. Indian commissioner David Taitt decided to visit a militia drill on the frontier near Augusta, Georgia, in June 1772 and noted that "the men made a very Sorry Appearance, some having old rusty firelocks, others Riffles, and some being well Clothed an Others with Osnaburgh Shirts and Trousers; they fired platoons as ununiformly as their Accuttrements and dress." Although some southern militia units such as the First (militia) Regiment in Savannah were well turned out and disciplined, in reality it was the fear of attack from the still powerful Cherokee and Creek Indian tribes or runaway slaves that seemed to motivate the southern militia more than anything else. If these threats were not present, their militia system was likely to become moribund in short order.[12]

THE ARMY OF OBSERVATION

So what was it like to be a member of a militia company in the New England Army of Observation? What sort of people were they? How long did they remain under arms? And, most important, what became of them?

First, it was clear that following Lexington and Concord, the militia had won respect from their adversaries. Lord Hugh Percy, writing to Adjutant General Edward Harvey in London, stated that

> whoever looks upon them as an irregular mob will find himself much mistaken. They have men among them who know very well what they are about. . . . You may depend upon it, that as the rebels have now time to prepare, they are determined to go through with it, nor will the insurrection here turn out so despicable as it is perhaps imagined at home.[13]

The daily lives of American soldiers in the first year of the war largely revolved around three general events, after the fighting at Bunker Hill ended with a pyrrhic victory for the British in June 1775: (1) observing the British force then securely penned up inside Boston from their camps around Cambridge, Massachusetts, (2) participating in a highly successful campaign into the Lake Champlain region to seize Fort Ticonderoga, and (3) floundering in the wilderness of Maine during an abortive winter attempt to seize Canada.

In the Cambridge camps, the initial issue was not so much about actual warfare but a more esoteric subject—food. Massachusetts General William Heath observed soon after Lexington that "how to feed the assembled militia was now the great object." Heath immediately sent foraging parties into the countryside surrounding Cambridge. His men were temporarily able to purloin enough food and some casks of sea bread bound for the Royal Navy. He even commandeered the cooking pots and kettles of Harvard College.[14]

In reality, it was evident to one and all that the Army of Observation lacked military stores in nearly every category. No shoes, arms, tents, cooking utensils, fodder, blankets, and provisions were to be had. The Massachusetts Committee of Safety even appealed to other colonies for help. New York responded favorably and sent 650 pounds of precious gunpowder "guarded by four to six trusty men" who were instructed to travel only at night. Even weapons were apparently difficult to come by in these early days. Just two days before Bunker Hill, Massachusetts towns ordered their townsmen to "deposit firearms with their town treasurers—each piece to be paid for. The total set forth in this quota was 1065 muskets"—a large number for an army preparing for a possible engagement with a well-armed enemy. One observer of the American camps at

Cambridge noted that all the "Houses were full, and the Provincial Troops are not yet in Tents, and uncertain when they will be." Soldiers neglected their clothing, and another noted that the men chose "to let their linen, etc., rot upon their backs than to be at the trouble of cleaning 'em themselves."[15]

Supply, it seemed, remained a consistent problem for the Army of Observation. Nathanael Greene and his Rhode Island Regiment arrived shortly after the fighting ended at Lexington. On May 23, 1775, Greene wrote to General John Thomas, commander of the Massachusetts militia in the Roxbury–Dorchester area from 20 April 1775 until March 1776, that he "concluded to incamp upon the forfeited Lands of the Arch-Traitor [Governor Francis] Barnard." Greene selected the ground and then applied to Thomas for permission to remain there. Just six days later, Greene lamented to Joseph Clarke, general treasurer of Rhode Island, that "[t]here is no mode of supply agreed upon by the Government."[16]

Even when the army did receive supplies, there was no guarantee that they were adequate. Greene observed that casks of bread sent to his men from Providence, Rhode Island, did "not have much more than one half and two thirds the quantity they ought to Contain. . . . A quantity of Bread arrivd from Providence last Week and today the much greater part was mouldy and unfit for use. . . . There was a quantity of Beef condemned last Week as being horse meat." Greene did not believe this last charge and convened a jury of butchers to determine the nature of the "mystery meat." The jury agreed that a "considerable part" was, indeed, "horse flesh."[17] It should be noted, however, that the Rhode Island Deputy Governor, Nicholas Cooke, did not ignore Greene's complaints and ordered the Committee of Safety to "re-pack and weigh all kinds of salt provisions, by you purchased for the use of said army, that you mark each barrel; and that you are very careful with respect to the flour and bread, and all other provisions purchased for the use of the said army." Most militia units in camp at Cambridge were supported either by their local towns or ultimately by their provincial governments. The farther colonial troops were from their base of supply, the worst their situation in camp seemed.[18]

As far as Greene was concerned, the poor quality of the food made his men difficult to command. Writing to his brother Jacob, Greene observed the near mutiny of his troops, who had been in camp for just over two weeks:

> The want of government, and of a certainty, had thrown everything into disorder. Several companies had clubbed their muskets in order to march home. I have made several regulations for introducing order, and composing their murmurs; but it is very difficult to limit people who had had so much latitude without throwing them into disorder.

In fact, Greene lamented having the militia there at all, and the day following the Battle of Bunker Hill he implored Cooke to not send anymore of the "Providence militia" until he could figure out what to do with them. Greene also had other problems. He informed the Rhode Island Committee of Safety that he only had "[e]leven casks of powder and four hundred weight of ball" for his entire unit. Greene was also not happy with the quality of officers who were being sent from Providence and remonstrated with the deputy governor to "be careful in the appointment of Officers not only the Field Officers but the Captains and Subalterns—for there are many inconveniences that arise from the bad conduct of Officers that you cannot conceive of unless you had ocular demonstration of the evil." Later, he noted that "there are some captains and many Subaltern officers that neglect their Duty, some through Fear of offending their Soldiers, some through Laziness and some through Obstinacy." Greene also bluntly noted that "there can no offensive Opperation go forward untill we are better supply'd with Ammunition." The troops, he believed, were "raw, irregular, and undisciplined. . . ."[19]

With himself as a notable exception, Lieutenant Ebenezer Huntington of Connecticut clearly agreed with Greene about the quality of company grade officers in camp. He thought that "three fourths of the Captains in Province Pay are as unfit for their Station as I Should be for a Gen'l in Command, not flattering myself would venture to say that I look upon myself as fit for a Captaincy." Huntington also noted that by late November 1775:

> [T]he Universal determination of the Soldiers from Connecticut seems to be for home at the Expiration of their Seven Months altho' they have been repeatedly Solicited in Gen'l Orders to tarry longer. We have reason to fear that our Enemies knowing our Situation will Endeavour to take the Advantage of it which if they do the Consequences will be worse than is Generally thought.

In early January, Huntington observed that the competition for recruits was so keen that one sergeant whom he had sent home to recruit returned to camp with twenty-two men. Unfortunately for Huntington, the sergeant was immediately offered "an ensigncy" by another officer hard up for troops if the sergeant and his new recruits would join his company. Huntington lamented that he "could not hold [the sergeant] or his men."[20]

TICONDEROGA

Although poor food and lax discipline may have been prevalent in camp for the Army of Observation, the situation on the western and northern frontiers for the militia was somewhat different. Out there, what motivated them was how to settle old scores. In a region known as the New Hampshire Grants (modern day Vermont), a single family, the Allens, controlled local politics. The Grants had a particularly bad prewar reputation as a "den of outlaws" and inhabited by a "mob of land thieves and banditti." The leader of this so-called "banditti" was Ethan Allen. Allen was described by Tory Peter Oliver as being "of a bad Character, & had been guilty of Actions bad enough to forfeit even a good one." In truth, well before the Revolution, violent disagreements over land claims between the colonies of New York and New Hampshire prevailed over reasoned debate concerning parliamentary taxation. At the center of this conflict was the "admittedly charismatic" Allen. Just prior to the outbreak of fighting at Lexington, Allen and his cousin Seth Warner formed a local militia called the "Green Mountain Boys," whose initial purpose was to provide military muscle to back Allen's schemes to keep New York colonial officials and land surveyors from establishing control over the Grants (and possibly abrogating Allen and his family's own land claims).[21] In this effort he was highly successful. Allen's Green Mountain Boys repeatedly intimidated New York officials on a variety of occasions in the months leading up to the spring of 1775. Allen himself deftly created the impression that New York was the "crown's favorite government" and was able to link Sons of Liberty ideology with that of "the Grant's settlers claims to their own land and institutions."[22]

Allen used the New England colonial militia model as a blueprint for forming his Green Mountain Boys. "Officially, there were five companies of Green Mountain Boys, organized by vicinity." In reality, however, "anyone could account himself a member by sticking a fir twig in his hat." This meant that more and more regional men could claim themselves to be a Green Mountain Boy and all were "firmly committed" to protecting their land titles in the Grants. Thus, with little or no effort, the locals became powerfully dedicated to opposing both authority of the colony of New York and, by association, authority of the Crown. And being the only organized force in the region for hundreds of miles around, they generally got their way without too much resistance from anyone who opposed them.[23]

When fighting broke out, Allen freely admitted that his argument was more with New York than with the Crown. However, most of those in the Grants had emigrated there from Connecticut and Massachusetts and felt a natural allegiance to family members and former neighbors to the east and nearly unanimously voted to throw-in with the patriot cause. Soon after receiving word of the outbreak of fighting at Lexington and Concord, Allen and the Boys quickly moved to attack the only British military posts in the entire region: Fort Ticonderoga and neighboring Crown Point. Allen reasoned that by attacking Ticonderoga, which was providentially located inside New York, he could reduce royal authority there and hopefully replace it with his own, embarrass the colony of New York, and, at the same time, curry favor with the Continental Congress and further solidify the land claims for himself and the Boys in the Grants. Clearly, if the British prevailed in the region, New York's claims in the Grants might win out over those of Allen and his men.[24]

However, before Allen could launch his attack, Benedict Arnold showed up with a colonel's commission from Massachusetts. Disregarding the long-standing New England tradition of militia serving under officers of their own choosing, and with express "secret" orders from the colony of Massachusetts to "take possession of the cannons, mortars, stores, etc, upon the lake," Arnold demanded overall command of Allen's force.[25]

The Green Mountain Boys absolutely refused to go along with this turn of events and threatened to go home if they were commanded by anyone other than Allen. Allen was able to defuse the situation by suggesting that Arnold place himself at the head of one of the storming columns. Arnold "reluctantly accepted," if only to ensure compliance with his orders that Massachusetts gain control of the fort's ordnance and war materials. Both he and Allen stormed the fort literally "side by side" and it "fell in less than 10 minutes" without bloodshed. Immediately thereafter, the Green Mountain Boys located the fort's store of rum and were soon drunk and looting the British officers and soldiers of their personal possessions. When Arnold tried to put a stop to this, some of the Boys allegedly snapped their flintlocks at him and threatened his life. Fortunately for Arnold, once there was no more plunder to be had, the Boys began to filter back toward their farms in the Grants, leaving Arnold and the recruits who eventually joined him in control of the fortifications at Ticonderoga and Crown Point.

Arnold immediately followed-up on his success at Ticonderoga and led a raid to the top of Lake Champlain and reduced another British fortification at St. Johns inside Canada before returning southward toward Crown Point. Not to be outdone by his rival Arnold, Allen and about a hundred of his Green Mountain Boys thought it would be a good idea to permanently occupy St. Johns and followed Arnold's lake-borne force in four bateaux. Nonetheless, once Arnold returned from the raid, the British were able to easily drive off Allen and the Boys, who rather ignominiously fled back to the Grants.

The easy conquest of the Lake Champlain region "electrified America." Just one week after the capture of Ticonderoga, the *Worcester Spy* reported, "the possession of this place affords us a key to all Canada. . . . *What think ye of the Yankees now?*" But Arnold's and Allen's spontaneous activity in the region presented Congress with another

Capture of Fort Ticonderoga by Ethan Allen and the Green Mountain
Boys, 1775. (*Courtesy of the North Wind Picture Archives*)

headache. Heretofore, Congress had argued that armed resistance was necessary to
defend colonial rights against oppression, that if the British behaved themselves and
admitted that the patriots had specific rights as Englishmen, then all would be well.
However, Allen and the Green Mountain Boys were clearly conducting *offensive* operations by their abortive attempt to occupy St. Johns. Thus, Congress quickly repudiated
the activity of Allen and instructed Arnold to deposit the cannon from Ticonderoga at
the south end of Lake George to await the final resolution of the dispute between the
colonies and the Crown.[26]

The lesson here, at least for New England frontier militia as compared with that of
the Army of Observation, was that militia commanders such as Allen were not beyond
exploiting provincial grievances against the Crown or other colonies in order to further
their own local cause. Persistent localism ruled in the Grants and on other places in the
northern frontier. Moreover, unless the Crown proposed to invade and physically occupy
this rugged region, it was the Green Mountain Boys who wielded all the authority

there—just as they had before the war started. Coming and going as they pleased, the frontier militia represented the only semiorganized military force in the area with the power to consistently compel people to do their bidding. Operating from local wayside taverns or semi-isolated individual farmsteads, the frontier militia could form relatively quickly in response to any emergency and just as quickly return home without incurring too much cost to the local authorities or to themselves, for that matter. But as witnessed at Ticonderoga and St. Johns, they could be tremendously difficult to control—especially by those they deemed "outsiders."[27]

IN CAMP AT CAMBRIDGE

The provincial army at Cambridge had little time to celebrate the victories of Allen and Arnold. With the British still threateningly nearby in Boston, there was no possibility of allowing their soldiers to go home for very long. Instead, provincial army commander Artemas Ward was more concerned about how to keep his force in the field. On April 24, 1775, Ward candidly wrote to the Provincial Congress that his "situation is such that if I have not enlisting orders immediately I shall be left all alone. It is impossible to keep the men here." Hundreds were leaving for homes and farms; hence, patriot leaders like Dr. Joseph Warren were soon begging the Continental Congress to tell them what to do.[28] As a result, Congress began taking more active interest in the army around Boston and quickly voted to send supplies and ten companies of riflemen from Pennsylvania, Maryland, and Virginia. More important, they agreed to appoint General George Washington of Virginia as commander in chief of all the Continental armed forces. John Adams saw this last move as extremely crucial to New England's cause. Not only would Washington's appointment further cement southern colonies to their brethren in the north, it would also provide Continental relief to Massachusetts. Adams noted in his autobiography that he was frequently "and pathetically" informed by Generals Warren, Ward, and Heath of "the impossibility of keeping their men together without the assistance of Congress." Adams believed that Congress had heretofore hesitated to assert control because of a "jealousy [mainly among southern delegates] of a New England Army under a New England General." As a result, Adams was ultimately able to convince Congress to appoint Washington as commander in chief and the army at Cambridge adopted as a Continental army at least at this point in the war, in name only.[29]

Although Washington's arrival in camp was certainly seen as a positive step toward creating an army capable of sustaining itself, the soldiers themselves seemed more preoccupied with living from day to day. One such soldier was seventeen-year-old David How of Methuen, Massachusetts. On December 27, 1775, How "listed" with a Sergeant Barker for one year. However, owing to provincial regiments being reformed on January 1, 1776, so that the entire army could be converted to Continental service with longer-serving soldiers, How was apparently discharged. While he never mentioned receiving a bounty for his original enlistment, he took advantage of his temporary leave of absence from the army and on January 8, 1776, hired himself as a laborer to a Mr. Watson. How worked for Watson for two solid weeks, cutting and hauling wood to the nearby town of Lexington and was paid 6 pounds, 5 shillings for his efforts.

During his original twelve-day stint as a soldier in the Army of Observation, How did not receive much in the way of training or discipline. Soon after arrival in camp, he was placed on "fatigue duty" at Lechmere's Point, building a fortification. The common practice for new soldiers was to give them duties that the "older" soldiers generally sought to avoid. But How seemed to be an especially enterprising "yankee" and quickly earned himself $2 for the sale of a blanket to another soldier. On December 30, How and his mates were paraded by their officers and had their weapons taken from them to be appraised as to their worth. This was done so that the army could be more uniformly equipped. However, soldiers such as How did not see it this way. According to Heath, this action was a source of major discontent among the men in camp. Many believed that they would not get a fair deal from the Continental authorities.[30]

On January 22, 1776, How again "listed" to serve in Colonel Paul Dudley Sargent's Massachusetts regiment for one year. This was his second enlistment in less than a month. How's diary entries for the next several weeks noted the sort of activity most of the men of his unit must have been constantly engaged in. He mentioned that "Colonel Bricket paid me Eight Dollars for my gun" and that he received "one month's pay of the Colonel and Twelve shillings for a blanket." Initially, How made so much money, thanks to the conversion to Continental service and perhaps his fortuitous ability to enlist twice, that he was able to send $16 home to Methuen in a letter carried by a friend. How and his messmates were also able to purchase a 17¼-pound "wild turcy" and "had it for supper" one evening. While How was a soldier, he was also an entrepreneur. He noted that during the week of January 30, he and his squad had been engaged in selling "Nuts and Cyder every day" and that he made enough profit to buy "4 Bushels of Apels" paying "12 shillings a Bushel for them." Washington lamented the amount of "stock-jobbing" that seemed to predominate among the soldiery in this still very New England army, but at this point there was very little he could do about it.

Throughout his time in camp, How thought it was important to note who broke out with smallpox and who was in the hospital. He mentioned the accidental deaths of comrades from drinking bad liquor or simple mishaps. Life for How revolved around finding adequate provisions, occasional rifle drill, keeping his weapon in good working order, supplementing his pay and those of his comrades through the sale of nuts and cider, and going on working parties ("for teag") to build fortifications or unload ships, standing guard, washing clothes, and making cartridges. How also noted the military discipline sometimes meted out in camp. On September 27, 1776, he observed that "Robbard Higings was Whipt 20 Lashes For geting Drunk and Dening Duty. Thomas Brimblecom was whipt 10 Lashes for geting Drunk. The Drummajor was whipt 15 Lashes for Theft." How saw very little military action beyond hearing cannon and mortar fire being exchanged between both sides as the British prepared to abandon Boston on March 17, 1776. When the British did finally evacuate, How and his squad mates were more interested in seeing the "Ruens of the Town" of Charlestown and the now abandoned British fortifications on Bunker Hill than anything else. Ominously, for the first time, How noted five men being "whipt 20 Lashes" for "Deserting" and another ten given the same punishment for "being Absent at rool Call With out Leave."[31]

Most soldier diaries of this period casually noted those who were punished. They seemed to accept the fact that military discipline was a necessary peril of soldier life. What stands out, however, is that the flogging was strictly limited in this very American army. Although their British opponents could and would receive sentences of one hundred to five hundred lashes for crimes such as drunkenness, stealing, and disrespect to their officers, the Americans followed a more religious example: limiting the number of lashes that could be given to thirty-nine, the same number proscribed in Mosaic law. The various diarists were amazed at the number and frequency the lash was used against the common redcoat. However, Washington and his military secretary Colonel Joseph Reed of Pennsylvania thought that thirty-nine lashes for his troops were too few. Reed, not impressed with army discipline, stated that:

> [H]e was sorry to say that we have too many who would equal, if not exceed, the Kings troops in all kinds of disorder and irregularity. To men of this stamp thirty-nine lashes is so contemptible a punishment that it is very frequent for them, in the hearing of their comrades, to offer to take as many more for a pint of rum.[32]

The original American army in Massachusetts must have been a shock to Washington. When he arrived in July 1775, "the Massachusetts legislature apologized for the state of discipline in the army." Washington was amazed to see soldiers firing off their muskets for the sheer joy of hearing the sound. There were so many varied styles of dress among the soldiers that Washington immediately suggested to John Hancock, the then-president of the Continental Congress, "that a Number of hunting Shirts not less than 10,000 would in a great Degree remove this Difficulty in the cheapest and quickest manner." The camps were foul and dirty. The army "sat amid a smoky miasma rising from green wood fires, gunpowder smoke, urine, feces, and animal offal." Soldiers were very careless with firearms. Washington noted as late as 1776 that "[s]eldom a day passes but some persons are shot by their friends."[33]

Private Samuel Haws of Wrentham, Massachusetts, confirmed Washington's complaint about carelessness with weapons. He wrote that on April 28, 1775:

> [T]his day our regiment paraded and went through the manuel exesise then we grounded our firelocks and every man set down by their arms and one abial Petty axedently discharged his peace and shot two Balls through the body of one asa cheany through his left side and rite rist he Lived about 24 hours and then expired . . . this young man was but a few days Before fired at by one main guard in attempting to pass the guard and was not hurt in the least.

Just two months later, Haws recorded another accidental shooting death—this time, a soldier named "Wood" who was "killed by a gun going off accidently of, he was shot about Seven o'clock and died nine o'clock the same night." Nonetheless, just a few days later, Haws wrote that he participated in a "rifle frolick [a shooting contest for liquor]."[34]

The day after Asa Cheney was accidentally killed, Haws heard a "very suitable sermon" preached by the Reverend Amos Adams, a minister at Roxbury, Massachusetts. Adams was a graduate of Harvard College and was soon to die himself not from a gunshot wound but of that other great killer of soldiers in the Cambridge camps—dysentery. Army surgeon Dr. James Thacher noted that by November 1775 "our hospitals [were] considerably crowded with sick soldiers from camp; the prevailing diseases are autumnal fevers and dysenteric complaints, which have proved fatal in a considerable number of instances." Thacher was quick to point out that while in the hospital the men were well provided for, but he was embarrassed to note that some others of his medical profession had taken to robbing soldiers' graves "for the purpose, probably of dissection, and the empty coffin left exposed." He believed that this gave the soldiers the impression that "a soldier's body is held in no estimation after death. Such a practice, if countenanced, might be attended with serious consequences as it respects our soldiers." Thacher gratefully noted that "this practice in the future is strictly prohibited by the commander-in-chief."[35]

Camp sanitation proved to be a huge problem for the army at Cambridge. Open latrines, a lack of general cleanliness among the soldiery, and the belief of many men of that era that frequent bathing was actually unhealthy were difficult to overcome. One Massachusetts soldier wrote in 1777 that "this day, the old carter, Brown, washed his face and handes he Desired to have it seat down in the Journal the first time since he Come in." After a few weeks of sleeping in such camps and in unusually close quarters, soldiers began to suffer from "the itch," which meant that they were crawling with lice. They would treat this particular problem with a variety of home remedies such as applying hog's lard or pine tar and brimstone. It was true that you could hear and smell the American camps from miles away for a variety of reasons.[36]

Clothing, rations, and pay were significant issues with the Army of Observation. Although for uniforms Washington wanted hunting shirts—a style he was very familiar with in his native state of Virginia—many men received, instead, dyed brown cloth coats "to be provided for, by stoppages out of the soldier's wages, at 1 [and] 2/3rds dollars per month." At least there would be some approximation of uniformity. As for pay, Congress established the private soldier's wage at $6.66 (or 40 shillings) per month. Compare this for a moment with the 3 pence a day a British private received and one can understand why colonial elites in Congress believed, at least at this early period of the war, the men were more than adequately compensated. As for food, Washington established the following ration:

> One pound of beef or three-quarters of a pound of pork, or one pound of salt fish, per day; one pound of bread or flour per day; three pints of peas or beans per week, or vegetables equivalent, at six Shillings per bushel for peas or beans, one pint of milk per day, or at the rate of one Penny per pint; one half pint of rice, or one pint of Indian meal, per man per week; one quart of spruce beer or cider per man, per day, or nine gallons of molasses per Company of one hundred men, per week; three pounds of candles to one hundred men, per week, for squads; twenty-four pounds of soft, or eight pounds of hard soap, for one hundred men per week.[37]

Although it was more of an ideal ration than reality, the soldiers were well aware of what was "due" to them and would loudly let their officers know if they were being shortchanged in this particular area because they could sell or trade what they did not use or eat.

WILDERNESS HELL

Although the Army of Observation struggled to turn into what Washington termed "a respectable army," a long-talked-about campaign to seize Canada in the summer of 1775 was seen by many of the bored soldiers in camp at Cambridge as a promising adventure and a welcome break from the tedium of camp. Ever since easily taking Ticonderoga, Arnold had been in favor of attacking Canada. Most believed the report of Connecticut Governor Jonathan Trumbull, who believed Canada to be lightly defended and not all that enamored of its British rulers since it fell to them just twelve years earlier. However, it was not until August 20, 1775, that Washington proposed to Philip Schuyler, commanding officer of the Northern Department, a plan to attack Canada. He believed that a dual thrust against British forces in the St. Lawrence region would force them to fall back to defend Québec and thereby ensure the security of the northern borders of New England and New York. And if all things worked out the way he hoped, even Québec might fall to them, which would, according to Washington, "have a decisive Effect and Influence on the publick Interests."[38]

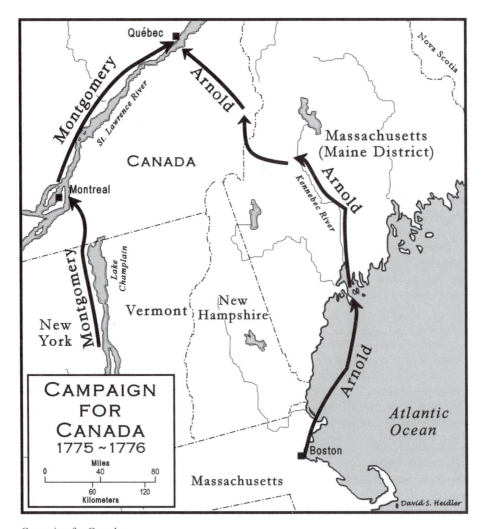

Campaign for Canada

Washington selected the enterprising Arnold to lead one of the two invasion prongs. Philip Schuyler fell ill and asked his second in command General Richard Montgomery to lead the other. Arnold was to take an overland route through the howling Maine wilderness with about seven hundred "volunteers" recruited from the camps at Cambridge. Washington later added three companies of recently arrived "riflemen" from Pennsylvania and Maryland to accompany Arnold, who, according to Sergeant William McCoy, a rifleman in "D" Company, of Colonel William Thompson's Rifle Battalion, their captains "cast lots who should go, and it fell to Capts. Hendricks and Smith of Pennsylvania, and Captain Morgan of Maryland." Since McCoy was a member of Hendricks' company, he was slated to go as well. Arnold wanted only "experienced men" on this mission. General Orders read that "as it is imagined the Officers and Men, sent from the Regiments both here, and at Roxbury, will be such Volunteers, as are active Woodsmen, and well acquainted with bateaus; so it is recommended that none but such will offer themselves for this service."[39]

One soldier who accompanied Arnold on the trek through Maine was seventeen-year-old Jeremiah Greenman of Newport, Rhode Island. By September 19, 1775, Greenman found himself in Newburyport, Massachusetts, along with the other volunteers from the Army of Observation. He was soon joined by the "riflemen" from Pennsylvania, Maryland, and Virginia. Greenman was certainly not a "woodsman," but being from the Narragansett Bay county, Rhode Island, he must have been relatively familiar with boats—although not necessarily the shallow draft bateaux used in the Maine backcountry. And if anyone had any concerns about starting toward Canada so late in the campaign season, it seems to have been forgotten in the excitement of "the Canadian temptation." Embarking on ships bound for the mouth of the Kennebec River, Greenman described the departure as thrilling, with "Drums a beating fifes a plaing the hils and warfs a Cover [with People] biding their friends fair well." Dr. Isaac Senter, a volunteer surgeon on the expedition, noticed something else—a large number of deserters from the British army in Boston among the boat crews.[40]

While traveling up the Kennebec, the going was relatively easy until Greenman and his comrades ran into the first of what proved to be dozens of grueling portages with their bateaux. Another soldier on the march, Caleb Haskell, admitted that carrying bateaux "was a new sort of work to us." Shifting their boats and supplies from "pon to pon," Greenman described in mid-October a wilderness hell where the terrain "in sum places half a leg deep in mud and mire / ware it wasn't mud and mire it was roks and hills as steep as a hous Side almost." He observed that the Dead River, which Arnold's force was then traversing to get into Canada, was of little help to them. He noted that the river was "so still you can't but jest procive wich way it runs / its black and very deep now." Private George Morison, a rifleman in Captain William Hendrick's company, described the travel as absolutely tortuous. He thought that the bateaux they were required to use "were so badly constructed, that whether in or out of them we were wet. Could we have then come within reach of the villains who constructed these crazy things, they would fully have experienced the effects of our vengeance." Morison

Drawn by Sydney Adamson.   Half-tone plate engraved by H. Davidson

WORKING AGAINST THE FLOOD ON DEAD RIVER

Working against the flood on the Dead River, troops, under the command of Benedict Arnold, portaged with boats, en route to the invasion of Canada. (*Courtesy of the Library of Congress*)

believed that the contractors who provided the shoddy bateaux did so on purpose in order to make a greater profit and directly accused them of being "an accessory to the death of our brethren, who expired in the wilderness."[41]

In a series of especially trying days in a single week in mid-October, Greenman described getting lost in the woods with some other soldiers, having several "battoes" overturn and numerous packs lost, having a flash flood carry away a barrel of precious food and gunpowder, and their provisions growing increasingly scant. On October 24, Greenman noted an internal disaffection that took place. Lieutenant Colonel Roger Enos had decided to turn back with three companies of men and "took with them large Stores of provision and ammunition wich made us shorter than we was before." The defection of Enos while Arnold was absent was especially galling to many of the soldiers who elected to go on with the expedition. Apparently, as supplies ran short, officers in the main body convened a "council of war" and voted on whether to stay with Arnold or turn back. The vote between the senior commanders was about evenly split. Although Enos was credited by Dr. Senter as having voted to stay, he believed that his true intention was to abandon the expedition as soon as he could—which in fact turned out to be the case. Senter was disgusted that Enos refused to order the "returners" to settle upon a "just division" of the remaining provisions. Enos pleaded that he had lost control of his men and that "they had determined to keep their possessed quantity [of food] whether they went backward or forward."[42] Those who elected to continue onward with Arnold received only two and a half barrels of flour before Enos and more than a third of the original expedition returned to the Maine settlements and eventually to the camp at Cambridge.

When Enos finally returned to Cambridge, Washington placed him under arrest, pending an investigation into his egregious conduct in the Maine wilderness. Unfortunately, all those, such as Dr. Senter and Arnold, who might have testified in a more negative light were still in Canada. Enos alleged that he was forced to turn back because of low provisions. However, unlike those who elected to stick it out with Arnold, no one starved on the way back. With fellow officers in his command backing up his side of the story and no one around to testify to the contrary, the court-martial voted to "acquit him with honor." Nonetheless, Enos and others perhaps knew the real truth and he soon resigned his commission in the Continental service.[43]

By the end of October, Greenman and his comrades had been forced to abandon their "battoes" and proceed on foot "over such hils mountain & Swamps such as men never passed before." By October 31, Greenman's company was forced to kill dogs for their provisions. Sergeant William McCoy noted that by November 1, he was so hungry that he "staggered around like a drunken man" and passed by two other "musket-men" he observed "eating two dogs, which they roasted skins, guts, and all." Dr. Senter saw soldiers eating candles "by boiling them in water gruel" and noted that dysentery (and, after eating the candles, constipation) was very common among the men. Fortunately, the very next day, thanks to the foresight of Arnold, Greenman stated that "we came in Sight of the Cattle wich the advance party had sent out it was the Joifulest Sight that I ever saw & Sum could not refrain from crying for joy."[44]

There was more good news for the remaining stalwarts who elected to continue on to Canada. First, by the end of October and at the exact moment that many of the men were running out of food, Arnold received intelligence that Canadian British Governor General Guy Carleton had moved most of his troops to the Montréal area to meet the other Montgomery-led prong of the American offensive against Canada, then coming up the St. Lawrence River from northern New York. Thus, Québec appeared to be lightly defended. Next, Arnold was also informed by a scout he had earlier sent forward named "Jaquin" that "the French inhabitants appear very friendly and were rejoiced to hear of our approach." Nonetheless, despite Arnold's careful preparations to the contrary, his men kept getting lost in the swamps and bogs around Lake Megantic on the Canadian border. One man drowned after a bateau belonging to Captain Morgan's rifle company overturned, with Morgan himself barely escaping this accident. The sick had to be left behind. Dr. Senter noted that "[l]ife depended on a vigorous push for the inhabitants." This was the worst part of the march.[45]

However, by early November, Arnold and his remaining men finally emerged from the Maine wilderness and were now among the French *habitants* on the south side of the St. Lawrence River. Near the town of Sartigan, Québec, Arnold met with the local Native Americans and urged them to join with the Americans in their effort to defeat their English overlords. Arnold apparently offered them "one Portuguese per month, two dollars bounty, and find them provisions, and their liberty to *chuse* their own officers." Nonetheless, with the exception of the Caughnawaga tribe, their response to his entities was decidedly lukewarm and Arnold could muster only fifty warriors.[46]

Arnold actively proselytized among the Canadians to get them to rise up against the British. Despite his vigorous efforts, he was met with cold rejection. Although the ragged and emaciated appearance of the Americans may have contributed to a lack of confidence the Canadians had in "*Les Bostonnais*," the deficiency of Canadian enthusiasm was more likely related to a fear of reprisal many of the inhabitants had if the Americans failed in their effort to take Québec. Since the 1763 Treaty of Paris, the British had wisely allowed the French Canadians much leeway in maintaining their Catholic religion and its traditions without interference from the new government. Moreover, the staunchly Protestant and highly anti-Catholic New Englanders had been at war off and on with the French and Indian *habitants* of southern Canada for more than a hundred years. Now they were being told that they would get a better deal by allying themselves with their former historical enemies. Many did not see how this change would benefit them. When Arnold addressed a French Catholic congregation on November 5, 1775, which he ironically did on Guy Fawkes Day, he was politely listened to and just as considerately ignored. November 5 was the traditional date that commemorated the foiling of a "popish plot" to blow up Parliament by a saboteur named Guy Fawkes. Boisterous anti-Catholic demonstrations and commentary were the order of the day throughout the British Empire. To further seal the loyalty of the French *habitants*, the British spread the rumor that they "were determined to burn and destroy all the inhabitants in the vicinity of Quebec, unless they came in and took up arms in defense of the garrison."[47]

Further, the local militia commander Gabriel Taschereau had threatened to arrest all male inhabitants "unwilling to perform militia service in defense of the province." To make matters worse, the British had captured some of Arnold's Native American couriers. Several other natives may have even informed the British and Canadians that Arnold was headed their way. It was clear that Arnold had lost the element of surprise. Now, the British were hurrying regular troops back to the walled city of Québec and seizing all the boats on the south shore of the St. Lawrence (to deter a river crossing by Arnold's force). The British also controlled the river with the recently arrived frigate HMS *Lizard*. As a result, more than seven hundred local habitants "warmly" responded to the call of Lieutenant Governor Hector Cramahé, to turn out to defend Québec. Upon being apprised of this situation, Arnold decided to wait for help from Montgomery's western wing of the American advance. Arnold informed Montgomery that he intended to isolate

Québec from the surrounding countryside and keep its defenders cooped up inside the town "in close quarters until your arrival here, which I shall wait with impatience."[48]

Although the enterprising Arnold was able to cross the river on canoes and barges in early November without being detected, his ragamuffin force was in no condition to take on the defenders of Québec. Dr. Senter noted that the condition of their arms and ammunition was very poor and "in much disorder. No bayonets, no field pieces and upon an average of the ammunition there amounted only to about four rounds per man. Under the circumstances it was thought proper to raise the siege, and proceed up the St. Lawrence, 8 leagues to Point Aux Tremble."[49] General Richard Montgomery finally caught up with the Maine refugees on December 1, 1775. While Montgomery and Arnold made plans to seize the town by assault, many New England companies talked openly of going home. John Pierce of Worcester, Massachusetts, was one of the disgruntled soldiers. He noted on December 23, 1775, that a group of officers met at the "Minute Tavern" and, led by malcontent captains Hanchett, Hubbard, and Goodrich, implied that they would soon be marching their companies for home. Pierce himself stated that he "intended to make the best of [his] way home as Soon as may be." He noted that the "Greater Part of Capt Hubbards Company is Determined for New England at all adventures."[50]

The American attack on Québec on New Year's Eve ended in ignominious failure. During the attack, Montgomery was killed and Arnold wounded. Several hundred soldiers were captured by the British and French Canadians, including the redoubtable Virginia rifle commander Daniel Morgan and many of Arnold's heretofore recalcitrant company commanders. Some of the causes of the failure of this assault may be related to the discontent in Arnold's companies or the fact that many of the soldiers' enlistments were due to expire on January 1, 1776. In fact, such was the case with Rhode Island Private Caleb Haskell, who was sick with smallpox during the actual fighting for Québec. When later ordered out with the rest of his company to guard a ferry crossing, they refused to go. As Haskell put it, they "looked upon themselves as freemen, and, have been so since the first of January." Faced with being punished with "39 stripes" and allowed only "two minutes" to cease their impromptu strike, Haskell and his comrades "found that arbitrary rule prevailed" and they agreed to go to the ferry.[51]

Private Jeremiah Greenman of Newport, who had left on the expedition with such high hopes in September 1775, was one of those captured. He stated that at the beginning of his captivity, he and his comrades were shut up inside houses in the city of Québec. Their cells were cold and so crowded that there was "Not a nuf [room] to lay down to sleep." He noted that "Stinking Salmon is [the] provision we have." The prisoners were frequently placed in irons. Greenman noted that many "old countrymen" (recent immigrants from the British Isles) were offered an opportunity to get out of prison by enlisting in the British forces. He recorded that many of these men promptly deserted the British as soon as they were able. Those who remained behind in captivity kept themselves "ha[r]ty in playing ball in the [prison] yard." After being a prisoner for nearly six months in Québec, Greenman and many of his fellow prisoners of war (POWs) were finally paroled. However, he admitted that he was not too interested in the conditions of his parole and stated that "we would sign'd anything thay braught to us if that would carry us home."[52]

By early spring, Dr. Senter observed that smallpox was now ravaging the entire army and was especially prevalent among the New England troops. Although Arnold and David Wooster, who had taken over for the deceased Montgomery, had about 2500 soldiers— a force larger than the one that attempted to seize the town on New Year's Eve—"786 (31 percent) were unfit for duty." Senter noted that officers and soldiers would sometimes attempt, "contrary to orders," to self-inoculate against smallpox—often with fatal consequences. Moreover, those who were formally inoculated and quarantined were unable to perform duty for several weeks. Such was the case with Seth Warner's Green Mountain contingent. These men, enlisted for just a few months, were immediately inoculated and spent most of the rest of their enlistment in a quarantine house—all the while drawing army pay and eating army rations. Even so, Arnold complained that his orders for soldiers to faithfully remain in quarantine camps and "pest houses" were "repeatedly disobeyed or neglected."[53] Often, still infectious soldiers wandered about the American camps and spread the pox among those not yet been inoculated.

In early May, a small relief fleet of four British ships reached Québec with provisions and reinforcements, and the decision was made by the Americans to retreat. According to Dr. Senter, they left Canada "in the most irregular, *helter skelter* manner. All the camp equipage, ammunition, and even our clothing, except what little we happened to have on us." He noted that "no provisions could be obtained but by the force of arms. No conveniences for ferrying our troops over the rivers emptying in upon either side of the St. Lawrence, except a canoe or two, and these are rare." Smallpox was still rampant within the ranks, and General John Thomas, who had relieved David Wooster of command of the army in the spring of 1776, caught the disease himself and soon died.[54]

By June 1776, what was left of the pox-ridden American army and Arnold's "famine-proof" veterans of the Maine wilderness straggled back into the Lake Champlain county. Meanwhile, British General John Burgoyne had landed at Québec with eight thousand regular troops, and all thoughts of easily seizing Canada were soon forgotten.

A RESPECTABLE ARMY

From nearly the moment of his arrival at camp in Cambridge, Washington was concerned with establishing an army that was not solely reliant on short-termed militia or provincial troops. During the fall and winter months of 1775–1776, while Arnold and Montgomery were toiling away before Québec, soldiers in the camps at Cambridge continued to come and go largely as they pleased. Few men had enlistments terms longer than a month and most expired at the end of the calendar year. Samuel Adams was aghast at the sudden cooling of revolutionary fervor. He noted in a letter home, "Do our Countrymen want animation at a time when [all] is at Stake! Your presses have been too long silent. What are your Committees of Correspondence about? I hear Nothing of circular Letters—of joint Committees, etc."[55]

Besides the heretofore mentioned chronic issue of supply, Washington had one other major problem with enlisting this hodgepodge militia and provincial force into something resembling a standard army. The men simply did not want to enlist for a long period of time, and there was no real mechanism in place, other than drafting from the established militia, to make them do so. Joseph Plumb Martin of Connecticut was one such recruit. Martin worked as a farm laborer for his grandparents. As the war completed its first year and tired of the farm and his very strict "grandsire," he toyed with the idea of becoming a soldier. However, Martin balked at signing up for even one year's service, stating that "it was too long a time for me at first trial. I wished only to take a priming before I took upon me the whole coat of paint for a soldier." As a result, Martin's initial "primer coat enlistment" was for only six months.[56]

One reason for the hesitancy of the "old soldiers" to reenlist was their very keen sense of obligation that occurred when one agreed to become a soldier—even for a very limited period of time. Historian Fred Anderson's very thorough study of the New

England militia during the Seven Years War revealed why this might be so. It seemed that "British army officers who served in North America [were] never tired of reminding one another that the American colonists made the world's worst soldiers." They believed that the Americans lacked discipline, were fainthearted, and could not endure the rigors of life in the field because they were, by nature, soft. These stereotypes missed a critical point about New England society. This region of colonial America was "fairly stepped in covenants: marriage covenants binding husbands to wives, church covenants among members of congregations, and the great covenant of salvation between God and his cho- sen people." Thus, unlike their regular British army counterparts who often enlisted in a regiment for fifteen years or more, the contractually minded New England men sought to limit their "terms of indenture," a frequent way many termed their enlistments. It was fairly common to find contemporary soldiers' diaries beginning with a "formalized entry" that denoted the officer they had enlisted under and the terms of their enlistment as it related to its length and promised pay and rations. Hence, we see soldiers like Haskell, before the walls of Québec, refusing to turn out to guard a ferry—and not because he was necessarily lacking in patriotism or virtue. Rather because both he and his company mates believed they had fulfilled the contractual requirements of their terms of enlistment and that to continue to serve would be akin to "perpetual servitude," a class and condition slavery-ridden America was very familiar with.[57]

At this point in the war, New Englanders John Adams and Roger Sherman both believed that soldiers could not be convinced to sign terms of enlistment for longer than a single year. In early 1776, Continental Congress diarist Richard Smith noted that Washington complained that "he cannot get Men or Arms enough, that at least 2000 Men in this camp [Cambridge] are without Firelocks and the New England Men are averse to inlisting for a longer Term than One Year and not fond of serving under any but Officers of their own choosing."[58]

Getting the army to enlist for the 1776 campaign season became a much-debated topic in Congress. Congressional delegate James Duane observed that members such as Samuel Adams and Elbridge Gerry were concerned that forming an army "for the war" had never been tried before and, if attempted, might not meet with much success. Roger Sherman of Connecticut stated what many soldiers in camp must have been thinking: "that long enlistment is a state of slavery." More shocking was the idea of Benjamin Harrison of Virginia, who saw the war as New England's fight. He argued that all non–New England troops and officers be withdrawn and the war should be left up to the New England governors to conduct in the way they saw fit. However, he thought that the Continental Congress should provide them an annual stipend of $3 million. He was of the opinion that the local governors, if appropriately financed, would be able to attract enough soldiers from inside and outside New England to fight the war with longer- termed paid mercenary soldiers, thus achieving the desires of Washington (and coinci- dentally limiting the war liability to his own state). John Adams was against enlisting on principle but was all right with those who would freely agree to do so. He believed that enlistment was lagging because many currently serving soldiers had heard rumors of a Continental bounty to be provided for new enlistees. James Wilson of Pennsylvania objected to giving money to the New England governors because no one really knew whether $3 million was too much or too little a sum for maintaining an army either in or out of New England, but he agreed that it was "dangerous to have a standing army."[59]

Washington, however, had other internal issues to deal with in camp. Continental officers were constantly fighting over rank and precedence. The saga of junior officer

Ebenezer Huntington is an excellent example of what Washington had to put up with during the first months in command. Huntington was a well-connected subaltern who was also highly ambitious. Hearing that his home state of Connecticut was forming a new regiment to be commanded by a friend, Samuel B. Webb, Huntington wrote to his father Jabez that "he would be Extremely happy in having a first Lieu' Birth under him at the same time would say that I would not Except of a Second Lieu' Birth under him nor any other man in the world and Quit my business." In a postscript, Huntington reminded his father that he "Should be Glad you would show the lines [of his letter] to some member of the lower house that would try to get me the birth above mentioned."[60]

Huntington's strategy apparently worked as he was given a first lieutenant "Birth" in Captain John Chester's company. Chester just happened to be married to Huntington's sister. What Huntington had not counted on were all the other officers of his regiment signing a strong letter of protest to General Spencer, commanding officer of the Connecticut troops, that he had received his position through connection vice any military competence or seniority. Later, in March 1776, Huntington was again upset over issues of rank. This time, a vacant company command that came with the rank of captain was given to another officer after Huntington had spent much time recruiting for it. He firmly believed that the company should have been his and in a huff went directly to "his excellency," Washington with the intention of tendering his resignation over the matter. What he got instead was a dose of the famous Washington temper, and he received a "very severe reprimand" from the commander in chief for bothering him with such a matter. Washington then brusquely waved Huntington away and told him to go think about the impact of his decision before asking him again. The next day, Ebenezer's brother, Colonel Jedidiah Huntington, commanding officer of the 17th Continental Regiment, was able to smooth things over with Washington and got himself and his brother a furlough instead. While Ebenezer was eventually given a company command, he was again subject to complaints from other officers in the regiment, who, in another petition, threatened to resign en masse if he were given the captaincy over another officer who they thought was more deserving of the position. Huntington began to carry his sword and a brace of loaded pistols with him at all times "as I expected to be Insulted."[61] However, the pending New York operations of the army seemed to have mercifully ended the resignation imbroglio.

Washington even had trouble with troops from his own state of Virginia (and that of Pennsylvania and Maryland). The much touted and feared "riflemen," the first non–New England troops raised for the new Continental army, soon proved to be as recalcitrant as any "yankee" soldier in Washington's command. When a popular sergeant in Thompson's Rifle Battalion named John Seamon was arrested and confined for unruly conduct, his fellow "rifflers" began to riot on Prospect Hill. As a result, a further thirty-two men were arrested. Greene in a note on the incident to Washington wrote that "rifflers seems very sulky and I am inform'd threaten to rescue their mates tonight." Greene strengthened the guard, and the issue was quickly resolved. However, there was a report that Generals Washington, Greene, and Charles Lee had to personally ride out to ensure that the men settled down. The next day, Sergeant Seamon and his fellow rioters were brought before a General Court Martial presided over by Colonel John Nixon of Massachusetts. The men were fined 20 shillings a piece for their behavior in the affair, and Seamon was given a further six days in the guardhouse.[62]

During the fall of 1775, Washington decided he needed to crack down on camp infractions and to impose some regularity of discipline among the various units in camp.

Greene noted in his General Orders that in order to cut down on the "stock-jobbing" that the men seemed to be constantly engaged in, he appointed an officer to act as a "Clark [clerk] to the maquet [market]." He warned that

> no ma[r]keting what Ever is to be allowed in any oather part of the Camp but at that place So appointed by the Clark. He is also to Regulate the Prises of all produce Brought into Camp and no Parson to Exseed the prices on penalty of having their Porduce Saized and taken From them for the Benefit of the army.[63]

Washington kept the men constantly busy by having them work on the various forts and redoubts that surrounded the city of Boston. However, he remained aghast at the state of discipline within his still predominately New England army. He complained that the New England officers were:

> of the same kidney with the privates . . . as there is no such thing as getting of officers of this stamp to exert themselves in carrying orders into execution—to curry favor with the men (by whom they were chosen, and on whose smiles possibly they may think they may again rely) seems to be one of their principal objects of their attention.

During the fall, Washington had an officer drummed out of camp for shaving one of his men—an act that would not be unusual for the town barber but very demeaning for a commanding officer. He was especially severe with officers who were caught submitting false manning reports so that they could draw more pay and rations than they were actually due. On August 10, 1775, Washington published in his General Orders that he hoped that "the Example of Jesse Saunders, late Captain in Col. [Paul Dudley] Sergeants regiment will prove the last shameful Instance of officers embezzling money and food for their own self-aggrandizement."[64]

Thus, Washington also began to discipline his officers. By the end of August 1775, he wrote to Richard Henry Lee that:

> I have made a pretty good slam among such kinds of officers as the Massachusetts government abound in since I came to this Camp, having broke one Colonel and two Captains for cowardly behavior in the action at Bunkers Hill—two Captains for drawing more provisions and pay than they had men in their company—and one for being absent from his post when the enemy appeared there and burnt a house just by it. Besides these, I have at this time one Colonel, one Major, one Captain, and two Subalterns under arrest for trial. In short I spare none yet fear it will not do as these people seem to be too inattentive to everything but their interest.[65]

Washington was a whirlwind of activity in the fall of 1775. He issued orders against "futile firing" and the needless waste of precious powder and lead by the men. He stopped officers from employing soldiers on their farms. He worked on getting the men fed and paid promptly, and provided serviceable clothing, and "humane hospital care." He discouraged "vice in every shape" and sought to limit the use of alcohol and swearing by the men. He even advocated that the men not drink "new cider" because he believed that "nothing is more pernicious to the health of soldiers, nor more certainly productive of the bloody flux." He even forbid naked soldiers from jumping into the water off bridges near Cambridge because of the presence of "passengers, and even ladies of the first fashion" being nearby.[66]

However, two constant camp problems continued to plague the army: firearms and powder and, now that the winter had arrived, procuring wood for various soldier camps. On November 5, 1775, Greene prohibited "any person Cutting Apple trees or Locusts for the future." He posted sentries over his unit's rapidly dwindling supply of wood.

After being in the Prospect Hill–Roxbury area for more than seven months, Greene and other commanders were now forced to send their woodcutting parties as far away as Woburn, Massachusetts (a distance of more than ten miles from the army camps). Greene also had to remind soldiers (once again) to stop firing at passing flocks of wild geese and stated that "that any person that fires for the future be immediately put under guard. Every officer that stands an Idle Spectator and sees such a wanton Waste of powder and don't do his utmost to suppress the Evil may expect to be reported."[67]

Soldiers' weapons and cartridge accountability had become a major concern to the army. With the end of the year approaching and enlistments expiring, many of the soldiers attempted to take their weapons and ammunition with them. The idea was that if they could get out of camp with their equipment, they could possibly sell it when they got home and hopefully recover what they had originally paid for them in the first place. If very lucky, they might even make some money on the deal. Thus, Greene required his soldiers to turn in their weapons and cartridges before leaving camp for any reason. He also discovered that "the Soldiers have got into a practice of Stealing Cartridges from one another and those that go home on Furlough or are dischar'd, cary them home." Greene decided on a system of fining soldiers 1 shilling for every lost cartridge and 3 pence for every lost flint. The scarcity of serviceable weapons was so prevalent that Washington required all departing soldiers to sell their guns to the army. In early December, before the Connecticut troops were allowed to depart camp, Washington had General John Sullivan inspect their arms (with the intention of purchasing them at the going Continental rate) but warned him not to divulge the purpose of his inspection for fear that "some of the best Arms will be Secreted," by the men. Despite the discretion of Sullivan, the soldiers must have been rather successful in hanging onto the best weapons. Writing to the Massachusetts legislature, Washington lamented that the departing soldiers had "by stealth borne them away." Those who were skillful enough to hide their weapons from the officers probably had good reason to do so. Those arms purchased by the army were usually paid for in rapidly depreciating currency or provincial promissory notes. The weapons problem was so severe that Greene appointed "30 Men that are active, bold and Resolute to use the Spears in defense of the lines instead of Guns."[68]

By December 1775, the greatest crisis faced by the new Continental army was the growing reluctance of the original soldiers to reenlist for the coming 1776 campaign season. In late December, Washington reported to John Hancock that "not more than 2540 men [had] reenlisted," despite a last-minute effort by himself and other officers to convince the men to remain in the ranks. The Connecticut men seemed especially determined to leave. On the last day of 1775, Greene noted that:

> this is the last day of the old enlisted Soldiers service; nothing but confusion and disorder Reigns. We are obliged to retain their Guns whether private or publick property. They are prized [priced] and the Owners paid, but as Guns last Spring run very high, the Committee that values them sets them much lower than the price they were purchast At. This is lookt upon to be both Tyrannical and unjust [by the departing soldiers].[69]

Washington was forced to request that seven thousand New England militiamen be temporarily called out until more soldiers could be enlisted. But all was not totally dark. While Greene remarked to Samuel Ward Jr. that "the fatigues of the Campaign, the suffering for want of Wood and Cloathing, has made abundance of the Soldiers heartily sick of service," he also noticed that the Connecticut troops met "with such an unfavorable Reception at Home that many are returning to Camp again already."[70]

By the end of 1775, the hodgepodge force that drove the British back into Boston after Lexington and Concord was—thanks to the efforts of Washington, Greene, and others—fitfully evolving into a true "Continental" army. Some men were slowly, if begrudging, enlisting for at least one more year, although certainly not at the rate or level desired by Washington or Congress. This same timeframe also saw American hopes soar with the taking of Ticonderoga and Crown Point and then just as precipitously dip with the defeat at Québec and the death of the popular Richard Montgomery. "If it had not been what John Adams called it at the time—'half a war'—neither had it been a full-scale effort on the American side" or the British for that matter.[71] Clearly, both sides seemed to be preparing for a much more vigorous effort in 1776.

NOTES

1. Victor Brooks, *The Boston Campaign: April 1775–March 1776* (Conshohocken, PA: Combined Publishing, 1999), 101.

2. Virginia militiaman quoted in John Whiteclay Chambers II, *To Raise an Army: The Draft Comes to Modern America* (New York: The Free Press, 1987), 18.

3. Chambers II, *To Raise an Army*, 14.

4. "The Sudbury Companies of Militia and Minute," Maynard Historical Society, http://web. Maynard.ma.us/history/society/minutemen2000 (accessed October 4, 2006); Alfred S. Hudson, *The History of Sudbury: Massachusetts 1638–1889* (Boston: R.H. Blodgett, 1889), 370.

5. Robert A. Gross, *The Minutemen and Their World* (New York: Hill and Wang, 1976), 131; David Hackett Fischer, *Paul Revere's Ride* (New York: Oxford University Press, 1994), Appendix O, 319–20.

6. Fischer, *Paul Revere's Ride*, 319–20.

7. John Shy, "A New Look at Colonial Militia, " in *A People Numerous & Armed: Reflections on the Military Struggle for American Independence*, rev. ed. (Ann Arbor, MI: University of Michigan Press, 1990), 34–35; James M. Johnson, *Militiamen, Rangers, and Redcoats: The Military in Georgia, 1754–1776* (Macon, GA: Mercer University Press, 1992), 33; Chambers II, *To Raise an Army*, 20.

8. John R. Galvin, *The Minute Men: Myths and Realities of the American Revolution* (Washington, DC: Brassey's, 1989), 246; Town of Sudbury, *The War Years in the Town of Sudbury, Massachusetts: 1765–1781* (Sudbury, MA: Town Record Books, 1975; book 6, 1755–1790), 139–40; Hudson, *The History of Sudbury*, 370–2, 375–82.

9. Fischer, *Paul Revere's Ride*, 161–2.

10. Gordon S. Wood, *The Radicalism of the American Revolution* (New York: Vintage Books, 1991), 45; Frank W. Coburn, *The Battle of April 19, 1775*. 2nd ed. (Port Washington, NY: Kennikat Press, 1970), 170–1.

11. Norman Castle, ed., *The Minute Men: 1775–1975* (Southborough, MA: Yankee Colour, 1977), 105; Don Higginbotham, "The American Militia," in *War and Society in Revolutionary America: The Wider Dimensions of Conflict* (Columbia, SC: University of South Carolina Press, 1988), 111.

12. "Journal of David Taitt's Travels from Pensacola, West Florida, to and through the Country of the Upper and Lower Creeks, 1772," quoted in Johnson, *Militiamen, Rangers, and Redcoats*, 85; James Habersham to Governor James Wright, June 6, 1772, quoted in Johnson, *Militiamen, Rangers, and Redcoats*, 86.

13. Hugh Percy to Edward Harvey, April 20, 1775, in George F. Scheer and Hugh F. Rankin, *Rebels & Redcoats: The American Revolution Through the Eyes of Those Who Fought and Lived It* (New York: Da Capo Press, 1957), 43.

14. Ibid., 42.

15. Richard M. Ketchum, *Decisive Day: The Battle for Bunker Hill* (New York: John McCrae/Owl Book, 1999), 62, 64–65.

16. Nathanael Greene to General John Thomas, May 23, 1775, in Richard K. Showman, ed., *The Papers of Nathanael Greene, Vol. 1, December 1766 to December 1776* (Chapel Hill, NC: University of North Carolina Press, 1976), 80; Nathanael Greene to Joseph Clarke, May 29, 1775, in Showman, *The Papers of Nathanael Greene, Vol. 1*, 82.

17. Nathanael Greene to Deputy Governor Nicholas Cooke, July 4, 1775, in Showman, *The Papers of Nathanael Greene, Vol. 1*, 95.

18. Nicholas Cooke to the Rhode Island Committee of Safety, July 7, 1775, Rhode Island Historical Society, *Collections*, vol. 6 [1867], 112.

19. Nathanael Greene to Jacob Greene, June 2 [6–10] 1775, 85; Nathanael Greene to the Rhode Island Committee of Safety, June 18, 1775, 86; Nathanael Greene to Deputy Governor Nicholas Cooke, June 18, 1775, 87; Nathanael Greene to Deputy Governor Nicholas Cooke, June 28, 1775, 91; Nathanael Greene to Jacob Greene, June 28, 1775, 92 in Showman, *The Papers of Nathanael Greene, Vol. 1.*

20. Ebenezer Huntington to Andrew Huntington, October 3, 1775; Ebenezer Huntington to Jabez Huntington, November 23, 1775, and January 12, 1776, in "Letters of Ebenezer Huntington," *The American Historical Review*, vols. 1–5, July 1900, Reel 2, 705.

21. Michael A. Bellesiles, *Revolutionary Outlaws: Ethan Allen and the Struggle for Independence on the Early American Frontier* (Charlottesville, VA: University Press of Virginia, 1993), 1.

22. Ibid., 105–6.

23. Ibid., 83.

24. James Kirby Martin, *Benedict Arnold, Revolutionary Hero: An American Warrior Reconsidered* (New York: New York University Press, 1997), 66.

25. Martin, *Benedict Arnold, Revolutionary Hero*, 65.

26. Bellesiles, *Revolutionary Outlaws*, 120–1.

27. Martin, *Benedict Arnold, Revolutionary Hero*, 69, 71.

28. Artemas Ward to the Massachusetts Congress, April 24, 1775, in Peter Force, *American Archives*, 4th ser., II, 348; Scheer and Rankin, *Rebels & Redcoats*, 52–53.

29. John Adams to Abigail Adams, June 17, 1775, in Edmund C. Burnett, ed., *Letters of the Members of the Continental Congress, Vol. 1, 1774–1776* (Washington, DC: Carnegie Institution, 1921), 130–1.

30. *Diary of David How*, entries for December 27–30, 1775, 1–2, in Henry B. Dawson, *Gleanings from the Harvest-field of American History* (Morrisania, NY, 1865); William Heath, January 1, 1776, *Memoirs of William Heath* (Freeport, NY: Books for Libraries Press, 1970), 44.

31. *Diary of David How.*

32. Lynn Montross, *Rag, Tag, and Bobtail: The Story of the Continental Army, 1775–1783* (New York: Harper & Brothers, 1952), 44.

33. Charles Royster, *A Revolutionary People at War: The Continental Arm & American Character, 1775–1783* (Chapel Hill, NC: University of North Carolina Press, 1979), 58-60; George Washington, General Orders, August 30, 1776, in John C. Fitzpatrick, ed., *The Writings of George Washington*, vol. 5 (Westport, CT: Greenwood Press), 500; George Washington to the President of Congress, July 10, 1775, vol. 3, 322–9.

34. "Samuel Haws Diary," entries for April 28–30, 1775, July 20, 1775, and October 13, 1775, in Abraham Tomlinson, ed., *The Military Journals of Two Private Soldiers, 1758–1775* (New York: Da Capo Press, 1971), 54–55, 62, 77.

35. James Thacher, entry dated November 1775, in *Military Journal of the American Revolution* (New York: Arno Press, 1969), 33.

36. Royster, *A Revolutionary People at War*, 59–60; entry of March 9, 1777, "Revolutionary Diary Kept by George Norton of Ipswich, 1777–1778," Essex Institute, *Historical Collections* (1938), 339–40.

37. Montross, *Rag, Tag, and Bobtail*, 46–47; George Washington, "General Orders," August 8, 1775, in John C. Fitzpatrick, ed., *The Writings of George Washington*, vol. 3 (Westport, CT: Greenwood Press), 408–9.

38. George Washington quoted in Robert Bray and Paul Bushnell, *Diary of a Common Soldier in the American Revolution, 1775–1783: An Annotated Edition of the Military Journal of Jeremiah Greenman* (Dekalb, IL: Northern Illinois University Press, 1978), 5.

39. "Journal of Sergeant William McCoy of the March from Pennsylvania to Quebec, July 13, 1775 to December 31, 1775," in *Pennsylvania Archives*, ser. 2, vol. 15, 22–51; Bray and Bushnell, *Diary of a Common Soldier in the American Revolution, 1775–1783*, 6; Martin, *Benedict Arnold, Revolutionary Hero*, 108. McCoy was mistaken about Morgan, who was actually from Virginia and would become a very famous soldier in the Continental army before the end of war.

40. Greenman diary entry, September 19, 1775, in Bray and Bushnell, *Diary of a Common Soldier in the American Revolution, 1775–1783*, 13; "Isaac Senter Journal," entry dated October 1, 1775, in Kenneth Roberts, ed., *March to Quebec: Journals of the Members of Arnold's Expedition* (New York: Doubleday, Doran & Company, 1940), 201.

41. "Caleb Haskell Journal," entry dated September 29, 1775, in Roberts, *March to Quebec*, 474; Greenman diary entries, October 16–24, 1775, November 2, 1775, in Bray and Bushnell, *Diary of a Common Soldier in the American Revolution, 1775–1783*, 16–18; "George Morison Journal," entry dated September 28, 1775, in Roberts, *March to Quebec*, 511–2.

42. Greenman diary entries, October 16–24, 1775, November 2, 1775, in Bray and Bushnell, *Diary of a Common Soldier in the American Revolution, 1775–1783*, 16–18; Isaac Senter Journal entry, dated

October 25, 1775 in Roberts, *March to Quebec*, 212.

43.   Martin, *Benedict Arnold, Revolutionary Hero*, 133–4.

44.   Greenman diary entries, October 16–24, 1775, November 2, 1775, in Bray and Bushnell, *Diary of a Common Soldier in the American Revolution, 1775–1783*, 16–18; "Journal of Sergeant William McCoy," in *Pennsylvania Archives*, ser. 2, vol. 15, 22–51; "Dr. Isaac Senter Journal," entry dated October 24, 1775, in Roberts, *March to Quebec*, 210.

45.   Benedict Arnold, quoted in Martin, *Benedict Arnold, Revolutionary Hero*, 135; "Dr. Isaac Senter Journal," entry dated October 31, 1775, in Roberts, *March to Quebec*, 218.

46.   "Dr. Isaac Senter Journal," entry dated November 4, 1775, in Roberts, *March to Quebec*, 221.

47.   Martin, *Benedict Arnold, Revolutionary Hero*, 141; "Isaac Senter Journal," entry dated November 5, 1775, in Roberts, *March to Quebec*, 222. Guy Fawkes Day, 5 November, is the anniversary of the alleged Popish plot to blow up Parliament. This day was generally known through British North American as an occasion to express strong anti-Catholic and anti-papal sentiments. Whether or not this irony dawned on Arnold is unknown.

48.   Benedict Arnold to Richard Montgomery, November 8, 1775, quoted in Martin, *Benedict Arnold, Revolutionary Hero*, 143.

49.   "Dr Isaac Senter Journal," entry dated November 18, 1775, in Roberts, *March to Quebec*, 226.

50.   "John Pierce Journal," entries dated December 23–24, 1775, in Roberts, *March to Quebec*, 699. The Minute Tavern was actually Menut's Tavern, Arnold's Headquarters.

51.   "Caleb Haskell Journal," entries dated January 30–31, 1775, in Roberts, *March to Quebec*, 488–9.

52.   "Jeremiah Greenman Journal," entries dated January 9–21, 1776, May 26–31, 1776, August 6, 1776, in Bray and Bushnell, *Diary of a Common Soldier in the American Revolution, 1775–1783*, 24, 28, 30.

53.   Benedict Arnold to George Washington, dated February 27, 1776, in Martin, *Benedict Arnold, Revolutionary Hero*, 189. Self-inoculation against smallpox involved a soldier rubbing an open wound against the pustules of an already infected soldier or making a small incision with a hunting knife on the forearm and performing the same sort of action.

54.   "Dr. Isaac Senter Journal," entry dated January 6, 1776, in Roberts, *March to Quebec*, 238–40.

55.   Samuel Adams quoted in Royster, *A Revolutionary People at War*, 64–65.

56.   James Kirby Martin, ed., *Ordinary Courage: The Revolutionary War Adventures of Joseph Plumb Martin*. 2nd ed. (St. James, NY: Brandywine Press, 1999), 12.

57.   Fred W. Anderson, "Why Did Colonial New Englanders Make Bad Soldiers? Contractual Principles and Military Conduct During the Seven Years' War," in *The Military in America: From the Colonial Era to the Present*, rev. ed., ed. Peter Karsten (New York: The Free Press, 1986), 36, 42–43. Charles Patrick Neimeyer, *America Goes to War: A Social History of the Continental Army* (New York: New York University Press, 1996), 110–2.

58.   "Richard Smith Diary," entry dated February 22, 1776, in Burnett, *Letters of the Members of the Continental Congress, Vol. 1*, 359.

59.   James Duane, "Notes of Debate," entry dated February 22, 1776, in Burnett, *Letters of the Members of the Continental Congress, Vol. 1*, 360–1.

60.   Ebenezer Huntington to Jabez Huntington, June 29, 1775, in "Letters of Ebenezer Huntington," *The American Historical Review*, vols. 1–5, July 1900, Reel 2, 705.

61.   Ebenezer Huntington to Jabez Huntington, March 24, 1776, in "Letters of Ebenezer Huntington," *The American Historical Review*, vols. 1–5, July 1900, Reel 2, 711–2; Ebenezer Huntington to Andrew Huntington, August 10, 1776, in "Letters of Ebenezer Huntington," *The American Historical Review*, vols. 1–5, July 1900, Reel 2, 712–3.

62.   Showman, *The Papers of Nathanael Greene, Vol. 1*, 117; Douglas Southall Freeman, *George Washington: A Biography*, vol. 3 (New York: Charles Scribner's Sons, 1951), 525. The report that the generals had to ride out to quell the "riflers" is related to a reference in Charles Martyn's, *Artemus Ward*, n 179, to a lost letter of Jesse Lukens.

63.   General Greene's Orders, September 19, 1775, in Showman, *The Papers of Nathanael Greene, Vol. 1*, 120–1. These orders were copied from one of his Orderly Books. The phonetic spelling is likely that of the officer of the day and not of the commanding general.

64.   Freeman, *George Washington*, vol. 3, 520; Fitzpatrick, "General Orders," August 10, 1775, in *The Writings of George Washington*, vol. 3, 412–3. Former Captain Saunders had been drummed out of camp following a court-martial for embezzling.

65.   Fitzpatrick, *The Writings of George Washington*, vol. 3, 451–2; Freeman, *George Washington*, vol. 3, 520.

66. Freeman, *George Washington*, vol. 3, 524–5.

67. Nathanael Greene, "General Orders," entries for November 7 and November 9, 1775, in Showman, *The Papers of Nathanael Greene, Vol. 1*, 148–9.

68. Nathanael Greene, "General Orders," entries dated November 12 and November 15, 1775, in Showman, *The Papers of Nathanael Greene, Vol. 1*, 150–1; John C. Fitzpatrick, ed., *The Writings of George Washington*, vol. 4 (Westport, CT: Greenwood Press), 152–3.

69. Nathanael Greene to Samuel Ward, Sr., dated December 31, 1775, in Showman, *The Papers of Nathanael Greene, Vol. 1*, 170–4.

70. George Washington, quoted in Neimeyer, *America Goes to War*, 116–7.

71. Robert Middlekauff, *The Glorious Cause* (New York: Oxford University Press, 1982), 311.

2 SUNSHINE SOLDIERS: THE TRANSITION BETWEEN THE ARMY OF OBSERVATION AND WASHINGTON'S NEW ARMY

In present-day Massachusetts, March 17 is a holiday. Although many assume that it is solely dedicated to Boston's traditional celebration of St. Patrick's Day, this would be incorrect. Instead, the day is known officially throughout the state as Evacuation Day—for it was on this date that the long-reviled redcoats finally departed Boston. While it took the British evacuation fleet some time to leave the outer harbor, it was soon clear to commanders like George Washington and Nathanael Greene that they would likely target another American town and use it as a base of operations. Newport, Rhode Island, or New York City seemed logical choices.

Thanks to crucial intelligence, Washington was able to quickly determine that New York was indeed their primary focus. If the British controlled this particular port, they could easily use it as a base to cut off New England to the north or invade the middle colonies toward the south. A second nearly simultaneous operation against Charleston, South Carolina, was also in the works. Thus, in one single campaign season, General William Howe, who had since replaced Thomas Gage as British commander in chief, planned to end the American rebellion once and for all.

THE CONTINENTAL ARMY

By January 1, 1776, the New England Army of Observation had been largely transformed into a Continental army. Washington announced that "this day giving commencement to the new army, [it is] in every point of View entirely Continental." While this was certainly true, army discipline was never far from his mind. He closed his New Year's Day greeting with a reminder to the officers and men that "an Army without Order, Regularity, and Discipline, is no better than a Commission'd Mob."[1]

American infantrymen in different uniforms. (*Courtesy of the Library of Congress*)

The previous November, Congress had "approved the reorganization of the infantry into 26 regiments." A Continental regiment was commanded by a colonel, and its complement of enlisted men resided in eight companies of approximately ninety officers and men (Figure 2.1). On paper and "at full strength," a Continental regiment represented a formidable battlefield organization of 728 officers and men, of which more than 88 percent were combat musket-wielding infantry. The regiment was also authorized thirty-two sergeants and thirty-two officers, more than adequate to exercise control in camp or on the battlefield.[2]

While Washington and other commanders had strongly desired that Congress raise an army of long-termed recruits, the army of 1776 had enlisted mostly for a single calendar year. The men were to be enlisted into new "continental regiments" and were numbered according to their commanding officer's seniority. For example, "New Hampshire's three regiments of 1775 under Cols. James Reed, John Stark, and Enoch Poor became the 2nd, 5th, and 8th Continental regiments." Moreover, since taking command of the army, Washington had made significant progress in its organization and discipline, although his letters clearly indicated he remained dissatisfied with some aspects of how his soldiers behaved. On January 10, 1776, he appointed William Marony the first Provost Marshal of the Main Army. Marony was now directly responsible for maintaining camp discipline, the guardhouse, and the supervision of the camp guards—something that up to this point Washington and his senior subordinates had

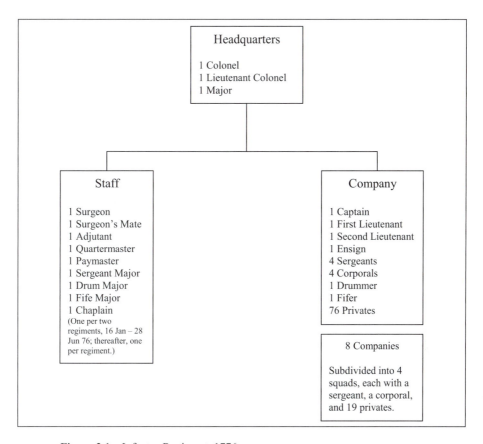

Figure 2.1   Infantry Regiment, 1776.

been doing on their own. The position also functioned as army executioner. This job was so hated that Washington usually could not find an officer willing to do it and had to "select a sergeant and confer upon him the temporary rank of captain." Unfortunately for Washington and the army, this office experienced a significant number of turnover and he was never fully satisfied with its performance in maintaining discipline.[3]

A comparison of the new 1776 American regiments with a British regiment is instructive, because of the fact that most Revolutionary War combat formations operated far below their official authorized strength. The size of the various staffs was about the same for both armies. However, the more pious American units provided for a regimental chaplain and a surgeon—two jobs largely missing in British forces. On paper, the "aggregate" strength of a British regiment was slightly larger than an American one at 809 men. Nonetheless, many of these men were on permanently detached assignment. For example, the standard British regimental unit contained twelve companies, "but 2 were recruiting depots (one each in England and Ireland)." Two others were known as "flank companies." One of these was the famous Grenadiers—large men who wore bearskin shakoes and typically used as shock troops. The other was a "light infantry" company. These select men were skilled and "agile" soldiers who, along with the Grenadiers, were more often than not organized into provisional battalions and served away from their home regiments. For example, Lieutenant Colonel Francis

Smith chose the elite "flank companies" of Grenadiers and light infantry from the British regiments in Boston along with a complement of Royal Marines from the fleet to make his ill-fated April powder raid on Lexington and Concord, Massachusetts. Thus, for all intents and purposes, the standard British regiments went into battle with just eight companies, often missing their best men. Moreover, their companies were comprised of only sixty-six officers and men as compared with the standard ninety-person American company.[4]

In reality, a British regiment was considerably smaller than its American counterpart. Further, American units contained more actual musket-wielding troops than their British counterpart: "(640 to 448) without sacrificing any control." The Americans deployed their regiments in two ranks, the British in three (although this changed for them as the war wore on). The rear British rank was rarely able to effectively fire their muskets. Instead, owing to their battlefield experience at Culloden (1745) and on the plains of Europe, the British army preferred to retain this third rank to increase the shock effect of a bayonet charge. Like a rugby scrum with larger and more numerous players, the sheer weight and force of three compact ranks hitting a thinner one would likely result in a break in the enemy line. Once broken, the enemy would logically flee or fall back in disorder and, if thoroughly stampeded, could be mopped up later by mounted dragoons. On the contrary, the Americans deployed in two ranks. This made their line longer and able to overlap that of the British but far less likely to withstand a bayonet charge, even if they had been trained to do so this early in the war. However, notwithstanding assertions by early Revolutionary War historians, most Continental regiments had more than enough bayonets. They were just not as disciplined or tactically arranged to use them to their advantage. The Americans preferred aimed musket fire over a bayonet melee and generally placed significantly more faith than the British in their musket men and "rifflers" to hit their targets well before the redcoats could theoretically close and deliver one of their feared bayonet charges. In the coming campaign at New York, however, the Americans would soon learn that it paid to be skillful with a bayonet.[5]

The Army in New York

Within days of the British evacuation of Boston, Washington began to transfer regiments to New York. After sending Generals William Heath and John Sullivan forward, he left Cambridge on April 4, 1776. And haste was the order of the day. Nonetheless, the army and its cumbersome train of baggage and artillery took more than two weeks to get to New York. By all accounts, soldier morale was high. As was the case with most of the officers, this was the first time many of the soldiers had been more than twenty miles from home. At first, many must have seen the change of scenery as quite an adventure. Some of the men went by land, and others were placed on transports at New London, Connecticut. The ubiquitous soldier Joseph Plumb Martin was one of the Connecticut six-month levies raised for the New York campaign. He "found himself on a sloop to New York; had a pleasant though protracted passage; passed through the straight called Hell Gate . . .; arrived at New York; marched up into the city, and joined the rest of the regiment that were already there." By the time Martin and his mates had arrived, more than one-third of the population of still strongly loyalist New York City had fled. Many of the newly arrived soldiers were billeted in the now-empty houses throughout the city.[6]

Martin bluntly described what life must have been like for one of the "new levies" in the army before the British arrived later that summer:

> I was called out every morning at reveille beating, which was at daybreak, to go to our regimental parade in Broad Street, and there practice the manual exercise, which was the most that was known in our new levies, if they even knew that. I was brought to an allowance of provisions which, while we lay in New York, was not bad. If there was any deficiency it could in some measure be supplied by procuring some kind of sauce, but I was a stranger to such living.[7]

Regimental Chaplain Ebenezer David accompanied James Mitchell Varnum's Rhode Island regiment and was one of those placed on barges at New London, Connecticut. He spent three cold and wet nights on Long Island Sound before arriving in New York harbor. *The New York Packet* noted with favor on April 18, 1776, the arrival of his unit and was especially impressed with their apparent piety:

> The behavior of the New-England Soldiers is decent, and their civility to the inhabitants very commendable. They attend prayers, with the Chaplain, evening and morning regularly, in which their officers set the example. On the Lord's day they attend public worship twice, and their deportment in the house of God, is such as becomes the place.

On May 4, David and another Rhode Island chaplain, Oliver Noble, preached to three regiments in Greene's brigade. At the time, Greene's unit consisted of Varnum's and Hitchcock's Rhode Island regiments as well as Edward Hand's now famous Pennsylvania riflemen. David concluded that he "hoped we shall live as Brethren." Varnum's men were soon spending most of the summer of 1776 digging fortifications in Brooklyn.[8]

David's experience in the summer of 1776 must have been similar to that of other soldiers the previous summer in the camps at Cambridge. Their daily lot consisted of drill, guard, fatigue duty, and digging fortifications. However, despite the initial similarity of duty and routine, the situation at New York was clearly not the same as Boston. Unlike Boston, New York and the surrounding countryside were rife with Tory sympathizers who kept General Howe informed on what Washington and his army were up to. In fact, "two thirds of the property in New York belonged to Tories." At Boston, it had been the other way around for General Gage. There, his officers had to talk in whispers at the end of the Long Wharf to keep their conservations from being reported by patriot spies. Moreover, while Boston was geographically situated on a single peninsula in a horseshoe-shaped harbor, New York was spread across several large islands and most notably Washington did not control the waterways. Charles Lee, at the time one of Washington's most trusted subordinates, asked, "What to do with the city? I own [it] puzzles me. It is so encircled with deep navigable water that whoever commands the sea must command the town." Washington, however, believed that he simply could not abandon the town without disastrous strategic consequences to the American cause and chose to put the men to work on field fortifications similar to those that had cost the British so dearly at Bunker Hill. He wrote to Congress that it was to be "a war of posts."[9]

Throughout the summer, Washington was concerned about getting enough men to man the posts that he had in mind. One soldier ordered into the theater during this eventful season was Private John Smith of Bristol, Rhode Island. Smith was a soldier in a battalion commanded by Christopher Lippit and noted that "some of the Company

Refused to goe Unless they were Paid their wages which was due them Befor they went out of town." This action got them into some hot water as he and his fellow soldiers were ordered on board a transport to immediately depart for New York. In a rather bizarre turn of events, Smith stated that no one in charge seemed to have remembered to bring any drinking water on board so that "being almost famished for something to Drink . . . some Soldiers Jumped over Board & Swam on Shore & Brought Some on Bord in Canteens which they Carried a Shore [before leaving Narragansett Bay] with them tied about their Necks for that Purpose."[10]

Smith recalled that the transport then returned to Newport harbor where he and his mates were "pushed of & Landed on Goat Island [a then desolate windswept island at the entrance to Newport harbor] as a further Punishment for the Sin of A Soldiers Standing out for his Right." Smith remained on Goat Island for two weeks and then was taken by transport to the other side of the bay where they proceeded by land to New York. During the trip, Smith described an almost leisurely march where he remembered occasionally sleeping in a "feather bed" and was treated along with other "Bristol Soldiers" by a Dr. Munro to a "half Gallon of west India Rum." During the march, Smith got into an argument with his captain and was confined along with fifer John Wilbur in a corn crib but was released the next day. He fondly recalled taking "five fat Geese" and "Asking no Questions with the Rest of my Brother Soldiers who Seamd Hearty in the Cause of Liberty of teaking what Came in the way first to their hand Being Resolv'd to Live By their industry." Later he humorously noted that on patrol "we took Up a Sheep & two Large fat turkeys [who] not Being able to Give the Countersign [were] Brought to our Castel where they was tryd by fire & Executed By the whole Division of Free Booters." He and his mates later liberated two bushels of oysters from an unguarded boat they found tied up to a river dock. Although certainly discouraged by the officers, soldier foraging was a common event on the march. Smith did not note whether there were any consequences to his foraging activities but was obviously smart about it. He wrote that the shells from the purloined oysters bushels "are to this Day Buried Under the floor [of the house where he and his squad mates were temporarily billeted] By the Hearth."[11]

Greene's troops had a rough voyage getting to New York. Washington had feared that some of the transports had been either captured or lost at sea. Nonetheless, by late April, he soon created five brigades under Generals "Heath, Spencer, Sullivan, Greene, and Lord Stirling." However, Washington soon felt compelled to detach Sullivan's troops to reinforce the pox-ridden remnants of the late Richard Montgomery's ill-starred Canadian invasion force now recovering in the vicinity of Crown Point. By mid-May, Greene was in command of the troops on Long Island and was desperately trying to find straw for his soldiers' bedding and enough firewood for his brigade. He kept his men busy working on fortifications originally started by General Charles Lee on Brooklyn Heights. Greene had to remind his men that "the Inhabitants [of Brooklyn] have enterd A Complaint that their Meadow Grounds are injur'd by the Troops going upon them to gather Greens," and he strictly forbids this practice and hoped that the men would not "sully their Reputation by any undue Liberty in Speech or Conduct, but behave themselves toward the inhabitants" with "decency and respect." He closed by admonishing that "the General would have the Troops consider We came here to protect the Inhabitants and their Property from the Ravages of the Enemy but if instead of support and Protection, they meet with nothing but insult and Outrage, we shall be considered as lawless Banditts and treated as Oppressors and Enemies." In addition to digging fortifications, Greene's troops also were active in rounding up known Tories in the vicinity and placing them under arrest.[12]

Problem Army Behavior

Some soldiers clearly did not remain fully engaged in digging trenches. Many were able to slip into New York City and visit a locale famous for prostitution and irreverently called "the Holy Ground" by the men. Pious New Englander Colonel Loammi Baldwin informed his wife that "the whores (by information) continue their employ which is become very lucrative." He went on to describe that whenever he was on duty as officer of the day, he had to, without fail, break up "knots of men and women fighting, pulling caps, swearing, crying 'Murder' & c—hurried them off to the Provost Dungeon by half dozens, there let them lay mixed till next day. Then some are punished and some get clear off—hell's work."[13] Lieutenant Isaac Bangs visited the Holy Ground as he stated "out of curiosity." He noted that at least forty men sent to reinforce the troops in Canada had previously contracted venereal disease as a result of their frequent visits to this infamous place. Bangs observed a riot occur when prostitutes or their henchmen apparently murdered and castrated two soldiers. "This so exasperated the Men that in the face of the Day they assembled and pulled down the Houses where the Men were thus treated, & with great difficulty the Guards dispersed them after they had leveled them to the Ground."[14]

As at Cambridge the summer before, soldiers on Long Island were in the habit of publicly swimming naked. While Greene did not want to discourage his men from bathing, he was also aware that many of them swam "in Open View of the Women and that they Come out of the Water and Run up Naked to the Houses with a Design to Insult and Wound the Modesty of female Decency." Like Private John Smith, Greene's men also had a penchant for oysters and noted that his soldiers had taken to robbing the local oyster beds. In order to stop such unauthorized foraging, Greene threatened such occurrences with "punishment of the utmost severity." He reminded his men that "Our Enemies have sought to Fix a Stigma upon the New England People as being Rude and Barbarous." He pleaded that "for Heaven's Sake don't let your Behaviour serve as an Example to confirm their Observations." If Greene appeared to be highly sensitive over what seemed to be relatively minor soldier indiscretions, it was likely due to his belief that his men needed to be on their best behavior in order to win over the numerous Tory sympathizers who lived in the vicinity of his camp.[15]

Drunkenness among the soldiery was a continuing problem with the army in camps so close to a major city but was usually strictly punished. Numerous regimental orderly book entries recorded numbers of soldiers being given lashes—usually between twenty and fifty—for being drunk on duty or in camp. In "one of the first 'Off Limits' designations in American military history," Washington ordered that "the gin shops and other houses where liquors have been heretofore retailed within or near the lines (except the house at the Two Ferries) are strictly forbidden to sell any for the future to any soldier in the army." He even regulated the authorized sale of liquor by camp sutlers and ordered that they not "sell to any soldier more than one half pint of spirit per day." Those that did were summarily drummed out of camp.[16]

Washington had decided to defend Brooklyn Heights and Manhattan. At the northern end of Manhattan was Kings Bridge, a critical point of defense as it was his sole link to Connecticut and possible reinforcement from New England. As a result, the city of New York slowly took on the look of an armed camp. On Long Island and Manhattan, trenches, forts, and redoubts formed various lines of defense. One resident lamented, "Oh the houses in New York, if you could be see the insides of them! . . . Kennedy's new house, Mallet's and the one next to it, had 600 men in them!" The soldiers slept on the hardwood floors in pairs so that they could lie on one blanket and share the other. As at Boston, they neglected personal cleanliness and camp police. Thus, it was not long before the "bloody flux" (dysentery) and various fevers broke out among the troops. King's College (Columbia) was soon converted into a hospital to house the sick.[17]

Alleged Traitors: The Hickey Plot

By late June 1776, the monotony of fortification building and camp life was broken by two events: the discovery of an alleged Tory plot to destroy the Kings Bridge at the northern tip of Manhattan and the long-feared arrival of a British invasion fleet. Many believed that Royal Governor William Tryon was behind the Tory plot and that he had been aided and abetted by Tory-leaning New York City Mayor David Matthews. The plot had been discovered when a counterfeiter named Isaac Ketchum was apprehended in the city. In order to minimize his own guilt, Ketchum offered that he had information about "two fellow prisoners, continental soldiers Thomas Hickey and Michael Lynch, [who] belonged to some 'Corps' that was receiving money from the British fleet and were preparing to 'cut down' the Kings Bridge." Alarmed at this "news," the Provincial Congress of New York quickly formed a committee to investigate the allegations. What they discovered was a rather amateurish plot that seemed to revolve around the mayor, a few soldiers in Washington's army, and a gunsmith named Gilbert Forbes, "a short thick man who wears a white coat." Upon questioning and with perhaps a view toward getting his life spared, Forbes revealed that he had indeed approached the mayor with a plan to destroy Kings Bridge. However, Mayor Matthews countered that he had told Forbes to forget about his plan but admitted that he had in fact previously met with royalist Governor Tryon and had carried money to Forbes for some guns that the gunsmith had previously made for the governor. Another implicated soldier, Drummer William Greene, "of the General's Guard," also confessed and alleged that he and the other con-spirators (Hickey and Lynch) were to be given "one dollar per man from Forbes" for every man they were able to get to sign on to their plot. Hickey and Lynch had been heard to boast that they had supposedly enrolled more than seven hundred men who stood ready to assist the British when they invaded New York. Later, rumors circulated among the soldiery that the conspirators had "a plan" to assassinate Washington, Israel Putnam, and several other generals and possessed a schematic of all the Continental defenses of New York. However, no hard evidence of either an assassination plot or defense plans were ultimately uncovered. Nonetheless, New York merchant Peter T. Curtenius, in a let-ter to army Captain Richard Varick, remained convinced that the plot "was a most damnable one & I hope that the Villains may receive a punishment equal to perpetual Itching without the benefit of scratching."[18]

The hapless Hickey was able to offer no reasonable defense other than to say that he meant to trick the Tories out of money by appearing to be in on the plot. Washington, however, thought that it was prudent to make an example of Hickey and quickly tried the deluded soldier by a military court and sentenced him to be hanged. Standing on the scaffold, thousands of Continental soldiers and throngs of New Yorkers assembled to witness his execution. Hickey stated that he had no need of clergy "on the grounds that all of them were cut-throats." Never one to pass up on a moral lesson to his troops, Washington later noted in General Orders that Hickey admitted during questioning that "dealing with lewd women had been the beginning of his downfall."[19]

Pursuing Tories in New York

Perhaps as a response to the Hickey plot, the army now vigorously pursued Tories in the city and on Long Island. Peter Elting noted in a letter to Captain Varick that "we Had some Grand Toory Rides in this City this week, & in particular yesterday, Several of them ware handeld verry Roughly Being Caried trugh the Streets on Rails, there Cloaths Tore from there becks and there Bodies pretty well Mingled with the dust." While Generals Putnam and Thomas Mifflin publicly disavowed such action by off-duty soldiers and civilians, there was little they could do about it. Nonetheless, the army actively sent patrols through the city and its suburbs with arrest warrants for the most active and notorious Tories that the New York Committee of Safety could name.[20]

Meanwhile, Dr. Solomon Drowne readied the hospital in anticipation of impending action. He noted that "tis thought [the British] will attempt landing on Long-Island, by some;—by others, that they will, with a fair breeze, run by the forts, up North River and land. We have things in pretty good Readiness at the Hospital for the horrid Effects of a general Action." Drowne remarked that "there has lately been a good deal of attention paid the Tories in this City. Some of the worst have been carried thro' the streets (at Noonday) on Rails, &c." Nonetheless, he told his father that he had obtained "as good a Berth as I coul'd have wished for." He revealed that he was able to draw "20 dollars a month and Two Rations per day" in compensation for his services. He also commented in his letter that the:

> Declaration was read, agreeable to general Orders, at ye Head of ye Brigade, &c. this week; and loud Huzzas express'd the approbation of ye Freeborn Bands. The Night following, the famous gilded equestrian statue of ye British King, in this City, was leveled with ye Dust: his head taken off, and the next morning, in a Wheel-Barrow carried to his Excellency's Quarters, I am told. There is a large Quantity of Lead about it, which is to be run into bullets to destroy his Myrmidons.[21]

For the most part, the Declaration was greeted with enthusiasm by most of Washington's soldiers—many of whom took part in the destruction of the equestrian statue of King George III. The statue itself, according to Lieutenant Isaac Bangs of Massachusetts, yielded ten ounces of gold leaf to some enterprising soldier and stated that he heard that the left over metal "will make . . . deep impressions in the bodies of some of his red-coated and Tory subjects. . . ."[22] The statue's head was eventually placed on a spike by some of the mob and placed outside a tavern. It was later recovered by the British when they occupied the town and sent on to London by Major John Montresor as an example of the perfidy of the patriots.[23]

However, Lieutenant Alexander Graydon of Pennsylvania was not so sanguine. Writing to a friend about the events surrounding the Declaration in Philadelphia, he noted that:

> The Declaration of Independency is variously relished here, some approving, others condemning it—for my own part, I have not the least objection did I know my rulers and the form of government. Innovations are always dangerous particularly here, where the populace have so great an ascendancy, and popular governments I could never approve of. However, I acquiesce in the measure as it becomes daily more necessary, although I am of opinion that delaying it awhile longer could have no bad tendency. On the contrary, it would still have kept the door open for a reconciliation, convinced the world of our reluctance to embrace it, and increased our friends on t'other side of the water—but the greatest danger is that subtle, designing knaves or weak insignificant

Americans tearing down the statue of George III in New York City to celebrate independence, 1776. (*Courtesy of the North Wind Picture Archives*)

blockheads may take the lead in public affairs. . . . However, the matter is now settled and our salvation depends upon supporting the measure."[24]

Dr. Solomon Drowne had more immediate concerns than the Declaration and noted with trepidation the ability of the British fleet to easily pass by the American forts in and around New York harbor. Heretofore, he believed that the American fortifications and especially the cannon at the Grand Battery were more than ready for any sort of challenge that the British fleet might pose. However, on July 13, 1776, he observed that:

two Ships & three Tenders came to sail, and stood towards ye City. They had not got fairly within shot, before our Forts & Batteries began to fire at them;—and, what was mortifying, they kept steadily along seemingly regardless of our constant fire, till they got almost abreast of our Works; then gave us a few passing Brodsides, and, with a fine Breeze, sailed stately up North River, I believe unhurt by us.

He added that during the action "thro' Carelessness or Ignorance," a number of American cannoneers at the Grand Battery had been killed or severely wounded when they had "neglected to swab ye Cannon at all, or doing it improperly, the cartridges took fire, and ye fatal Accidents ensued." Drowne himself amputated the arm of one wounded artilleryman.[25]

By early July, Howe had landed nine thousand troops without much opposition on lightly defended Staten Island. This event had an immediate effect on patriot morale. Elting related to Richard Varick, then in Albany, New York, with General Philip Schuyler, that "you would be surprised to see what Number of Empty houses here are in this place, Verry few of the inhabitants Remain in town that are not ingaged in the Service." And the formerly indefatigable Dr. Solomon Drowne now remarked that:

> our Wages were raised some time ago (in consequence of a Petition to Congress) to thirty Dollars per Month, or a Dollar per Day. The Pay wou'd be no Inducement to stay a moment in this shocking Place, at the Expense of Health, that best of Blessings. The Air of the whole City seems infected. In almost every street there is a horrid smell.[26]

THE ARMY IN CANADA: AGONY AT THE CEDARS, TROIS-RIVIÈRES, AND THE ISLE AUX NOIX

While Washington and the main army anxiously awaited the coming British attack at New York City, many held out hope in the summer of 1776 that the sickly force ostensibly commanded by Schuyler in the northern Lake Champlain country might still be able to do something about Canada. However, Schuyler's forces, at least since they had been driven from the walls of Québec in late 1775, had been exceedingly debilitated by smallpox, so much so that it made them militarily ineffective.

The role of smallpox during the campaign of 1776 deserves further investigation as it seemed to be constantly on the mind of commanders like Schuyler and Benedict Arnold. In fact, some historians have declared that smallpox had reached pandemic proportions in North America by 1775 and lasted throughout most of the war. Washington himself had been afflicted with a version of smallpox or "variola," as it was sometimes known, during a trip to Barbados with his half-brother Lawrence in 1751.

The disease itself had long been the great scourge of mankind, killing multitudes before a crude form of inoculation called "variolation" could be given to the uninitiated. Even then, doctors would sometimes release an infected soldier too early from quarantine or would botch the inoculation process. Early symptoms of the disease appeared to mimic influenza or "ague," as it was known then. After several days of high fever, the patient seemed to briefly rally only to relapse as the first "pustules" or smallpox sores "arose in the mouth, throat, and nasal passages. At this point the patient is contagious and would remain so for several weeks. Susceptible individuals risk their lives if they come near." In most cases, a rash soon envelops much of the body and "the soles of the feet, the palms of the hands, the face, forearms, neck, and back are focal points of the eruption. Elsewhere the distribution is lighter." Death usually occurs within "ten to sixteen days" of the onset of fever. Most soldiers remained contagious for upwards of thirty days, and the virus itself could remain active outside the human body for weeks on end. Thus, contact with affected floors of the hospitals where the soldiers were treated, clothing, bedding, and even the ground itself could often cause outbreaks long after the initial person affected had either died or slowly recovered. However, if a soldier was lucky enough to survive this dreaded disease, he was now immune for life.[27]

By February 15, 1776, Arnold thought that "Small-Pox at this Juncture" was going to cause "the entire ruin of the Army." When General John Thomas arrived to take command of the Canadian expedition in the first week of May 1776, "only 1900 American soldiers remained." John Thomas himself was to later succumb to the disease. It was noted that in their retreat from Québec, the "British rescued between two and five hundred men, nearly all in the throes of smallpox," who had been left behind or abandoned by their terrified comrades.[28]

During the spring of 1776, Dr. Lewis Beebe was a physician with the northern army. He noted on May 19, 1776, that Arnold had ordered the troops to be inoculated just a few days earlier. Upon arrival in camp, Beebe observed that this order was countermanded by General John Thomas, who announced "that it was death for any person to inoculate, and that every person [already] inoculated should be sent immediately to Montreal." Ominously, the next day, Beebe noted that John Thomas himself was beginning to show "symptoms of the small pox." By May 21, 1776, Beebe confirmed that John Thomas indeed had the disease. And true to form, a few days later, John Thomas felt well enough to "walk a half mile." However, as was typical of the disease, he would soon take an immediate turn for the worse. Beebe observed "large barns filled with men in the very height of the small pox." He noted that General John Thomas died on June 2, 1776, "the 13th day after the eruption first appeared."[29] Apparently not fond of General David Wooster, who temporarily took command upon the death of John Thomas, Beebe penned a short poem in his diary:

> Thomas is dead that pious man,
> Where all our hopes were laid.
> Had it been one, now in Command,
> My heart should not be greiv'd.[30]

Beebe was highly critical of most officers. When Arnold ordered Enoch Poor's regiment to reinforce the sick and dying men at Sorel, Québec, Beebe rather sarcastically complained in his journal that "there is not Ten men in the Regiment but what has either now got the small pox; or taken the infection. Some men love to command, however ridiculous their orders appear." Beebe lamented that "it is enough to confuse & distract a rational man to be Surg'n to a Reg't where nothing to be heard from morning to night, but Doct'r, Doct'r, Doct'r from every side 'till one is deaf, dumb & blind, and almost dead." Later, Beebe noted that Arnold was very busy "making experiments, upon the field officers and others," relieving some and placing others under arrest. Beebe "heartily wished some person would try and experiment upon [Arnold] and make the sun shine thro' his head with an ounce ball; and then see whether the rays come in a Direct or oblique direction."[31]

But Beebe was in for a worse shock when he was later sent with Poor's regiment to the Isle aux Noix in the Richelieu River in Canada, just over the present border with the United States. There he found "crowds of poor distressed creatures" infected with smallpox. He saw men "continually groaning & calling for relief, but in vain!" He noticed that several men "had large maggots, an inch long, Crawl out of their ears, were on almost every part of the body." Yet he admitted that at this point "in General [he could] effect greater cures with words than by medicine."[32]

Colonel Jeduthan Baldwin was one who decided that inoculation was a better risk than contracting the disease and allowed himself along with several other officers to be inoculated by a Dr. McKensey on May 17, 1776. Baldwin also noted at the same time that the "Army being very much neglected the supplies not being sent forward in season proper for the support of the army togeather with the distress ocationed by the spreading of Small pox in the army, & other distempers 2 thirds, were return'd unfit for Duty." He wrote that he heard "Col. Poors & Col. Porters Regt. Are retireing to St. Johns to fortify that place. If this is the case when none persues what may we expect when we are driven by the enemy."[33]

By May 23, the first signs of the pox appeared on Jeduthan Baldwin's forehead. He was able to describe his ordeal in detail and noted that he "had a hard pain in my head & knees." His "appetite and relish failed." As of May 28, he noticed "the Pox coming out thick." On June 6, he wrote that "I had a high fevour last night, my Boddy being all covered over with the pox, & an extreme fire and itching made me Very uncomfortable." In another week, Jeduthan Baldwin's smallpox was in remission, although he remained "covered in scales" and not fit to travel for several more days. On July 16, 1776, Baldwin lost most of his personal effects when he noticed that a chest that he kept in his tent had been broken open. The next day he reminded General Sullivan of his desire to resign as he was "heartily tired of this Retreating, Raged Starved, lousey, thievish, Pockey Army in this unhealthy Country." General Horatio Gates was later able to convince Baldwin to continue with the army a little longer by appealing to his sense of patriotism.[34]

Problems continued to plague the Canadian force throughout the late spring and summer of 1776. It was the same old story of disease and a deficiency of support. By early March, the patriot force had run out of money. Lacking hard currency, soldiers began to harass the local *habitants* with their muskets for the things that they needed to survive. The lack of specie also affected the ability of the Americans to recruit Canadians into the Continental army. Authorized to recruit two Canadian regiments, Colonel Moses Hazen and Lieutenant Colonel James Livingston were specifically tasked with this mission, and after weeks of trying "Hazen's regiment could muster fewer than 250 troops, slightly more than one-fourth of its authorized strength. Livingston's numbers were even smaller." In truth, without "hard money," there was little hope that Arnold and John Thomas could augment their pox-ridden army with Canadian recruits. Hence, the Americans slowly retreated southwestward up the St. Lawrence River before the forces of Canadian Governor General Guy Carleton, taking successive positions at Deschambault, Trois-Rivières (Three Rivers), Sorel, and St. Johns (at the head of the Richelieu River–Lake Champlain invasion corridor). To maintain a rear guard against a possible British foray from the Lake Ontario region, Arnold ordered Colonel Timothy Bedel and approximately four hundred New Hampshire soldiers to fortify a place known as "the Cedars."[35]

By mid-April, the first of several Continental regiments ordered north to the Canadian campaign arrived under the command of Brigadier General William Thompson. However, the lack of supplies now made these reinforcements more of a liability at present than anything else. Arnold told John Thomas that "men indeed we have, but almost every other requisite for war is wanting." Being at the end of winter, Arnold's main concern was to find enough food for this fresh influx of manpower. Moreover, the men coming from New York carelessly mingled with the northern pox-affected survivors of Québec and they soon were coming down with the dreaded disease by the hundreds.[36]

In early May, John Thomas tried one more attempt at taking Québec but found that smallpox had ravaged at least half of the two thousand troops he had at his disposal.

John Thomas, who would soon be dead from smallpox himself, had no choice but to retreat toward the American posts at Sorel and St. Johns. Meanwhile a three-hundred-men force of redcoats, Canadians, and Indians under the command of "Captain George Forster, of the 8th Regiment" took "dead aim" at possibly driving the Americans from Montréal. However, he first had to reduce Bedel's force at the Cedars. Unfortunately for the Americans, Bedel, without orders, left the Cedars and returned to Montréal after turning over his command to Major Isaac Butterfield. Moreover, many of the men at the Cedars also suffered from smallpox, including Major Butterfield. Apparently, the pro-American Caughnawaga Indians had warned Bedel of the approach of Forster's relief force. Rather than remain at his post, he had decided to personally return to Montréal to ask for reinforcements. To Continental Congress commissioners Charles Carroll and Samuel Chase, sent by Congress to help entice the Canadians toward the American cause (Carroll was a Roman Catholic from Maryland), they were incredulous at Bedel's apparent craven behavior. He appeared (to them) to be "disoriented and confused" and possibly still suffering from his own recent bout with smallpox. Forced by circumstance to take charge of a rapidly declining situation, Carroll and Chase informed Congress that "your commissioners who have neither abilities nor inclination, are constrained to act like generals." They quickly organized an emergency relief force under Major Henry Sherburne and had him march for the Cedars on May 17, 1776.[37]

Captain Forster's force reached the Cedars the next day, and he immediately besieged Butterfield's force inside their wooden stockade. Throughout the night of May 18, Indian warriors screamed blood-curdling war cries and soldiers fired their weapons at the fort. This activity had the effect of unnerving Butterfield, who, without having even a single man wounded (and not knowing that a relief force was on its way), surrendered the post to Forster in order possibly to save his men from being scalped by the Indians if they took the place by assault. By May 20, Sherburne's relief force approached the village of Quize Chiens and he also soon found himself attacked by Forster's force. Unlike Butterfield, however, Sherburne actually suffered twenty-eight casualties before he surrendered. Now even more aggressive thanks to their easy twin victories over substantial American forces, Forster's Indians quickly stripped and robbed Sherburne and his men of everything they possessed, including the clothing on their backs. The "physically imposing" Sherburne himself was "humiliatingly" forced to stand naked "before his captors until a French-speaking soldier took pity on him and draped a cape around his beefy body." However, since the Indians took the pox-infected clothing of Butterfield's and Sherburne's soldiers, they likely carried the virus deep into the Great Lakes country and unwittingly infected unexposed tribes further west. In just two days, Forster and his pick up force of redcoats, Canadians, and Indians had captured more than five hundred American soldiers with little or no loss to themselves. While Arnold later gave chase to the British column now burdened with controlling their huge haul of captives, Forster was able to keep Arnold at bay by threatening to allow his Indians to kill his captives if the rescue force pressed him too hard. At a "council of war," Arnold's own officers opposed his plan to continue to attack Forster's column.[38]

At 2:00 A.M. on May 27, Major Sherburne and Captain Andrew Parke suddenly appeared out of the darkness and presented to Arnold their captors' terms that once again reiterated the threat of unleashing the Indians on the prisoners of war (POWs) and included a clause that offered a prisoner exchange of an equal number of British troops in American hands. The major exception in this document was that the terms would not allow the American repatriates to fight again in the war, whereas the same rule did not

A view of St. Johns, upon the River Sorell, with the redoubts and works, 1776. (*Courtesy of the Library of Congress*)

apply to the released British prisoners. Arnold flat out refused to agree to these unequal terms and bluntly told Forster that "if our prisoners were murdered," he would order his men to "sacrifice every soul who fell into our hands." Unsure that he could continue to control his own Indian allies, Forster eventually agreed to an equal exchange of prisoners. Arnold had successfully called his bluff.[39]

After the death of John Thomas, a second wave of reinforcements led by Major General John Sullivan arrived from New York City. Upon arrival at St. Johns, Sullivan, as senior officer, immediately assumed command. Instead of retreating, Sullivan rather arrogantly went on the offensive and ordered Brigadier General William Thompson and his initial contingent of two thousand soldiers to secure Trois-Rivières. Unfortunately for Thompson, the town was strongly defended with British reinforcements under the overall command of British Major General John Burgoyne, who now outnumbered Thompson's assault force at Trois-Rivières by more than 3 to 1. As expected, Trois-Rivières became another bloody debacle in a long line of disasters that seemed to mark American efforts to seize Canada. Losing more than four hundred men, Thompson himself was captured. The shattered American forces fled back toward St. Johns. Arnold admitted that "the junction of the Canadians with the colonies—an object that brought us into this country—is now at an end." He convinced Sullivan that he has no other choice but to retreat back toward northern Lake Champlain. The Americans abandoned Sorel, burned Fort Chambly, and retreated south of St. Johns. Arnold and Sullivan were now focused on moving the large number of disease-ridden troops to Isle aux Noix (just north of the present-day border between Canada and New York state). In some cases, according to Jeduthan Baldwin, the men were simply abandoned by their officers.[40]

An "Island of Death"

If any place could be truly called an island of death, it was the Isle aux Noix. Hundreds of sick and dispirited soldiers were temporarily deposited there during the retreat. Soon, mass graves were being dug by those still healthy enough to lift a shovel.

Many of the dead had been some of the most recent arrivals under Thompson and Sullivan. It was estimated that three-fourths of the New England troops had never been exposed to smallpox. However, when they arrived at Sorel and personally witnessed the devastation of the disease on the soldiers who had been at camp, for awhile many of them, contrary to orders, practiced self-inoculation. "Québec veteran" John Joseph Henry stated that "great numbers of the soldiers inoculated themselves . . . by laceration under the finger nails by means of pins or needles." No one wanted to contract the disease in "the natural way." Within days, Sullivan sent bateaux to the Isle to transport his surviving soldiers back down Lake Champlain. The campaign for Canada was truly over.[41]

However, the fight to control further outbreaks of smallpox continued. Major General Horatio Gates, who had come north to take over from General Sullivan, ordered all infected men to quarantine themselves on the west shore of Lake Champlain and "by no Means to Stop at Tyconderoga or at any house on the East Side of Lake Champlain." Soldiers who exhibited any symptoms of the disease "had to swear solemnly by the Ever Living God" to General Horatio Gates, who was fearful that his men were still practicing self-inoculation, that they had not practiced self-induced variolation. This methodology of quarantine must have worked, since by mid-July 1776, smallpox outbreaks among the soldiery began to rapidly abate.[42]

DISASTER AT NEW YORK

Although Howe had landed nine thousand troops on Staten Island in late June 1776, he awaited further reinforcements before taking on Washington's fortifications on Long Island and Manhattan. He would soon receive his first installment of "Hessians" hired by George III from German princes anxious to improve their treasuries. In order to offset the growing British buildup in the region, Congress authorized on June 3, 1776, the creation of a "Flying Camp" of ten thousand militiamen from New Jersey to Maryland. A further 13,500 were ordered by Congress to reinforce Washington in New York City. However, by late July, the Flying Camp, commanded by Brigadier General Hugh Mercer, had only three thousand men on hand instead of the required ten thousand. Many had remained behind to harvest summer crops instead of reporting for duty with the militia. In Hunterdon County, New Jersey, for example, militiamen attacked their colonel and captains with clubs rather than be forced to leave their crops to rot while they waited on Howe to attack.[43]

By August 22, 1776, Howe was finally ready to move and began landing fifteen thousand troops at Gravesend, on the western tip of Long Island. Washington had about nine thousand men on Long Island to initially oppose Howe. He had decided to defend the Heights of Guana, a wooded ridgeline that roughly parallels the north shore of Long Island itself. The heights were rocky, steep, and heavily wooded, thus making it an ideal location for the Americans to fight their war of posts. However, the heights extended for nearly ten miles and there were four distinct "passes" through this natural barrier. This forced Washington to stretch his Long Island forces fairly thin. Three of the passes— Gowanus, Flatbush, and Bedford—were fairly well defended. The fourth pass, Jamaica, had been largely forgotten by the inexperienced Americans. General Henry Clinton proposed to Howe to take the majority of British forces on an envelopment march and force the Jamaica pass while Howe demonstrated with the rest of his force in front of the American lines. Anxious to avoid another Bunker Hill, Howe readily agreed.

Clinton, who in his youth had lived in New York for a time, took about ten thousand men on a sweeping end run of the entire American line and was able to capture the few

American scouts sent to observe the pass. He had neatly turned the entire American flank. To make matters worse, the demonstration troops under British Major General James Grant had also nearly simultaneously forced the Gowanus Pass, and by the late morning of August 27, American troops under Generals John Sullivan (now returned from Canada) and Lord Stirling were in full treat toward Brooklyn Heights. In order to hold the British back, Stirling sacrificed his elite Maryland Continentals commanded by William Smallwood. Sullivan and Stirling were forced to surrender, and they had more than two hundred men killed and nine hundred troops captured by the British by early afternoon.

One of the soldiers sent over to reinforce Sullivan's men on Long Island was Connecticut "levy" Joseph Plumb Martin. The engagement on Long Island was Martin's first combat action, and rather than being afraid, the fifteen-year-old soldier wrote that he felt a sense of elation when an officer pointed him out as an example of how to behave as a battle approached. Martin observed soon after landing, the first casualties coming back from the firing line. While waiting for orders, he wrote disgustedly of a lieutenant who "ran round among the men of his company, sniveling and blubbering, praying each one if he had aught against him, or if *he* had injured anyone that they would forgive him. . . . A fine soldier you are, thought I." Martin remembered that he would have rather died than behave as this officer did. He also noticed the officers tearing the various cockades of rank from their hats before going into action. They did this out of fear of being shot by British sharpshooters. His unit arrived at the edge of Gowanus Creek in time to witness the Marylanders emerging from the water. He noted that those who survived looked:

> like water rats, it was a truly pitiful sight. Many of them were killed in the pond, and more were drowned. Some of us went into the water after the fall of the tide, and took out a number of corpses and a great many arms that were sunk in the pond and creek.[44]

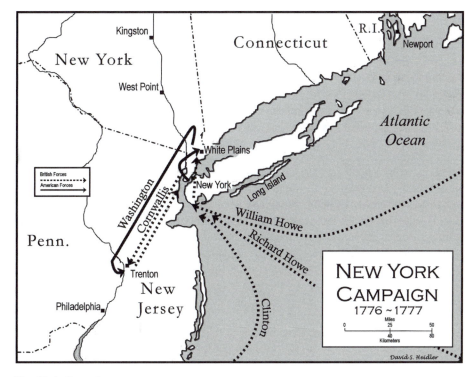

New York Campaign

Fortunately for the Americans now penned up on Brooklyn Heights with their backs to the East River, contrary winds kept the British navy from sailing up the river and sealing their fate. On the evening of August 29, Washington held a Council of War and made a determination to retreat to Manhattan. Ordering flat barges and boats to Brooklyn, Washington was fortunate to have a regiment of Marblehead fishermen under Massachusetts Colonel John Glover available to man the boats. However, the wind that kept the British out of the East River also threatened to blow the retreating American boats right into their midst. Nonetheless, the withdrawal went as well as could be expected, and thanks to an early morning fog and the strong backs of Glover's oarsmen, on August 30, Washington had been able to pull off a miracle retreat to Manhattan.

About two weeks later, Howe successfully used his naval superiority and once again outflanked Washington's lines by landing at the nearly undefended Kip's Bay near present-day 34th Street on Manhattan. Martin's unit was also there, and he described being raked by British naval gunfire as he and his mates fled toward the northern end of Manhattan Island. He bitterly recalled being stopped in the road by an officer and a sentinel assigned to stem the rout. After the officer left, Martin and his comrade were able to slip by the sentinel and rejoin their unit.

Howe continued to press northward, and Washington fought another engagement at Harlem Heights on September 16. Here, however, Washington fared somewhat better. The fight started between the British light infantry and a group of American rangers led by Lieutenant Colonel Thomas Knowlton, who had earlier distinguished himself at Bunker Hill. While the gallant Knowlton and his men were driven in to their main line by the stronger British force, Washington's aide, Colonel Joseph Reed, noted that the pursuing British and Hessians sounded their bugles "as is usual after a fox chase."[45] This act made Reed especially angry and he urged Washington to attack them with a force larger than Knowlton's. Demonstrating in front of the exultant British with Colonel John Nixon's Massachusetts brigade, Washington sent Knowlton's rangers on a flanking maneuver to get into their rear. The plan worked perfectly and the British were forced to retreat to the cover of their naval frigates in the Hudson River. Unfortunately, the enterprising Knowlton was killed during the action, but the check bought Washington more time to safely continue his retreat into Westchester County, New York.

Martin and his unit, once again, found themselves in the center of action. In his diary, Martin extensively recounted the post–Harlem Heights court-martial of a popular Connecticut Sergeant named Ebenezer Leffingwell. This seemingly minor affair had a significant impact on the soldiery at large. Apparently, Leffingwell had been arrested by Washington's adjutant, Colonel Joseph Reed of Pennsylvania, who witnessed the Sergeant leaving the ranks at Harlem Heights. Leffingwell argued with Reed to no avail that he had been ordered by his officers to leave the ranks to find a supply of ammunition. Reed did not believe him and had the sergeant convicted of cowardice and sentenced to be shot. However, Martin and most of the rest of the soldiers believed Leffingwell's side of the story. Wisely, Washington issued a gallows reprieve for Leffingwell on the same day as Nathan Hale was hanged in Manhattan. Martin stated that the reprieve was fortunate because the troops showed "what their feelings were by their lively and repeated cheerings after the reprieve, but more so by their secret and open threats before it."[46]

On September 21, a major fire broke out in Manhattan, allegedly set by American incendiaries. It apparently started in the southern portion of the town near the White Hall pier around 2:00 A.M. The *New York Mercury* newspaper noted that since the retreating Americans had carried off all the bells in the town, there was no effective way to sound the alarm to fight the fire. The newspaper noted that:

> the fire raged with inconceivable violence, and in its destructive progress swept away all the buildings between Broad street and the North River [the Hudson], almost as high as the City Hall; and from thence, all the houses between Broadway and the North River, as far as King's College [Columbia], a few only excepted.

The venerable Trinity Church with its 140-foot steeple became a towering inferno. The *Mercury* editors alleged that several rebels had been caught with "large bundles of matches, dipped in melted rosin and brimstone." Hundreds of British soldiers and sailors were rowed ashore to aid in putting out the fire which was brought under control the next day.[47]

Howe directly accused his opponent Washington of having ordered the fire set, and there was no direct evidence that this charge was true, although Washington had previously admitted to his cousin, Lund Washington, that he had earlier asked Congress permission to fire the town if he was forced to retreat, but they had denied his request. Washington told Congress President John Hancock that the fire had been "an accident." Most likely, retreating soldiers acting on their own volition, set the city buildings ablaze.

Unfortunately for an intrepid American officer named Nathan Hale, he had been asked by his commanding officer, Lieutenant Colonel Thomas Knowlton, just prior to the fire to venture behind British lines disguised as an out-of-work school teacher and possibly learn of Howe's next objective. It was a poorly planned mission from start to finish, and Hale was quickly seized soon after he landed on Manhattan. Caught red-handed with military intelligence, Howe, in his anger over the fire, ordered that Hale be

Several buildings along the street engulfed in flames during the New York fire on September 19, 1776. Citizens were beaten by redcoats and African slaves looted. (*Courtesy of the Library of Congress*)

immediately hanged without the benefit of a court-martial—a significant departure from eighteenth-century military protocol. Moreover, they denied him the benefit of clergy and left Hale's body to hang as a deterrent to other nearby rebels who might also be in Washington's intelligence service. While it is still debated whether Hale actually uttered his famous gallows epitaph, British Major John Montresor, in whose tent Hale was confined on the eve of his execution, noted that upon the scaffold, Hale stated that: "I only regret that I have but one life to lose for my country."[48] The Yale-educated Hale was clearly paraphrasing a line from Joseph Addison's *Cato*, and the British officers in attendance noted his calm and courageous demeanor as he faced his end. Although the British steadfastly claimed that Hale had been hanged for his alleged role in the fire, the evidence surrounding his mission suggests otherwise, since Hale had been ordered to initially scout Long Island before entering the city. If his mission had been to burn the town, he would have likely not have been sent to Long Island at all.

Private Joseph Plumb Martin observed that during the retreat from Manhattan, starvation and nakedness returned as constant companions for the army. Martin noted that at one point all he had to eat was a "sheep's head," which he had begged from some butchers who were carving the animal up for an officer's meal. Foraging in a farmer's field for some "English turnips," Martin and some of his friends were surprised by the landowner. They made a deal with the farmer and stated that they would help him pull up the turnips free of charge if they could keep the turnip tops to eat. Not having any other available labor handy, the farmer readily agreed to this bargain. After the farmer left, however, Martin stated that "we had pulled and cut as many as we wanted, we packed them up and decamped, leaving the owner of the turnips to pull his share himself."[49]

By late October 1776, Howe, in cooperation with his brother Admiral Richard Howe, using his sea lanes of communication once again, outflanked Washington's lines near White Plains, New York, and, after a short sharp engagement at Chatterton's Hill, forced the Continental army to continue its retreat. During the retreat, American soldiers, to the disgust of Washington, also set fire to the village of White Plains. Martin noted the growing despondency of the soldiers and commented that he had caught a violent cold as a result of standing in trenches with standing water. He observed that immediately following the battle he had nothing to eat but "some boiled hog's flesh (it was not pork) and turnips, without bread or salt." Martin's situation immediately after the battle was not unusual. Combat nearly always disrupted the rickety American supply system and sometimes it was several days after an action before it could be efficiently restored. Martin was sent with the sick to Norwalk, Connecticut, to act as a nurse for the more seriously ill. He wrote that he remained with the army surgeons, "moving from place to place as the occasion required, undergoing hunger, cold, and fatigue until the 25th day of December, 1776," whereupon "his time being up" he received his discharge. He felt he had learned much in his six months as a soldier, and although he had several offers to reenlist, he declined and went home (for the time being) to his grandparents' farm.[50]

The Fall of Fort Washington and Fort Lee

There was to be one final humiliating scene for the American army in what was clearly turning out to be a debacle for Washington and his soldiers in late 1776. While Putnam had attempted to sink obstructions in the Hudson River, his efforts had been largely unsuccessful. Thus, Washington wanted to evacuate his last strongpoint on the east bank of the Hudson before the British could use their ships to once again wreak havoc on the American east bank defenses. Following the battle of White Plains, Washington had successfully crossed the bulk of his army to the west bank opposite Peekskill, New York. Major General Charles Lee was sent with seven thousand Continentals to occupy Fort Lee nearly directly across the river from Fort Washington. It was thought the forts and the obstructions would impede British ships from sailing further up the Hudson. They did not. However, Washington was talked out of evacuation by his normally astute subordinate Nathanael Greene. Greene wrongly believed that the garrison under Colonel Robert Magaw was in little danger and that "the men can be brought off at any time." It was not a good sign that Magaw's own adjutant William Demont had deserted to the British just two weeks earlier. As a result of key intelligence the British had conveniently received from Demont, Howe was determined to seize Fort Washington and capture or kill the Americans defending it and sent Magaw an ultimatum that within two hours, he must surrender Fort Washington "*at discretion*, or every man being put to the sword." Greene ordered Magaw to defend the place, and Magaw informed Howe he was prepared to defend the fort to the last man.[51]

Greene had recently reinforced the garrison to about 2800 men. Still, this was not enough to defend the various outworks, trench lines, and strong points in and about Fort Washington. It was a job better suited for a much larger force, and in the early daylight hours of November 16, in a coordinated attack using the Hessians as his main assault force, Howe's army stormed the American works. It was during this assault that American Margaret Corbin allegedly took her fallen mate's place as a cannoneer. During the fight, Corbin was wounded in the shoulder. Forcing the Americans to crowd into the main fort and actually trapping a number outside against the fort walls, the Hessians gave Magaw thirty minutes to surrender. In order to avoid having his men brutally bayoneted, Magaw decided to surrender the garrison to Hessian General Wilhelm Van Knyphausen. Lieutenant Frederick MacKenzie witnessed the Americans as they filed out of the fort and noted the run down and unimposing appearance of the new POWs. He stated that "few of them appeared to have a second shirt, nor did they appear to have washed themselves during the campaign. A great many of them were lads under fifteen and old men, and few had the appearance of soldiers. Their odd figures frequently excited the laughter of our soldiers." Washington, Lee, and Greene bitterly observed the surrender from the opposite shore. Many of Magaw's men ended up in the disease-ridden jails of New York City or onboard the notoriously lethal prison hulks the British had reserved for them. Quite a few of them had been bayoneted by the charging Hessians during the assault on the outer works of the fort.

Sixteen-year-old John Adlum of York, Pennsylvania, was one of the POWs. Not knowing when he would get his next meal, he cut the lining of his coat open and "filled the skirts with from a peck [to] a half bushel of biscuit and I advised my companions to do the same." As Adlum and his mates were being marched off, he bitterly recalled how they were abused by the locals and noted that very few "seemed to sympathize with us, but numbers were disposed to say ill-natured things to us by saying that we ought to be or would be hanged and called up by opprobrious names of rebel with a damn added to it by some." As the POWs were marched into the city, the abuse increased, especially as they passed by the "Holy Ground Ladies" or women attached to the Hessian regiments. Many believed that Washington's entire army had been captured and repeatedly asked the soldiers, "Which is Washington? Where is he?"[52]

Howe quickly followed up his success at Fort Washington and launched an attack four days later against Fort Lee on the opposite shore. Guided by loyalists and using a little-known and unguarded landing spot on the west bank, Washington was unaware of the danger to Fort Lee until the British were nearly upon the fort. Thus, instead of an orderly planned withdrawal, the Americans precipitously abandoned the fort with the loss of all their guns, baggage, and material. Allegedly, the British stormed the now empty fort only to discover the American camp kettles boiling over onto their fires. Greene noted in a letter to Nicholas Cooke that:

> about Ninety or a hundred Prisoners were taken [by the British] but these were a set of rascals that Skulkt out of the way, for fear of fighting. The Troops at Ft. Lee were mostly of the Flying Camp—irregular and undisciplined. Had they obeyed orders not a man would have been taken.[53]

With more than 2600 men captured, hundreds of cannon and stands of arms, and, more importantly, crucial camp and military stores, the twin losses of Forts Washington and Lee were hammer blows to the American cause. It was a hard end to the campaign.

The Crisis

By the end of November 1776, Washington privately wrote to a kinsman that he believed "that the game is pretty near up." Never able to get an accurate account of his army strength, he nonetheless estimated for Congress that he would soon be left with a mere handful of men by January 1. In reality, he was soon down to just more than two thousand men and the notoriously unreliable militia was soon departing by companies as quickly as possible. The situation for the army was even more desperate than the previous December when the Connecticut troops had marched for home. To make matters worse, during the retreat across New Jersey and despite continued entreaties from Washington for his forces to join the main army, a dilatory Charles Lee foolishly allowed himself to be captured by British dragoons (members of his former regiment in the British army) near Basking Ridge, New Jersey. Moreover, the New Jersey militia failed to turn out and members of the "Flying Camp" of militiamen formed during the summer of 1776 enlistments were expiring, soon to be followed by many of the "continental" regiments formed for a single calendar year in January 1776. Washington wrote to Congress on December 12, 1776, and bluntly stated that he feared for the survival of the rebellion:

> Perhaps Congress have some hope and prospect of reinforcements; I have no intelligence of the sort and wish to be informed on the subject. Our little handful is daily decreasing by sickness and other causes, and without considerable succors and exertions on the part of the people, what can we reasonably look for or expect, but an event that will be severely felt by the common cause . . . the loss of Philadelphia.[54]

During the retreat across New Jersey, Washington's rapidly shrinking army grew weaker by the day. In their haste to get away from the British and Hessians, the soldiers had been forced to burn their tents, lost accoutrements such as canteens and haversacks and were literally left with the clothes on their backs and perhaps a wool blanket.

Soldiers began to take from the local population anything that came to hand. Greene, in a letter to his wife on December 4, noted that the soldiers were so desperate that "their footsteps are markt with destruction wherever they go. There is no difference made between the Whigs and Tories—all fare alike. They take the Cloaths off of the Peoples back. The distress they spread wherever they go exceeds all description."[55]

Washington now endeavored to place the Delaware River between the British and his rapidly dwindling forces. The artist Charles Willson Peale, a lieutenant in the Pennsylvania forces, observed the early December night crossing with some trepidation. He noted that it was the most hellish scene I ever beheld. All the shores were lighted up with huge fires, boats continually passing and repassing, full of men, horses, artillery and camp equipage. . . . The Hollowing of hundreds of men in their difficulties of getting Horses and artillery out of the boats, made it rather the appearance of Hell than any earthly scene.

While watching, Peale was met by his own brother James, who had earlier enlisted as a junior officer in Smallwood's Maryland regiment that had suffered so greatly during the New York campaign. He was virtually unrecognizable and Peale noted that his brother had lost all his clothes and was able to cover himself with a single dirty blanket.[56]

By December 8, Washington had conclusively lost the state of New Jersey, and on this same day, General Henry Clinton, with a force of British and Hessian assault troops, seized Rhode Island and the city of Newport without a fight—the third colony to fall to the British in just four months. Thomas Paine had not exaggerated when he wrote the political tract, *The Crisis*, during the dark days of December 1776. These were indeed "times that try men's souls." Paine first published the tract on December 19. He purposely only charged 2 pennies to recoup the cost of publication so that it could be widely distributed to one and all during this critical moment in the war. Soon it was being read at nearly every army campfire and had a very positive effect on army morale. As historian David Hackett Fischer noted, *The Crisis* "was more than an exhortation. It was program for action." It laid out in detail exactly what was expected of the country in order to rebuild its failing army. Paine called for a revival of spirit, and for the most part, the country responded.

VICTORY AT TRENTON AND PRINCETON

With the approach of winter and Howe and his redcoats clearly gaining the upper hand over Washington and his hapless Continental army, the British decided to go into winter cantonments. Unfortunately, Washington and his men were forced to stay mostly outdoors without much in the way of covering since they had lost much of their camp equipage in the retreat across New Jersey. Captain Enoch Anderson's Delaware troops solved this problem by lying in the leaves "with [their] feet to the fire." He noted that "we had nothing to cook with but our ramrods, which we run through a piece of meat and roasted it over the fire, and to hungry soldiers it tasted sweet." Sergeant Joseph White of the Massachusetts artillery was a bit luckier than Anderson. He was billeted in the back of a Bucks County tavern along with some of his battery mates, and they believed that they would soon be able to at least get some warm food. However, to his consternation, White noted that the tavernkeeper "refused to take rebel money, as he called it." White decided to elevate this disagreement to higher headquarters and informed General Putnam about the situation. Putnam replied that if the tavernkeeper would not take Continental money, then the soldiers were authorized to take whatever they wanted without payment. The stubborn tavernkeeper refused to give in, and White and his mates soon looted his back storeroom. However, White was thoughtful enough to send Putnam a portion of their ill-gotten gains, which the general received "with thanks."[57]

As the end of the year approached, the Pennsylvania militia did not turn out as expected and only sent about 1200 men to reinforce Washington. Nearby Bucks County added another two hundred, but other than that no more men appeared to be coming from the state. Many patriot leaders in Philadelphia, Pennsylvania, were absolutely incredulous at this turn of events. Congress even left town and resided for awhile in the town of Baltimore, Maryland.

By December 23, Washington recognized that he must do something with the few forces that he had or risk it withering away by the New Year. Member of Congress Benjamin Rush visited Washington's headquarters and observed the commander in chief doodling on a piece of paper, which fell to the floor. He noted that he had written on it, "Victory or Death." Rush believed that Washington had an attack in mind. Indeed that same day, Washington ordered his soldiers to cook rations for three days—a sure sign of impending action. He intended to attack a detachment of about one thousand Hessians at Trenton, New Jersey, under the command of Colonel Johann Rall. He would use "victory or death" as his countersign. However, Rall had little regard for the Americans he had seen so easily beaten at New York and referred to them as "country clowns." His disrespect was so great that he did not even bother to build defenses and used two of the six cannons at his disposal as ornaments for his headquarters—one on each side of the entryway. It was to be a fatal mistake on his part.

Washington crossed with the main body of the army at McConkey's Ferry, about ten miles above Trenton and sent another small force under Philadelphia Colonel John Cadwalader toward Burlington, New Jersey, to keep other Hessians at nearby Bordentown from coming to Rall's assistance. Washington ordered the infantry to cross the river in the strictest silence and stated that once across, it was death for any man to leave the ranks for any reason. The officers were ordered to have white paper fixed into their hat bands for easier recognition as Washington hoped to launch a predawn attack on the Hessians. However, owing to the fog and friction of war and perhaps the bitterly cold, wet blustery night of December 25, 1776, the army quickly fell behind schedule. Washington had also ordered a central crossing of about eight hundred Pennsylvania militia nearer the town of Trenton, but this operation failed because of huge chunks of floating pack ice piling up just below Trenton Falls. The jagged broken ice made it impossible for either boats or foot-traffic to cross the river at that particular point. Although Cadwalader's men did not have to face an ice jam, the river was so turbulent that he was forced to cross his men further south at Dunk's ferry. However, no sooner had they had crossed the now extremely choppy river than Cadwalader made the decision to return his force to the Pennsylvania shore. It was even more difficult getting back across the river. Thus, by the early morning hours of December 26, two of the three prongs Washington had envisioned attacking the Hessians were still on the Pennsylvania side of the river. Only the force that crossed at McConkey's Ferry seemed to have met with any success. Using big "Durham Boats" that carried cargo and ore from the nearby Durham Iron Works, the troops and equipment, including fourteen pieces of Henry Knox's artillery, were slowly ferried across the river. In reality, the army put men and equipment in just about anything that floated. Again, John Glover's Marblehead fishermen and numerous Philadelphia maritime workers, longshoremen, and river pilots manned the oars of the boats. They would be rowing nearly all night long. Nonetheless, Washington was at least three hours behind schedule.

Washington was finally on the march on the Jersey side by 4:00 A.M. However, it was clear that his plans of a predawn attack had been dashed by the ice and weather. Using local New Jersey militia as guides, Washington's men struggled toward Trenton in a heavy sleet, snow, rain mix combined with a bitterly cold wind. The route was slippery and treacherous especially as the men crossed the steep ravine leading over Jacob's Creek. Here they had to use up more precious time unhitching the artillery pieces and using drag lines to lower them to the creek and then manhandle them up the other side. It was brutal work. As the men approached the town and began to form up for the attack, Washington rode along the lines and quietly encouraged the men to keep by their officers.

General George Washington standing with a group of soldiers looking at the flags captured from the British during the Battle of Trenton. (*Courtesy of the Library of Congress*)

At slightly past 8:00 A.M., Washington's tired, frozen columns began their attack. To his amazement, he had achieved nearly complete surprise as the Hessians tumbled out of their bunks and tried to make a stand. However, surprise was certainly not a fore- gone conclusion. Incredibly, during the march to Trenton and just about thirty minutes prior to beginning the actual attack, Washington was informed of the approach of about fifty men who appeared to be coming from the town. Thinking that the vital element of surprise had been lost, Washington rode forward to see who these men were, only to shockingly discover they were an element of Adam Stephen's 4th Virginia regiment being led by a Captain George Wallis. In Washington's mind, these men had no earthly reason to be where they were at that particular time. Apparently, Wallis and his men had been ordered by Stephen to take a party across the river to avenge an earlier shooting death of one of the Virginians by a Hessian sharpshooter on the opposite shore. Wallis chose the night of December 25, the same one as his commander in chief, to retaliate against the Hessians. It apparently never occurred to Stephen that this action gravely jeopardized the operational security of the entire Continental army. Most likely, he casually gave the order to Wallis and simply believed that at some point, the revenge attack would take place and in the meantime got caught up in the planning for the Trenton operation. Needless to say, Washington was furious with Stephen, who had earlier served with him during the French and Indian War and did not have an exactly sterling reputation as a military commander. Nonetheless, Washington was determined to press on toward the nearby town of Trenton and launch his attack at all costs.[58]

At Trenton, the American regiments attacked on a dead run and quickly overran the few outposts that Rall had ordered as security outside the confines of the town. Another wing under New Hampshire General John Stark closed the trap from the other side of town. It was soon all over. Rall had been mortally wounded and had surrendered his garrison of more than nine hundred soldiers. The Americans did not lose a man in the engagement—in all, it was an incredible feat of arms and the victory came precisely at the lowest ebb in the war for the patriot cause. With the weather worsening, Washington later recrossed the river that same day and immediately made plans for how he was going to field an army after New Year's Day.

In sum, and despite the last-minute heroics of Washington and the Continental army, the year 1776 had been nothing short of disastrous for the American cause. While Boston had been liberated and independence declared, the war was not going especially well for the patriots. Washington had been literally driven out of New York City and its environs, and the loss of the entire state of New Jersey soon followed. Nearly simultaneous to Washington's defeat at New York, the pox-ridden American army that had attempted to seize Canada crawled back to Fort Ticonderoga and was now awaiting the next move by the British in the Lake Champlain region. But help was clearly on the way. Congress and Washington would raise a new model army in 1777, one based on long-termed enlistments. However, it remained to be seen whether recruiting officers could find enough men to fill out the eighty-eight battalion force (plus sixteen additional regiments) that was ordered by Congress in September 1776. State governments needed to reorganize their lines, and these units would have to be placed into brigades and divisions commanded by competent officers. Nonetheless, despite the losses incurred during the retreat across New Jersey, the men remained hopeful. Just ten days before the battle of Trenton, twenty-three-year-old Lieutenant Colonel Samuel Blachley Webb of Connecticut and aide de camp to the commander in chief noted in a response to letter from Joseph Trumbull about the state of the army after the fall of 1776 that:

> It has been the Devil, but is to appearance better. About 2,000 of us have been obliged to run damn'd hard before 10,000 of the enemy. Never was finer lads at a retreat than we are. . . . No fun for us that I can see; however, I cannot but think we shall drub the dogs.[59]

It was this sort of optimistic attitude that enabled Washington to turn the tide at Trenton and Princeton.

NOTES

1. John C. Fitzpatrick, ed., *The Writings of George Washington*, vol. 4 (Westport, CT: Greenwood Press, 1931), 202.

2. Robert K. Wright Jr., *The Continental Army* (Washington, DC: Center of Military History, 1986), 39–40, 47.

3. Ibid., 39–40, 51.

4. Wright Jr., *The Continental Army*, 48.

5. Ibid., 48–49.

6. James Kirby Martin, ed., *Ordinary Courage: The Revolutionary War Adventures of Joseph Plumb Martin*. 2nd ed. (St. James, NY: Brandywine Press, 1999), 13.

7. Martin, *Ordinary Courage*, 13–15.

8. Jeanette D. Black and William Greene Roelker, eds., *A Rhode Island Chaplain in the Revolution: The Letters of Ebenezer David to Nicholas Brown, 1775–1778* (Port Washington, NY: Kennikat Press, 1949), 20–21.

9. David McCullough, *1776* (New York: Simon & Schuster, 2005), 117–18; Lee, quoted in McCullough, 118; John C. Fitzpatrick, ed., *The Writings of George Washington*, vol. 6 (Westport, CT: Greenwood Press), 28.

10. Louise Rau, ed., "Sergeant John Smith's Diary of 1776," in *The Mississippi Valley Historical Review*, vol. XX, June 1933–March 1934, 249–52.

11. Ibid., 252.

12. Fitzpatrick, *The Writings of George Washington*, vol. 4, 512–13, 526, 536, 537; Richard K. Showman, ed., *The Papers of Nathanael Greene, Vol. 1, December 1766 to December 1776* (Chapel Hill, NC: University of North Carolina Press, 1976) "General Orders," May 2, 1776, 211, Greene *Papers*, "General Orders," May 5, 1776, 212.

13. "Loammi Baldwin letter to his wife, 17 June 1776," quoted in Douglas Southall Freeman, *George Washington: A Biography*, vol. 4 (New York: Charles Scribner's Sons, 1951), 85.

14. Journal entry, April 25, 1776, in *Journal of Lieutenant Isaac Bangs, April 1 to July 29, 1776* (New York: New York Times & Arno Press, 1968), 29.

15. "General Orders," May 18, 1776, Greene *Papers*, 213–14.

16. George Washington, quoted in George F. Scheer and Hugh F. Rankin, *Rebels & Redcoats: The American Revolution Through the Eyes of Those Who Fought and Lived It* (New York: Da Capo Press, 1957), 146–47.

17. Quoted in Barnet Schecter, *The Battle for New York* (New York: Penguin Books, 2002), 90.

18. Freeman, *George Washington*, vol. 4, 115–19; Peter T. Curtenius to Richard Varick, June 22, 1776, and Solomon Drowne, MD, to Miss Sally Drowne, June 24, 1776, in *New York City During the American Revolution* (New York: Mercantile Library Association of New York City, 1861), 66–69.

19. Freeman, *George Washington*, vol. 4, 120.

20. Peter Elting to Richard Varick, June 13, 1776, in *New York City During the American Revolution*, 97.

21. Dr. Solomon Drowne to Solomon Drowne Sr., June 17, 1776, Solomon Drowne to William Drowne, July 13, 1776, in *New York City During the American Revolution*, 79–80, 98–99.

22. Lieutenant Isaac Bangs, "Journal," in New Jersey Historical Society, *Proceedings*, VIII (1856–1859), 125.

23. Schecter, *The Battle for New York*, 102–3.

24. Alexander Graydon to John Lardner, July 18, 1776, quoted in Scheer and Rankin, *Rebels & Redcoats*, 155.

25. Solomon Drowne to Sally Drowne, July 13, 1776, 100–1.

26. Peter Elting to Richard Varick, July 30, 1776, and Solomon Drowne to Solomon Drowne Sr., August 9, 1776, in *New York City During the American Revolution*, 103–5.

27. Elizabeth Anne Fenn, *Pox Americana: The Great Smallpox Epidemic of 1775–82* (New York: Hill & Wang, 2001), 15–20.

28. Fenn, *Pox Americana*, 67–68.

29. Journal entries, May 19, 1776, May 21, 1776, May 23, 1776, June 2, 1776, in *Journal of Lewis Beebe* (New York: New York Times & Arno Press, 1971), 328–32.

30. Beebe *Journal*, 332.

31. Ibid., 333, 341–42.

32. Ibid., 336.

33. Journal entries, May 17, 1776, May 22, 1776, in *The Revolutionary Journal of Colonel Jeduthan Baldwin, 1775–1778* (Bangor, ME: The De Bernians, 1906), 43, 45.

34. Baldwin *Journal*, 59–60.

35. James Kirby Martin, *Benedict Arnold, Revolutionary Hero: An American Warrior Reconsidered* (New York: New York University Press, 1997), 194, 200–4.

36. Benedict Arnold to John Thomas, quoted in Martin, *Benedict Arnold, Revolutionary Hero*, 207–8.

37. Fenn, *Pox Americana*, 73; James Kirby Martin, *Benedict Arnold, Revolutionary Hero*, 208–10; Carroll and Chase, quoted in Martin, *Benedict Arnold, Revolutionary Hero*, 210.

38. Fenn, *Pox Americana*, 74; Martin, *Benedict Arnold, Revolutionary Hero*, 210–2.

39. Benedict Arnold quoted in Martin, *Benedict Arnold, Revolutionary Hero*, 214.

40. Martin, *Benedict Arnold, Revolutionary Hero*, 217–8; Benedict Arnold quoted in Martin, *Benedict Arnold, Revolutionary Hero*, 218; Journal entry, 16 June 1776, *The Revolutionary Journal of Colonel Jeduthan Baldwin, 1775–1778*, 55.

41. Fenn, *Pox Americana*, 70–71, 76; John Joseph Henry, quoted in Fenn, *Pox Americana*, 70.

42. Fenn, *Pox Americana*, 77; Horatio Gates quoted in Fenn, *Pox Americana*, 77.

43. Mark Kwasny, *Washington's Partisan War: 1775–1783* (Kent, OH: Kent State University Press, 1996), 57, 60.

44. Martin, *Ordinary Courage*, 17–18.

45. Joseph Reed, quoted in Schecter, *The Battle for New York*, 198.

46. Martin, *Ordinary Courage*, 29.

47. *New York Mercury*, September 30, 1776.

48. Mary J. Ortner, "Captain Nathan Hale (1755–1776)," The Connecticut Society of the Sons of the American Revolution. http://www.connecticutsar.org/patriots/hale_nathan_2.htm (accessed October 13, 2006).

49. Martin, *Ordinary Courage*, 32.

50. Martin, *Ordinary Courage*, 33–34.

51. Nathanael Greene to George Washington, November 9, 1776, and Robert Magaw to Nathanael Greene, November 15, 1776, in Showman, *The Papers of Nathanael Greene, Vol. 1*, 344, 351.

52. John Adlum, quoted in William M. Dwyer, *The Day is Ours* (New York: The Viking Press, 1983), 6–8.

53. Nathanael Greene to Nicholas Cooke, December 4, 1776, in Showman, *The Papers of Nathanael Greene, Vol. 1*, 362.

54. George Washington to John Hancock, December 12, 1776, in Fitzpatrick, *The Writings of George Washington*, vol. 6, 355.

55. Nathanael Greene to Catherine Greene, December 4, 1776, in Showman, *The Papers of Nathanael Greene, Vol. 1*, 364–5.

56. "Journal of Charles Willson Peale," *Pennsylvania Magazine of History and Biography* 38 (1914): 271–3; David Hackett Fischer, *Washington's Crossing* (New York: Oxford University Press, 2004), 133.

57. Captain Enoch Anderson and Sergeant Joseph White, quoted in Dwyer, *The Day is Ours*, 115.

58. Fischer, *Washington's Crossing*, 231–2.

59. Samuel Blachley Webb to Joseph Trumbull, December 16, 1776, quoted in Fischer, *Washington's Crossing*, 159.

3 CREATING A RESPECTABLE ARMY

Robert Morris wrote to George Washington on New Year's Day, 1777. He was glad that the previous year had finally ended and sincerely wished that neither Washington nor "America will ever be plagued again with such another." This was an amazing admission and one that contemporary historian David Hackett Fischer noted rang "strangely" to modern ears—since we extol the spirit of 1776 today.[1] But it was true; 1776 was one of the worst times of the war for the patriot cause and the soldiers fighting for independence. Despite the last-minute twin victories at Trenton and Princeton, New Jersey, Washington had been ejected from New York City, repeatedly beaten on a variety of battlefields, lost thousands of men killed or captured, and had been driven out of New Jersey and across the Delaware River into Pennsylvania. His army was dissolving before his very eyes, and there seemed nothing he could do about it until a new one was recruited.

As the war deepened in 1777, the experience of the army of 1776 made it clear to Washington and Congress that several issues needed to be addressed. First and foremost was recruiting a new army to replace the one that had been based largely on a single-year enlistments (1776). Washington earnestly hoped that a new army would be raised by Congress, with enlistments "for the duration" of the war. Next, after nearly twenty months of fighting and dozens of engagements, both sides had captured significant numbers of the opposite side. The question of what to do about prisoners of war (POWs), especially now that the Americans had captured nearly a thousand Hessians following their victory at Trenton, became readily apparent.

Moreover, in late 1776, reports began filtering back to Washington and Congress about the barbaric treatment of Americans captured during the New York campaign, including the 2600 taken at once with the fall of Fort Washington. Captain John Chester wrote to Colonel Samuel B. Webb of Connecticut of the suffering of the troops captured during the New York campaign. "The inhuman treatment our prisoners met while in New York is beyond all description. . . . They are mere skeletons, unable to creep or speak in many instances . . . and they are dying all along the road. . . . Is this proof of the much boasted humanity of Britons?"[2] Finally, it was revealed, especially after the considerable sickness experienced by American troops during the Canadian campaign,

George Washington on horseback during the Battle of Princeton. (*Courtesy of the Library of Congress*)

that it was necessary to professionalize a plan for the hospitalization of sick and wounded troops and to deal with the scourge of smallpox that had played such a large role in the stupendous American failure to seize a lightly defended Canada. The hospital plan of 1775 was no longer effective and in urgent need of immediate reform.

THE NEW MODEL ARMY

No one more than Washington was more keenly aware of the pernicious effects of short-termed enlistments. Writing to Congress in September 1776, Washington asked for and received from Congress an army of enlistees who would join their regiments for at least three years or the duration of the war. He strongly desired to avoid the annual meltdown of American military power at the end of each calendar year and the uncertainty of having enough available troops to oppose the British the following spring.

Congress's Improvements for Soldiers' Lives

To its credit, Congress resolved to improve things for the soldiers and voted to provide them with an annual suit of clothes, raise the pay of officers, and reorganized the army into an eighty-eight-battalion force—each state being given a quota based on its prewar population. Moreover, Washington himself was empowered to raise an additional sixteen regiments with artillery and cavalry support. This was an extraordinary admission by Congress of their growing trust and confidence in the commander in chief. On paper, this meant that Washington would have nearly seventy-five thousand troops to oppose the British in the coming 1777 campaign season. Further, in answer to Washington's pleas for help in disciplining the army, Congress revised the original and clearly antiquated 1775 Articles of War and quickly mirrored much of what was contained in the British army version, with the notable exception that the maximum number of lashes that could be given to a court-martialed soldier was capped at hundred. British soldiers could still receive five hundred (or sometimes more). Moreover, Congress also greatly increased the number of military crimes that could be awarded the death penalty. Finally, Congress was forced to admit that the "rage militaire" of the first year and a half of the war was over. Congress and Washington finally had to recognize that the "virtuous" army of citizen-soldiers that had been recruited with such high hopes in 1776 had likely run its course. Washington believed that he could get men to serve but only if Congress could make it in their interest to enlist. Logically, he concluded that such self-serving men could not be disciplined by love of country alone. Rather, long-termed enlistees needed to be governed by a strict enforcement of reinvigorated Articles of War. This new system would hopefully give Washington the "respectable army" he had longed for.

Even before the debacle of New York, Congress was concerned that it needed a disciplined army of longer duration. John Adams wrote to General William Heath in August 1776 and stated that he was convinced "that the Prosperity of a State depends upon the Discipline of its Army. This Discipline reared the Roman Empire and the British: and the American will Stand or fall, in my Opinion, according as it adheres to or deviates from the Same Discipline. . . ." Adams further noted that "we shall never do well, untill We get a regular Army, and this will never be, untill Men are inlisted for a longer Duration, and that will never be effected untill We are more generous in our Encouragement to Men."[3]

The "encouragement" Adams mentioned came in the form of a Continental bounty. Initially, the bounty was set at $20. This sum would eventually approach nearly $1000 late in the war. The bounty was soon augmented with a further offer of one hundred acres of land, to be awarded at the conclusion of the war, and if the soldier were killed or died in camp before he could collect, his next of kin would be given the land certificate. Soldiers were to be also given, by contract, an annual suit of clothes and a specified daily ration. However, state militia units offered shorter-termed opportunities and essentially provided the same bounty or sometimes a higher one. This competition for military manpower put them at odds with the establishment of a truly national army, and Washington continued throughout most of the war to remonstrate with Congress and the State governments over this pernicious practice. The unintended consequence of this national–state competition was the likely cause behind Washington's continued and long-standing Continental army recruiting difficulties.

However, the bounty seemed to be the last thing on the minds of most soldiers in camp on New Year's Day, 1777. A good example of their changed attitude was expressed by Private Josiah Burr of Connecticut, who had earlier boastfully written home in 1775 to his mother that he could "eat raw Pork & drink white fac'd Rum with the best of them." Yet just a year and a half later, this same soldier whined to his commanding officer that "it is really surprising to me that a person sick & infirm as . . . I am should be consider'd as an able bodied Man & and as such drag'd by force & Arms & be obliged to join the Army dead or alive."[4]

Despite the bounty, many of the men were like Private Burr and had their fill of "soldiering." Entire regiments and companies still marched for home. Edmund Phinney's 18th Continental Regiment, stationed near Lake Champlain, "marched for home" en masse on New Year's Day, 1777. No amount of cajoling or encouragement from General Philip Schuyler could convince them to stay another moment. In a rather extraordinary departure, Charles Burrall's Connecticut Regiment was reported by Anthony Wayne as having "went off in the Night" on the very evening (January 31, 1777) that their enlistments expired.[5]

A few in Congress believed that the requirement for a longer enlistment was beyond the reluctance of many soldiers to reenlist. James Sullivan wrote to Adams and Elbridge Gerry and stated that:

> There is not in my mind the shadow of a probability of [Congress] raising two thousand men on the proposed Establishment. . . . [The soldiers] will not Engage for an indefinite Term of Time, and those who are Engaged in the Family way [married] are by no means willing to inlist for a Term the End whereof they are not able to see. Indeed few Americans would choose the Life of a Soldier and be willing to be bound during Life.[6]

Nevertheless, the proposed new army of 1777 was extraordinarily ambitious and represented perhaps some wishful thinking on the part of Washington and Congress. It was clear that the Americans had decided to build a new, professionalized army along the lines of their British opponents. Creating a new, standing army was anathema to many of the upstanding Whigs in Congress who feared the professionalization of the army. However, they really did not have much of a choice. Either they attracted enough men to replace the departing veterans of 1776 or the war would be over for lack of interest on the part of the Americans.

One person who remained concerned about this new army was John Taylor of New Jersey. Taylor was an ardent patriot militia officer who happened to see part of the main army drilling near Princeton in the early spring of 1777. He was not impressed with the quality of the men in the ranks. He noted that "the Yeomanry," or the average American citizen, were no longer prevalent in the ranks and had been replaced by what he called "mostly foreigners." He stated that "they were mostly mercenaries with no attachment to the country except what accrues from the emoluments of service." He was worried and concluded to "hope for the best but at the same time fear the worst." Although Taylor was certainly overstating the case that the army was largely made up of foreigners, it was true that the Americans were desperate in the early spring of 1777 to fill its ranks as quickly as possibly with just about anyone willing to take the bounty and enlist for three years or the duration of the war.[7]

Recruiting Problems

Recruiting for the war at this point was a particularly tough assignment. Alexander Graydon of Pennsylvania set out into the suburbs of Philadelphia, Pennsylvania, in 1776 with orders to recruit a company of men. He noted that unlike in Europe where the recruiting service was largely conducted by sergeants and corporals, in America the men expected to actually *see* the officer who was to command them. This meant that the officers themselves, like Graydon, had to make the rounds when trying to fill out a company or regiment. Graydon freely admitted that 1776 was certainly not a time of "universal patriotism" and after weeks of traveling about the countryside had only about half his company recruited. Another officer suggested that he venture down to the Maryland eastern shore to find "some *long shore* men there, out of employ." Graydon quickly met up with a man named Dan Heath near the Maryland village of Warwick. He hoped that Heath would agree to take the bounty and become a soldier but quickly surmised that he had more of the "sportsman" in him than any desire to be a soldier. However, in a surprise move, Heath volunteered to direct him to another man whom he said "would do to stop a bullet as well as a better man, and as he was a truly worthless dog, he held, that the neighborhood would be much in indebted to us for taking him away." Graydon quickly snapped this man up. Going further to Chestertown, Maryland, Graydon was informed that he was not welcome to recruit Marylanders for a Pennsylvania regiment in their town, and he and his party had to reverse course and return to Pennsylvania. Graydon admitted that his whole trip netted only "three or four men." However, his prospects brightened up a bit when two of his lieutenants returned with 21 "stout" recruits from Little Egg Harbor, New Jersey. By the spring of 1776, Graydon could boast that he had forty recruits signed up. It only accounted to half of what he had hoped to recruit, but this was at least a start.[8]

On January 13, 1777, Washington sent out specific recruiting instructions and admonished his officers to "inlist none but Freemen above the Age of Seventeen, and under that of fifty, of sufficient Stature and Ability of body, to discharge all the Offices of a private Soldier, to be free from lameness, or other bodily infirmities . . ." He also told them to be careful to not enlist deserters from the British, but the recruiters did anyway. They especially wanted to entice the newly acquired Hessian POWs from Trenton to join the American cause, in hope that others still in the employ of the British would follow their example.[9]

One of those who had decided to reenlist was former Connecticut "levy" Joseph Plumb Martin. Martin had returned to Connecticut after serving as a six-month levy

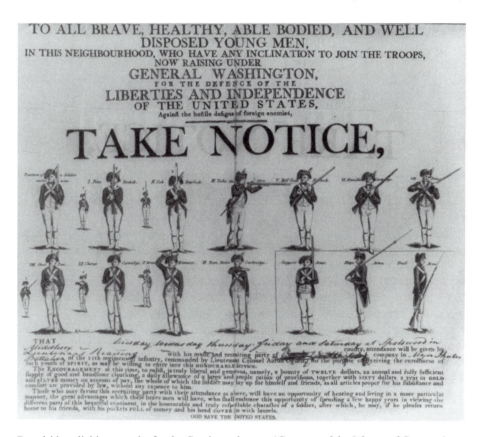

Broadside soliciting recruits for the Continental army. (*Courtesy of the Library of Congress*)

during the New York campaign. He had heard that: "orders were out for enlisting men for three years, or during the war. The general opinion of the people was that the war would not continue three years longer; what reasons they had for making such conjectures I cannot imagine, but so it was." Martin bluntly confessed that he had trouble saying no to anyone and without thinking about it agreed to sign up when the first army recruiter came to his neighborhood. Remembering perhaps the hardship and privation of the New York campaign, he stated that he immediately regretted his decision. But fortunately for him and perhaps due to his youthful appearance and since he had not yet taken "the bounty money," he was allowed by a kind recruiting sergeant to get out of his enlistment. Nonetheless, young Martin was still a highly sought after commodity. He noted that the town had been organized "into what were called squads, according to their ratable property." Martin stated that these squads were then required by the town to provide one man for army service "either by hiring or sending one of their own number." This "back door" draft proved quite successful for the squads. Martin believed that since his grandfather had been earlier convinced by a relative with an army commission that he should return to the army that "[he] might as well endeavor to get as much for my skin as I could; accordingly, I told them that I would go for them and fixed upon a day when I would meet them and clinch the bargain." While not specifically mentioned by Martin, he did not make this generous decision for free.[10]

Muster days in any town were usually times of great excitement. With drums beating, sergeants bellowing, and men in various stages of going off to war, it was very much a carnival-like atmosphere. Martin described what took place:

> I went to the parade where all was liveliness, as it generally is upon such occasions; but poor *I* felt miserably; my execution day was come. I kept wandering about till the afternoon among the crowd, when I saw the Lieutenant [his relative], who went with me into a house where the men of the squad were, and there I put my name to enlisting indentures for the last time. . . . The men gave me what they had agreed to; I forget the sum. . . . They were now freed from any further trouble, as least for the present, and I had become the scapegoat for them.[11]

Enticing the Foreign Born and Hessians into the Continental Army

With states trying and not often succeeding in filling up their Continental quotas and with enthusiasm for the rebellion clearing waning at this particular point in the war, it was no wonder that Washington's recruiting instructions were somewhat set aside by recruiters in the field. Large numbers of men were enlisted without regard to race, creed, or national origin. And in fact, Washington eventually was won over to the idea of encouraging Hessian POWs to enlist in the service of the United States and even employed his German-born Continental army baker Christopher Ludwig in several schemes to get Hessians to abandon the British. Congress even published a broadside that did not require Hessian prisoners to enlist against their former employers. Rather, by deserting the British they would be given fifty acres of land and "all foreign mercenaries who chose to leave the British army free exercise of their respective religions, all the rights, privileges, and immunities [that] American citizenship offered."[12]

However, initial American efforts to recruit captured or deserted Hessians did not meet with much success. Only about 2 percent of the Hessians were willing to exchange captivity for a place in the American army in late 1776. Their decision made sense, in that if they were recaptured, they likely faced the death penalty at the hands of their former comrades. As a further encouragement to them, the Hessian POWs were treated more liberally than their British counterparts. At a prison camp location near Winchester, Virginia, the Hessians were given an opportunity to mix with the local population of German Americans, while the British POWs were imprisoned in buildings. In fact, Hessian prisoners were often colocated near large concentrations of German Americans, such as Reading and York, Pennsylvania, or Frederick, Maryland. The idea behind this policy was the hope that the locals could convince them to desert and either join the Continental army or at least leave the British army permanently. Thus, as the war ground on, more and more Hessians were willing to desert. In 1780, a Hessian POW officer named Wiederhold observed the passage of an American unit led by Charles Armand de Tuffin, a French volunteer officer who specialized in the enlistment of foreign-born troops and commanded what was called "Armand's Legion." As these troops marched by, Wiederhold noted that Armand's Legion of about four hundred men was entirely composed of "former Hessians."[13]

Recruiting foreign-born soldiers seemed to be prevalent in the middle colonies where prewar immigration levels had been high and especially in Pennsylvania. So many Irish seemed to permeate the ranks that one British observer exclaimed that "great numbers of Irish emigrants were in the army for mere subsistence." Fragmentary muster rolls reveal that the Irish presence in Pennsylvania regiments was indeed quite extraordinary. At least 46 and 45 percent, respectively, of the 1st and 11th Pennsylvania regiments were Irish. The majority of at least four companies of the 7th Pennsylvania "claimed Ireland as their birthplace." An examination of the April 1779 muster records of the Pennsylvania State Regiment of Artillery showed that 32 percent of this 205-men organization were Irish, "including its commanding officer" Colonel Thomas Procter. What is more amazing was that only forty two men or 20 percent of Procter's unit were even from Pennsylvania.[14]

Late in the war, General William Smallwood of Maryland was sent home to help replenish the decimated ranks of the formerly elite Maryland Continental line. Smallwood's instructions from the Maryland General Assembly warned him to closely scrutinize any foreign-born recruits because "many of this class of men make a practice of enlisting with no other view but to go off with the [bounty] money." Nonetheless, Smallwood's new recruits comprised nearly 50 percent of the total 308 person body he was able to gather at this point in the war. Of this half, over 80 percent claimed Ireland as their place of birth. At least fifty-nine simply listed "America" as their place of origin.[15]

African American Recruits

One subset of military manpower that was not overlooked by army recruiters was that of the African American community—both free and unfree. In July 1775, Horatio Gates required recruiters to not enlist "any deserter from the Ministerial army, nor any stroller, negro, or vagabond." Substantial numbers of free African Americans who had initially joined the army in the heady days after Lexington and Concord, Massachusetts, were told that they were no longer wanted in the army. However, by early 1777, the military manpower crisis of the new army overrode any prior prejudice recruiters might have once had about accepting African Americans as combat soldiers. One Hessian officer noted that "the Negro can take the field instead of his master; and, therefore, no regiment is seen in which there are not negroes in abundance, and among them there are able-bodied, strong and brave fellows."[16]

Army muster records bear this observation out. One particular muster roll reported by Alexander Scammell, adjutant-general of the army on August 24, 1778, revealed the number of African American soldiers present by regiment. Comparing for a moment the total number of soldiers Washington had fit and present for duty on that particular day, we can arrive at a reasonably accurate figure for the number of African Americans in the ranks at the time. For example, about 10 percent of Parson's Brigade was African American. "Muhlenberg's Virginia battalions were 13 percent African-American." In sum, African Americans were about evenly spread throughout the army (at least in 1778) at a rate of one for every ten soldiers (ten percent). Moreover, black Continental soldiers served for longer enlistments than many white soldiers and therefore would represent an even higher cohort at any given time in the new army of 1777.[17]

However, few militia muster rolls revealed any significant numbers of African American soldiers present for duty. In an examination of the Philadelphia militia, only a single African American could be found on any muster roll. Therefore, it is clear that African Americans helped "fulfill the onerous continental manpower quota for the states but were still discriminated against on the local level" (especially south of New England). It is also important to note that military service during the eighteenth century was a traditional route for African American manumission. Thus, if a slave or a runaway could get into the army, it most often enabled him to win his own freedom (if he survived the war). Although there were some very notable exceptions to this tradition, most courts after the war felt morally compelled to set former slave-soldiers free after surviving an eight-year war for national liberty (at least for most whites). In fact, "free African Americans became a permanent legacy of the Revolution. Maryland's free African American population, which was 1817 in 1755, reached 8000 by 1790." African Americans, both slave and free, made significant contribution toward manning the Continental army.[18]

By 1778, the state of Rhode Island had some moderate success in raising its own regiment of predominately black soldiers. "On February 28, 1778, the first three American Americans" enlisted in this particular unit. "Cuff Greene, Dick Champlin, and Jack Champlin, all former slaves residing in South Kingstown, Rhode Island, joined the Continental army. The state of Rhode Island reimbursed their former owners for the maximum value of 120 pounds (Jack was purchased for 10 pounds less)." Although the exact number of African Americans who had enlisted cannot be precisely determined, "taking into account all the incomplete muster rolls, treasurer's lists, payrolls, and casualty lists, the most probable number was between 225 and 250." This regiment, which had enlisted for the duration of the war, played a major role in the successful retreat of the American army during the Battle of Rhode Island in August 1778.[19]

Both Connecticut and Massachusetts were known to have raised at least a company-sized unit of African Americans. The only extant remains of one such company, "the Bucks of America," was a green battle flag which featured a running stag and had been "presented to the unit by John Hancock." In general, however, unlike later nineteenth-century civil war–era units, most African American soldiers served side by side with their white comrades throughout the war and were fully integrated as combat soldiers into each state line, with the notable exceptions of South Carolina and Georgia.[20]

Smallpox Prevention

Continental army recruiters did learn one thing from their experience of the previous year. Recruits were to be inoculated for smallpox *before* they came on to join the main army. Recruiting in Connecticut, Brigadier General Samuel Parsons noted in a letter to Washington that "he had established Hospitals in several Parts of this State for inoculating the Recruits; most of those who had not the Small Pox before are now in the Hospitals: Some will come out in about ten days." Moreover, Parsons found the recruiting business steady but slow. As late as March 1777, writing to Washington, Parsons noted that of the nine "regiments" that Connecticut listed as being actively recruited, the most complete were the regiments commanded by Jedidiah Huntington and Samuel Wyllys, who had raised 250 men each, a far cry from the seven hundred plus "on paper" figure of the standard 1776 regiment. The regiments of John Chandler, Charles Webb, and Samuel B. Webb had only eighty men each in their particular units. In reality, they were not much bigger than a standard Continental army company. However, Parsons believed that four of the regiments had gotten a late start on recruiting and that the bounty money was late in getting to Samuel B. Webb, and now that he had finally received it, he expected him to "soon fill that regiment."[21]

But it was not until May 15, 1777, that Parsons was able to forward the now smallpox-inoculated recruits on to the Continental army depot at Peekskill, New York. Between March and May, Charles Webb increased his regiment to 257 men; Samuel B. Webb reported 205. Chandler had 297. Huntington's regiment was the only one that barely approached paper strength at 480 men. Parsons also asked Washington whether it was advisable to stop inoculating the troops in "this Advanced season" and simply send recruits along as they came in.[22] By mid-June Washington issued orders that threatened to punish anyone, including army doctors, who continued to inoculate against smallpox.

PRISONERS OF WAR

During the Revolution, the problem of POWs ran squarely into eighteenth-century military warfare traditions. First, in European-style combat, it was left up to the victor of an engagement and often to the individual soldiers themselves to whether they would grant quarter to a defeated enemy. Granting quarter meant taking enemy soldiers prisoner. This usually occurred in the heat of battle or in the immediate aftermath of overrunning or dispersing an enemy position. However, this situation could be different, at least in the eyes of the British in 1775, to those they deemed "rebels." For example, on the exceptionally bloody battlefield of Culloden in 1745, the Duke of Cumberland ordered his men to dispatch any wounded Highlanders they found. The Duke believed that they, as "rebels" against the crown, did not merit any quarter, and he was heard to have personally ordered the execution of several wounded Highlanders found immediately after the battle.

During the French and Indian War, British Lieutenant Colonel George Munro, commanding officer of the garrison at Fort William Henry (1758), was given favorable terms by the besieging French General Marquis de Montcalm to surrender Fort William Henry or risk having any men captured "at discretion." This meant that the garrison *could* be put to the sword if Montcalm were required to take the place by storm. The garrison was bombarded by French artillery for five straight days and nights and was nearly out of ammunition, and this was enough to convince Munro to surrender the garrison in order to spare his men. Unfortunately for Munro and his men, however, such military conventions did not make sense to the French Indian allies, who thought themselves cheated out of the spoils of war by Montcalm's European ideals of granting "quarter" to a defeated enemy, and Munro's men were viciously attacked and slaughtered by Indians after Montcalm lost control over them. General Henry Clinton demanded the same sort of surrender conditions of Colonel Robert Magaw, the American commanding officer at Fort Washington. Unlike Munro, however, Magaw refused Clinton's demand, but the British and Hessian assault was so swift and the American collapse so rapid that quarter was granted (for the most part) anyway and over 2600 captured Americans were marched off to POW camps and prison ships in New York City.

The second issue revolved around the status of the Americans as belligerents. To admit that the Americans were combat soldiers and not rebels along the lines of the Scottish Highlanders of 1745 was to nearly confirm the status of the United States as a nation independent of the mother country, something the British were clearly trying to prevent. Moreover, for rebellion, the British had a particularly harsh reputation for how they treated "rebels," whether they were Scotch, Irish, or American. Brutal public treatment of rebels dated back centuries in British history, and they believed that this had a deterrent effect on others of like minds. They held so strongly to this position that it was "not until six months after Yorktown did parliament enact that 'rebel prisoners' might be lawfully 'held and detained' in Britain as prisoners of war." Further, when Washington protested to Howe about the treatment of the four hundred captured New Hampshire soldiers at the Cedars, William Howe returned the letter addressed to "George Washington, Esq." rather than recognize the military rank of the "rebel" leader. William Howe did so out of concern that referring to Washington as "General" imputed an equality between the belligerents that might provide further legitimacy to the American cause. Because the letter did not follow military protocol, Washington wisely refused to receive it.[23]

Another prisoner issue was created over the large number of American privateers roaming the seas carrying "letters of marque" from Congress or individual states that authorized them to take British shipping when they came upon them. When the American privateers were captured by the British, the question of whether they were legitimate combatants or mere pirates worthy of the gallows perplexed the British for years. In fact, during the war, many more "marine prisoners" would be taken than those captured on land. The major difference in their treatment was the ambiguity of their status and that they were usually (but not always) taken back to Great Britain rather than detained and housed in North America. Many were "encouraged" to join the British navy by various devices but often in order to merely survive.

Fifteen-year-old New Englander John Blatchford was one of the unlucky ones captured at sea by the British. Blatchford had shipped aboard the Continental sloop *Hancock* as a fifteen-year-old cabin boy. After a hard fight, the *Hancock* captured the small British frigate HMS *Fox*. Unfortunately for Blatchford, his ship was later captured by a larger frigate, the HMS *Milford*, which had also recently taken the American brig *Cabot* as well. Blatchford and over three hundred American sailors were then taken to Halifax, Nova Scotia, where they were all confined in a sugar house.

During the Revolution, sugar houses frequently doubled as prisons in a number of towns because of their open warehouse style of architecture and ease with which newly captured prisoners could be confined and guarded. One captured American soldier imprisoned in the New York sugar house for three months was Joseph Rundel. Rundel noted that:

> [A]s I was young and small of my age, they permitted me in the daytime to be out, and I was sent to bring water and do chores about the yard. Some of the other prisoners were also permitted to be out. It was the custom at night to lock us up. The names were called over, and care taken to see that we were all in.

Fortunately for Rundel, he was able to gain the confidence of a Hessian guard named Michael Hilderbrand, and both men later made their escape to the American garrison at West Point, New York.[24]

In order to get out of the Halifax sugar house, Blatchford and five of his mates dug a hole under the wooden floor planking and made a small tunnel. However, before they could pull it off, another sailor named Knowles, a former midshipman on the American frigate *Boston*, "basely" informed the guards of their plan. As a result, Blatchford and his friends were placed in irons. The guards filled up the hole and placed an armed sentinel inside the sugar house. While being kept in "close confinement," Blatchford noted that "two of my fellow-sufferers Barnard and Cole, died; one of which was put into the ground with his irons [still] on his hands." Eventually, Blatchford was permitted to walk in the yard but remained affixed with his irons. He was taunted by Knowles, who, according to Blatchford, "took every opportunity to insult and mortify me, by asking me whether I wanted to run away again and when I was going home, &c." Unfortunately for the perfidious Knowles, during one of these sessions, Blatchford was able to work a hand free and punched him square in the mouth, "knocking out two or three of his teeth. . . ." As a result of his earlier escape attempt and his attack on the prison informer, Blatchford was forced aboard an outbound East Indiaman, where he soon found at least eighty other American "marine" POWs on board. They were bound for Batavia on the island of Java. After taking on provisions at Batavia, the ship approached the island of Sumatra, and soon all the Americans were put ashore and informed that they were now required to serve as soldiers for five years (it was then June 1780). With disease and poor diet, Blatchford and the others knew that this was a virtual death sentence for them. Instead, Blatchford offered himself to his captain as a sailor, but his request was refused. Forced to learn the manual of arms, Blatchford and three of his friends feigned stupidity as a way of getting out of their predicament. However, this simply caused them to get severely beaten on a daily basis by their British drill sergeant.[25]

As predicted, Blatchford noted that "Americans died daily with heat and hard fare" working in the "pepper gardens" as laborers and impressed soldiers. Out of desperation, he and two other Americans attempted a second escape to the Dutch harbor of "Croy," on the opposite side of the island. After a period of four days, Blatchford and his friends were surprised by "seapoys" (native born soldiers in British employ). An American named Folgier, originally from Nantucket, Massachusetts, had killed one of the seapoys with an old bayonet he had found. Nevertheless, Blatchford and company were soon overpowered and brought back before the British governor, William Broff, Esq. The three men were confined in irons once again and condemned to be shot at dawn the following day. The next morning Blatchford and his fellow escapees were marched out and stood in front of "three white coffins." Blatchford stated that he could not "describe [his] feeling upon this occasion." However, to his everlasting joy, he found that at the last moment he and one other prisoner named Randall had been reprieved by the governor. Nonetheless, the Nantucketer, Folgier, who had killed one of his pursuers, was not reprieved. Blatchford related that as Folgier was older it was assumed that he was the leader of the escape attempt. Blatchford and Randall watched as Folgier was executed by musket fire. But they did not get off easy either. Immediately after Folgier's execution, both men were then tied to a stake and sentenced on the spot to receive eight hundred lashes each. Normally, this would have been enough to kill a man. However, Blatchford recorded that the adjutant cut off the knots at the end of the whip before it was handed to the drummer for the execution of the sentence so that "it was not worse than to have been whipt with cotton yarn." Apparently the governor meant to terrorize the two men, who had been reprieved from the firing squad because of their youthfulness. They both got the message.[26]

Early in 1777, owing to reports coming in about the horrible conditions aboard the prison ships in New York harbor, Washington felt obliged to write to Lord Richard Howe, the admiral in command of the British navy in North America and older brother of British Commander in Chief, William Howe, and asked him to investigate these allegations. Even though Washington had trouble with the Howe brothers recognizing his status as commander in chief of the American forces, he was not totally powerless on the POW issue. He reminded Richard Howe that: "Remember my Lord, that supposing us Rebels, we still have feelings equally as keen and sensible, as Loyalists, and will, if forced to it, most assuredly retaliate upon those, upon whom we look, as the unjust invaders of our Rights, Liberties and properties."[27]

There is no doubt that the American soldiers captured at Fort Washington were particularly treated cruelly while in British hands in New York City. Not only did they fit the term "rebel" very well, but the large fire that had broken out in Manhattan following the American retreat up the island had made many New Yorkers homeless just prior to winter and they squarely blamed the Continental army for their situation. Finally, unlike Boston, New York had a substantially larger Tory population that became very aggressive especially after the British had occupied the city. New York City and its immediate environs were definitely "enemy territory" for any Americans who fell into their hands.

One of those who fell into their hands during the first engagement on Long Island was Connecticut Lieutenant Jabez Fitch of the 17th Continental Regiment, along with 208 others of his unit. For the first two days of his captivity, Fitch attended his mortally wounded commanding officer, Captain Joseph Jewett. Jewett passed away on the evening of August 28, 1776, and Fitch supervised his burial on August 29, 1776. Immediately thereafter, Fitch noted that "all the Officers & most of the Soldiers that were Prisoners here were order'd into the Flat bottom'd Botes & went down to the Fleet, where we were put on Board the *Pacific* a Ship of about 900 Tons." Fitch noted that the conditions on board were "Cours" and "being almost 400 in Number, were soon Drove under Deck together without Distinction." At the time, Fitch believed that despite the crowded conditions, on the whole the British aboard the *Pacific* were quite civil to him and the other prisoners.[28]

Fitch was soon transferred to the *Mentor*, a smaller ship that housed most of the captured officers of the 17th Regiment. He noted that the British offered freedom to those soldiers who would enlist in their service, and allegedly more than one hundred men took that offer. Fitch and other officers were even allowed to walk about the city from dawn to dusk and were on their honor to be back aboard ship before dark and were not allowed to talk to their men. The men, however, remained in close confinement and mostly on half rations. Thanks to the sudden influx of several thousand soldiers at the end of the New York campaign, the unanticipated burning of over one-fourth of the city, the lack of an appropriate cartel for exchange of prisoners at the time, the men, as noted by Lieutenant William McPherson of Mile's Pennsylvania regiment, "were very sickly and died fast." The huge numbers of captured men were confined in just about any building big enough to hold them in. Sugar houses, Quaker meeting houses, ship holds, and churches became the usual repositories. The Quaker meeting house on Crown Street just off Broadway was notorious as a place of great mortality.[29]

Some officers were not as liberally treated as Fitch. Lieutenant Jonathan Gillet, also of the 17th Regiment, recalled that he had been captured on Long Island by "a people called Heshens and by a party called Yagers, the most inhuman of all mortals I can't give Room to picture them here." Gillet bitterly wrote that the Hessians "first disarmed me then plundered me of all I had, watch Buckles money and sum Clothing after which they abused me by brusing my flesh with the buts of there guns. They knocked me down; I got up and they (kept on) beating me almost all the way to there (camp) . . ." Gillet was put on board one of the prison ships and promptly contracted severe dysentery. However, bad as his situation was, Gillet wrote that the enlisted men had it worse. He noted that the biggest problem during that first winter of captivity was finding fuel to keep warm. The British Commissary for Prisoners, Joshua Loring of Boston, an arch Tory whose wife was allegedly the mistress of Howe himself, informed Gillet that there would be no wood for prisoners that winter but that they might be able to provide them with some coal. Gillet went on to describe emaciated, vermin-covered, and ragged soldiers slowly wasting away in the prison houses and ships in the harbor. He stated that he longed to take revenge on the Hessians who had robbed and beat him.[30]

The Prison Ship *Jersey*

One of the most notorious places of captivity was the prison ship *Jersey*. The *Jersey* was a former sixty-four-gun ship of the line long past its prime. In 1780, the British condemned the ship and cut all its masts down, unhinged its rudder, covered over its gunports, and anchored the ship near "the Wallabout, a solitary and unfrequented place near the shore of Long Island." The ship had installed a series of small holes cut through its sides for ventilation about every ten feet, "being about 20 inches square, and guarded by two strong bars of iron, crossing at right angles." Thomas Dring of Newport, Rhode Island, had the unenviable distinction of serving time on two prison ships during the war. He was first confined aboard the *Good Hope* in 1779 but after a confinement of four months escaped to New Jersey. However, in 1782, he was again captured aboard the privateer *Chance* along with about 130 men from other ships and interned for five months on the infamous *Jersey*. By 1782, the *Jersey* had already earned a well-deserved reputation as a death ship. Dring noted that as he and his mates were rowed toward the hulk he could see hundreds of men crowding its deck.[31]

As Dring's longboat drew closer to the *Jersey*, the first thing that struck him was the strong odor emanating from the air holes. After a brief examination on deck, Dring and his comrades were quickly ushered below into the crowded main hold reserved for the general prisoner population. Dring tried to get a place to lie down near one of the air holes but found them already occupied. He had donned several layers of clothing to ensure that they were not stolen but was soon forced by the heat of hundreds of bodies in close quarters to divest himself of these garments. The next morning, as soon as he could see, Dring realized that he was surrounded by men in various stages of smallpox. Never having had the disease himself, he immediately approached a man "in the appropriate stage" of the illness and scraped some of the matter and inoculated himself against getting smallpox in the natural way. Dring happily noted that within a few days, his smallpox symptoms were very mild and that his medical experiment had been a remarkable success. However, he did note with concern that a small black silk handkerchief that he wore around his neck was now crawling with lice and that he realized that they would be his "companions" for the rest of his time aboard the ship.

An interior view of the *Jersey* showing prisoners and guards. (*Courtesy of the Library of Congress*)

Dring noted that one of the keys to survival on the *Jersey* was to get admitted to an established "mess." A mess was a grouping of prisoners (usually six men to a mess) who had their meager food rations issued to them as a group at a particular time of day. The ship steward would call out the mess numbers in rotation, and the men were fed in that order. New men not in a mess sometimes had to wait two or more days for their particular mess groupings to be officially formed and entered onto the steward's rolls. For the meantime, these men received nothing to eat. But Dring noted that getting into an established mess was not difficult because of the rapidity with which men died on board the ship.

For food, the men were given something called "sweet oil" as a substitute for butter. But it was anything but sweet and, as Dring noted, smelled foul and rancid, and most of the American prisoners refused to eat it. Instead, the men gave it to the French POWs who seemed to not mind its odor "and swallowed it with a little salt and their wormy bread." The average ration was two-thirds of what a British seaman received at sea. Each prisoner usually got a pound of wormy biscuit per day. On Sundays, in addition to the biscuit they received a half pint of peas, the only vegetable they would get all week and even this was irregularly provided. Occasionally, they would get some oatmeal or inferior-grade beef. The food was boiled all together using seawater in the "Great Copper" or galley cooking pot located at the forward part of the ship. Sometimes the men would not have time to cook their food and would have to wait another twenty-four hours for their turn at the pot. A bell was rung to put the food in and another rung to pull it out. Each mess had a string attached to its ration bag, and these were closely watched at all times. Dring noted that many prisoners preferred to cook their rations separately and believed that one of the reasons he survived was that his particular mess never cooked their food in the Great Copper but did so by scrounging pieces of wood to prepare their meals.[32]

The British guards never ventured out too frequently among the prisoners. Another sailor prisoner, Thomas Andros, recalled that once or twice during his captivity aboard the *Jersey*, "a bag of apples were hurled promiscuously into the midst of hundreds of prisoners crowded together as thick as they could stand, and life and limbs were endangered by the scramble." He stated that he always got himself out of the area when it looked like such activities were about to commence. Andros noted that yellow fever was prevalent among the prisoners, and in their derangement, they would run about the totally darkened gun decks at night shrieking and howling and stumbling over others packed together on the ship's deck. Since no one was allowed water at night, those with fever especially suffered. Andros recalled that no clergy and "no English Physician, or any one from the city, ever, to my knowledge came near us."[33]

Dring rank ordered the guards according to their level of brutality. In his opinion, the worst by far were the green uniformed "refugees" or loyalists who had enlisted in the British army. Clearly, most of them had a personal ax to grind against the patriots, and the POWs made convenient and stationary target for them to vent their anger upon. He did not hold a favorable opinion of Scottish soldiers who were mentioned by Dring as being only barely behind the loyalists in terms of brutality and heinous conduct toward the POWs.

The British built a ten-foot high "barricado" across the entire length of the quarterdeck and extended it out several feet beyond the deck rail with loopholes for muskets in case of a riot. No prisoner was allowed past the barricado unless ordered to be examined by ship officers. The guards nearly always stayed on their side of the barricado and the men on the other. The prisoners kept their meager belongings in wooden sea chests and arranged them on the prisoner deck by messes. Many men slept on top of the chests to keep them from being robbed by the other prisoners. Dring noted that the lowest prisoner deck seemed to be the worst: "From the disgusting and squalid appearance of the groups which I saw ascending the stairs which led to it, it must have been more dismal, if possible, than that part of the hulk where I resided." Dring observed that many were clothed only in remnants of rags and with matted beards and hair crawling with lice. He noted that the only way men could wash their clothes was to strip naked, wet them with seawater, and stamp up and down on them on the deck. At night, once the gratings were fastened over the prisoner holds, the noise from the sick and dying and the stench from the dirty packed-together bodies became almost unendurable. Below decks at night, it was pitch black and never quiet.[34]

One of the only events to relieve the monotony of prison life aboard the *Jersey* was to get assigned to a burial detail. Prisoners readily volunteered for such duty just to get to touch dry land. Dring described the work as especially heartrending. Each morning, the British would call the working parties to deposit those who had died during the night on the gratings of the hold. If a blanket was available and another prisoner did not want it, one of his messmates might sew it up around the deceased. The bodies of the dead were then lowered into a longboat and rowed ashore. A trench was dug in the sand on the shore and below the high watermark. Sand was then thrown over the bodies, and the working party was quickly returned to the *Jersey*. Dring sadly recalls taking off his shoes to feel the sand on his feet and pulling up some grass turf and taking it back to the ship for his mates to "smell." Human remains alleged to have been connected to men who may have died aboard the *Jersey* were still being uncovered well into the late twentieth century in and around the sands of "the Wallabout."[35]

Prison Alternatives for American Soldiers

While treatment of American POWs was certainly horrific during the war, one proven method to escape such conditions was to establish "cartels" for exchange of prisoners. As previously noted, this was difficult to do in the early part of the war when the British were adamant about not giving the Americans legitimate belligerent status. However, by 1777, the sheer volume of prisoners made it economically worthwhile for the British to consider exchanges. Moreover, guarding prisoners placed a strain on the number of forces available as combat soldiers. Often, recovering wounded soldiers or "invalids" who were healthy enough to stand guard but not able to accompany the British army on a campaign were detailed for such duty.

Another way in which soldiers could avoid prison camps altogether was to be paroled. Paroles were normally given immediately after being captured. Paroled soldiers were provided specific conditions by their captors under which they would be allowed to return to their homes to sit out the rest of the war or, if properly exchanged, could then rejoin their former units. One of the major components of a parole was that the person listed on it was subject to recall by their captors. For instance, Patrick Hughes was captured near Charleston, South Carolina, in 1780. His parole read:

> I Patrick Hughes private militia man from South Carolina do Acknowledge myself to be a prisoner of the British troops & do give my word of honor to remain quietly at my plantation neither saying nor doing anything against His Majesty's government. And do promise to deliver myself when called for.

> Patrick Hughes, Dorchester, May 16, 1780[36]

However, most POWs not fortunate enough to be paroled like Hughes lived in constant hope of an exchange. Congress had instructed Washington that exchanges would be conducted on the following terms: "Continental officers for those of equal rank, either in the Land or Sea Service, Soldier for Soldier, Sailor for Sailor, and Citizen for Citizen." Moreover, those captured first should be given priority over those more recently captured. Thus, in late 1776, Americans taken during the late Canadian adventure were given precedence over those taken at New York. Nevertheless, Howe did not necessarily play by these rules and often times sent out other prisoners vice the ones requested for exchange by Washington. Further, getting Howe to recognize American officers on an equal footing with their British opposites was especially tough. Washington threatened to break off all exchanges if Howe did not stop this arbitrary process. Sometimes, individual state commissaries undertook to conduct their own exchanges and did not bother to inform either Congress or Washington. Member of Congress James Duane noted to Washington that this procedure was causing "confusion and mischief." At one point, another member, Joseph Hewes of North Carolina, suggested to Washington that he exchange a soldier for one of his civilian friends then under British detention. This Washington steadfastly refused to do on the grounds that if this process became policy then the British could simply scoop up civilians at will and demand the repatriation of their captured officers and men.[37]

Elias Boudinot of New Jersey and later president of Congress toward the end of the war was appointed by Congress in 1778 to create a "cartel" for the exchange of prisoners. He was again advised to take only equally ranked officers for officers and to offer only an equivalent number of soldiers for captured Americans. Since the United States had essentially created two nearly completely new armies in 1775 and 1776, an exchange probably worked more in their favor since it meant getting "veterans" back into the ranks. While this certainly worked for the British as well, getting a POW back for them meant a bit less since the captured soldier or officer had most likely already been replaced by the Crown in order to keep an adequate force in the field.

Boudinot arrived in New York City during February 1778 to establish a mutual exchange of prisoners with Joshua Loring, the British Commissary for Prisoners. While he was there, Governor Jonathan Trumbull, without consulting Congress or Boudinot, also sent a delegation to negotiate for the exchange of Connecticut POWs. This group was led by Joseph Webb, brother of Colonel Samuel Blachley Webb of the Connecticut Continental line. Boudinot noted that he "was much surprised at this measure & opposed it." Nonetheless, he proceeded ahead with his own plans for exchange and visited "two hospitals & Sugar House, [finding] everything as decent as could be expected." Following the Congressional direction of trading rank for rank, Boudinot proposed "to exchange on Parole, Col. Lawrence for Col. Holden and Col. DeLancey for Col. Swoop [Swope]." Exchange on parole did not mean freedom to return to the army. Rather, it simply meant that these men would be allowed to return to their homes (on parole) until properly exchanged rank for rank by a later cartel. For example, the abovementioned Colonel Michael Swope, of York County, Pennsylvania, who had been captured at Fort Washington in November 1776, was not officially exchanged and able to return to service until January 1781, but at least he did not have to languish under guard in New York City. Exchanges on parole were rarely if ever offered to enlisted men, and both sides usually agreed to such arrangements for officers most likely to save on their cost of captivity.

Much of the business of the 1778 cartel revolved around the requirement for Boudinot to be the advocate of prisoners who believed they were being mistreated, being falsely charged with something, or not being accorded treatment due their rank and station. For example, Boudinot spent a considerable amount of time investigating the claims that Ethan Allen had been placed in close confinement after the British alleged that he violated the bounds of his provisional parole. Allen, who held a provincial colonel's commission, had been a captive of the British since being taken at Montréal in early 1776 and had frequently been placed in irons and abused for his role in the seizure of Fort Ticonderoga and the invasion of Canada. Boudinot reported that Allen admitted that he had violated the spirit of his parole while a prisoner in New York City but had done nothing that other parolees had not been doing and that his arrest had just been an excuse for them to put him back in close confinement. Other complaints came from American officers who were confined as enlisted men because of the claim by the British that the "officers" they captured held no "commissions." Boudinot frequently had to vouch for these officers or try to provide some form of proof from their state regiments, which could often take months to receive if it ever came at all. Some enlisted men confined in the Sugar House complained in writing to Boudinot about the brutality of one particular British guard sergeant who allegedly had refused the men food or water for over two days. However, when he went to investigate this charge, the men "all denied it with great resentment & threatened vengeance on the author." Boudinot was suspicious and believed that "the greater part of these fellows are great Villians and rob each other." In any case, Boudinot ordered that they each be given a gill of rum. Moreover, even if the charge were true, the men would likely be afraid to say so out of fear of retribution by the guards. Other officers were accused of theft, and a Captain Van Dyke was placed in "close and severe confinement" for his alleged role in the great New York City fire of September 1776, a charge he vehemently denied. Nonetheless, the British remained convinced that Van Dyke had a direct hand in the fire, and he was not included in Boudinot's proposed exchange of officers and enlisted men.[38]

Boudinot grew extremely frustrated with investigating various claims and charges, but he did his duty. However, like Washington, what he found especially trying was the policy of state governors to work out prisoner exchanges with Loring on their own. One such case revolved around Connecticut Governor Trumbull and his commissioner, the aforementioned Joseph Webb. Joseph Webb tried to exchange one of the principal leaders of the New York Tories, Colonel Oliver DeLancey, for a mere Connecticut militia colonel, named John Ely. "All this I objected to," stated Boudinot. Instead, he was eventually able to trade DeLancey for a far more important prisoner, the captured commanding officer of Fort Washington, Colonel Robert Magaw.[39] In the end, Boudinot's visit resulted in a fairly equitable exchange of prisoners.

CONTINENTAL HOSPITALS

While the POW issue was evolving, so was that of the Continental medical department. In 1775, Dr. Benjamin Church was appointed by Congress as the army's first "director-general and chief physician" of the hospital department. The fact that less than four months later Church was discovered to be a spy in the employ of the British should provide some understanding as to why this particular military function seemed to operate with such great difficulty throughout most of the war.

One problem that became immediately apparent with the Continental hospitals was that while Congress had empowered the director general to purchase "medicines, Bedding, and all other necessaries, [and] to . . . superintend the whole," including the appointment of subdirectors, nurses, and an apothecary, they neglected to delineate the functional relationship of the various regimental surgeons to the office of director general. As a result of this omission, the regimental surgeons quickly began operating independently of the director general, setting up their own independent hospitals, and refused to cooperate with him. Nevertheless, the regimental surgeons demanded Director General Church and later his successor, Dr. John Morgan, to provide them with medical supplies, while still claiming that "they were not subject to the director-general's authority." Thus, most Continental army hospitals were run as semiautonomous entities that varied in their degree of professionalism and support.[40]

As far as the medical department was concerned, the Americans were fortunate that the capital city of Philadelphia was also the center of American medicine. Philadelphia possessed the only professional hospital in all the colonies in 1775. The city also had a first-rate medical school (the College of Philadelphia), and at least eight of its thirty practicing physicians had been trained in Europe. As a result, following the arrest of Dr. Church, Dr. John Morgan of Philadelphia was appointed director general.[41]

Although Philadelphia could boast of having the highest-quality physicians of any American city, eighteenth-century medicine could hardly be called progressive. For example, mercury was prescribed for sick soldiers for nearly every sort of ailment encountered in camp, including venereal disease, pneumonia, yellow fever, and small-pox. Doctors still prescribed bleeding and purging for just about any internal illness, often doing more harm than good to the patient. At the same time, it was intuitively recognized by Continental doctors of the necessity of creating hospitals with airy, open spaces if available and maintaining sanitary conditions in and around the building itself.

Increased attention was paid by the army command to preventive medicine. Washington wrote frequently about such issues in General Orders and warned the soldiers to be mindful of their health and noted that he expected them to:

> keep themselves clean & neat, their Hair cut decently short & comb'd & avoid using unwholesome Food or that is partially cook'd, when they have the opportunity to cook it thoroughly. Also that they take Care not to lye upon the cold ground or in the damp night air when the Situation of the Army doth not make it necessary.[42]

One of the most influential preventive medicine pamphlets published in English translation both in Philadelphia and in Boston just as war broke out was Baron van Swieten's "Diseases Incident to Armies with the Method of Cure." Not only did van Swieten advocate the use of vegetables and fruit as the principal means of preventing scurvy, he also addressed common homesickness or "nostalgia," as it was known then. Homesick soldiers away from home for the first time in their young lives were prone to desertion and even suicide. He believed that soldiers must be given some sort of diversion in army camps in order to prevent these possible consequences.

The selection of proper camp sites was seen as paramount to preventing disease. Sites were selected for four principal features: relative dryness of the ground, open air, and proximity to wood and water. As already noted, by 1775, inoculation for smallpox was common for most soldiers. The problem of scurvy and diet deficiency had also been recognized. Thus, spruce beer was included as an initial item for soldier rations almost from the start of the war. Congress also strongly advised having an ample supply of vegetables or "garden cresses" and "sufficient antiscorbutics" on hand as they saw these items as crucial for preventing scurvy. Although scurvy has been traditionally associated as a disease that affected sailors on long voyages, such cases were not unusual in an army camp, especially in winter. An inability to stand, blackened gums, and loose teeth were the usual symptoms of scurvy.[43]

Revolutionary War surgery was very rudimentary. Surgeons and physicians had very little idea about antiseptic conditions. But surgeons in the Continental army were mainly called upon to perform amputations. The average lead ball fired at the Americans during the war was launched by the famous British "Brown Bess" musket. This ball was a .75-caliber round projectile, propelled out of a smoothbore musket barrel, and had a relatively low muzzle velocity. Thus, upon striking a human body, the ball tended to flatten out, especially when it came into contact with dense objects such as bones or even vital organs. The damage one of these musket balls caused was truly horrific. If one were hit in the body by a musket ball, it was usually always fatal. If you were hit in an extremity, and the ball did not hit a bone, the soldier could count himself as indeed fortunate and his chances of recovery greatly increased. However, if the ball hit a bone, amputation was usually called for in nearly every case because the bone is shattered into pieces by the heavy lead projectile. The surgeon's rule of thumb for such wounds was that the further the damage from the trunk of the body, the better the chance for recovery. The idea here was that if gangrene set in after amputation (as was frequently the case), a wounded soldier with more limb and tissue to remove could possibly recover with a second operation. Those wounded near the shoulder or hip often succumbed to subsequent infection.

There was no organized ambulance service or dedicated stretcher-bearers assigned during a battle. The men had to take care of themselves the best that they could under the circumstances or hope that some of their comrades might haul them off on blankets or sheets of canvass. Soldiers were not normally allowed to drop out of the ranks for any reason, and the injured were usually policed by camp followers and other rear-area personnel after the battle.

Surgeons were also frequently called upon to bleed their patients for a variety of ailments. Sometimes, patients would be bled for three consecutive days. Purging was another common medical procedure and was commonly referred to as a "physick." Opium and Peruvian bark were provided as internal medicines, and nearly all surgeons were very familiar with the use of tourniquets. Most army doctors were ignorant of disease pathology and remained wedded to the medieval theories of the famous physician Galen about bodily "humors—blood, phlegm, black bile, and yellow bile." Significant surgeries were largely limited to "trepanning" or taking out pieces of the skull to "relieve" pressure and clots from head injuries and amputation. It was very rare for a surgeon to even contemplate operating on regions of the body such as the intestines or stomach.[44]

The appearance of "laudable pus" on a wounded soldier was considered a good sign of his eventual recovery. Continental doctors believed that suppuration was the body's attempt at ridding itself of foreign and harmful material. However, "the average 18th century surgeon was so unaware of the causes and effects of infection that, when a colleague achieved an unusually low mortality rate, the explanation was sought in his surgical techniques and not in his standard of cleanliness."[45] In this "pre-scientific" era of medicine, mortality rates inside army hospitals were quite high and most of the men recognized this fact. Corporal James Fergus was ordered into a hospital near Charleston, South Carolina. He noted that he "had seen the [army] hospitals in Philadelphia, Princeton, and Newark and would prefer dying in the open air of the woods rather [than] be stifled to death in a crowded hospital."[46]

During the first year of the war, abandoned Tory homes frequently doubled as field hospitals for the army. Mass inoculations of men usually occurred in the early spring before the serious campaign season got underway, and these men were kept in "pest houses" away from the general populace until they recovered. While the Army of Observation was relatively disease free, with only a 12 percent overall sickness rate, the lack of serious campaigning and the relatively spread-out condition of the American forces in and around Boston likely contributed to their relatively better health. Nonetheless, sickness and not British muskets or bayonets caused the vast majority of American casualties that first campaign as it would throughout the war.

As Dr. Morgan slowly created his system of hospitals, his position as director general required him to accumulate medical supplies for the army. However, finding such supplies was a different matter—nearly all of it had to be brought in from Philadelphia. Adequate surgeon's tools were especially lacking. Most instruments were the personal property of the surgeon and varied as to completeness and serviceability. At one point, Morgan was reduced to suggesting to one surgeon to use a razor blade in place of a scalpel. Moreover, Morgan believed that his principal mission was to accumulate medical supplies in readiness for a general campaign, whereas the busy regimental field hospitals, which were more directly engaged in the day-to-day care of sick men, believed that they should be able to call upon the General Hospital for any supplies they thought necessary for their own day-to-day operations. Nathanael Greene wrote to Congress and complained about Morgan's stockpiling policy:

> The sick of the Army, who are under the care of Regimental Surgeons, are in the most wretched condition; the Surgeons being without the least articles of medicine to assist nature in her efforts for the recovery of health. . . . The Director General complains of want of medicines and says his stocks are but barely sufficient for the General Hospital. I can see no reason, either from policy or humanity, that the stores for the General Hospital should be preserved for contingencies which may never happen And the present regimental sick left to perish for want of proper necessities. It is wholly immaterial, in my opinion, either to the state or to the Army, Whether a man dies in the General or Regimental Hospital.[47]

The bureaucratic infighting between Morgan and the regimental surgeons gained the attention of the commander in chief, who complained that the "constant bickering among them, which tends greatly to the Injury of the sick; and will always subsist till the Regimental Surgeons are made to look upon the director-general of the Hospital as a Superior." He even went so far as to pronounce many of the regimental surgeons as "very great Rascals." Nonetheless, some of the line officers, closer to the situation in the regiments, sided with Greene. For example, General William Smallwood, commanding officer of the Maryland line, refused to send his men to Continental army hospitals and believed that they were better off being taken care of in private homes. Although during the summer and fall of 1776 Congress passed a number of resolutions intended to reform the medical department, it was too little and too late.[48]

Moreover, from nearly the beginning of the war, there was very little accountability of how supplies were obtained or disbursed both at the army and at the regimental levels. Further, getting consistent returns from the hospitals remained a continued thorn in the side of the director general. It was not until mid-July 1776 with the entire army fully ensconced in camps around New York City that Congress finally rectified this situation and officially clarified the relationship between the regimental surgeons and the General Hospital. The new Congressional act finally made the regimental doctors subordinate to the director general and increased the number of medical professionals dedicated to the army and provided for "one surgeon and five mates for every 5000 men and the hiring of as many storekeepers, stewards, nurses, and other hospital employees as deemed necessary, to be appointed by individual hospital directors." Although Morgan hoped that the Congress would allow him to deduct a percentage of a sick soldier's pay to offset the cost of his hospital stay, he was denied this but was allowed to stop the regular daily ration of each soldier admitted to the hospital and use it as he saw fit. Nonetheless, the tension between the regimental hospitals, the General Hospital, and the director general continued over supplies and their command relationship with each other. Morgan wrote to Congress about the regimental surgeons: "they all look to me, for supplies of every thing they want: I have no authority for that purpose." He begged Congress for orders on what he should do and noted that "every General, every Colonel of a Regiment, every surgeon in the army think I have full power, and ample instructions, and know not where to apply for relief of their men, if sick or wounded, and needing uncommon supplies, if I cannot afford them."[49]

However, the medical situation at New York quickly went from bad to worse. Although the army set up hospitals at King's College (Columbia) and at other significant town structures, by "early October, 8,000 of 20,000 troops were sick." By the end of 1776, Morgan's medical department was in a state of virtual collapse.[50] While Morgan was not entirely at fault for the abysmal state of Continental hospitals and the condition of the men, he was certainly not making much progress either, at least for Washington's and Congress's tastes, and he was soon replaced by Dr. William Shippen Jr. of Philadelphia.

Shippen had been originally appointed director general of the Flying Camp hospital in New Jersey and was later given complete charge by Washington of all hospitals west of the Hudson River. Morgan still retained the title of director general, but unclear to even him, he was given only operational control of hospitals on the east side of the Hudson. After Washington's retreat from New York, his position became moot, and with no explanation or word of thanks for prior service, Morgan was dismissed from his post by Congress in early January 1777. Morgan believed that his demise was directly attributable to no small amount of internal intrigue by Shippen, who was soon appointed the new director general. In fact, just two and a half years later, Morgan, aided and abetted by no less an eminent figure than fellow Philadelphia physician and member of Congress Dr. Benjamin Rush, charged Shippen with misconduct and malfeasance in office. Specifically, he was charged by Morgan with selling hospital stores as his own personal property, irregularity in hospital accounting procedures, and, most importantly, spreading rumors about his superior officers in order to supplant them. Nonetheless, after a lengthy and acrimonious investigation with Rush as Morgan's principal witness, Congress and Washington were anxious to put the battle of the director generals behind them, and despite some strong evidence that Shippen did indeed speculate in stores, he was found not guilty of all charges and ordered to be released from arrest. However, the damage to his reputation was done, and Shippen eventually resigned his office and returned to a medical teaching post in Philadelphia.

However, before he resigned, Shippen had established major army hospitals in the Pennsylvania backcountry at Bethlehem, Easton, and Allentown. In fact, Bethlehem became a major focal point for the sick and wounded of the 1777 campaign, and Dr. Shippen sent hundreds of men to this small village of about three hundred souls, most of whom were pacifist Moravians. Many of the sick were housed in the Moravian's large three-story "Brethren's House." The sick and injured of Washington's army were also evacuated directly to Philadelphia before it fell to the British. Hundreds of them died of typhus that winter, and cartloads of dead soldiers rolling through the streets of the city were not an unusual sight. Nancy Shippen exclaimed that "it is too dreadful a scene to attempt to describe. The poor creatures died without numbers."[51]

By 1778, major hospitals were established at two other Moravian towns: Lititz and Ephrata. Camp fevers spread to the local inhabitants. Ephrata's miller, a man named Hans Baer, stated that his parents died from a fever brought to town by sick soldiers and that "the disorder raged through the neighborhood and proved fatal to a great number of all ages." A major convalescent center was established at Yellow Springs, Pennsylvania, and sick and dying soldiers were soon spread out throughout the countryside. By the time of the Valley Forge encampment in late December 1777, "32 percent of Washington's men—sick present and sick absent—were listed as unfit for duty." So grotesque were the conditions in the hospitals that Anthony Wayne was heard to remark that he preferred to fight the British than have to perform hospital inspection duty.[52]

By late 1777, Rush complained to a fellow member of Congress William Duer that he believed that nearly one-half of the army was incapacitated. Although he was likely overstating the case in order to undermine William Shippen, Rush nonetheless noted

Brethren's House at Lititz. (*Courtesy of the Historical Society of Pennsylvania*)

that the crowding of so many soldiers into spaces designed for much smaller numbers was directly contributing to the rapid demise of the soldiers sent to such places. He observed that hospital diseases carried off soldiers but the surgeons as well, noting that "six surgeons have died since last spring of fevers contracted in our hospitals, and there is scarcely one who has not been ill in a greater or lesser degree with it." Two weeks later, Rush wrote directly to Washington and stated that "there cannot be a greater calumity for a sick man than to come into our hospital at *this season* of the year. Old disorders are prolonged, and new ones contracted among us." He was convinced that "a *great majority* of those who die under our hands perish with diseases caught in our hospitals." Like Smallwood, Rush advocated that the soldiers would be better off being housed in farmers' homes in exchange for their daily ration rather than risk a hospital stay. Looking at the hospital returns provided by William Shippen for the month of December 1777, Rush sarcastically observed that he apologized for perhaps overstating the level of mortality at the hospitals and that he had been:

> deceived by counting the number of coffins that were daily put into the ground. From their weight and smell I am persuaded they contained hospital patients in them, and if they were not dead I hope some steps will be taken for the future to prevent and punish the crime of burying the Continental soldiers alive.[53]

Yet all was not doom and gloom in the hospital service. Yellow Springs, Pennsylvania, was a prewar health spa and became a logical site for establishing a large army hospital. Washington ordered a large three-story building (later named Washington

Hall) erected as a hospital facility with plenty of porches and ventilation. The building itself was 106 feet long, 36 feet wide, and divided into individual sick rooms and large wards. It was the only facility of its kind so ordered during the course of the entire war. Yellow Springs quickly established a reputation as a place where a sick soldier might actually recover, in large part thanks to its efficient director, Dr. Bodo Otto and his physician sons.

Most of the Continental hospitals were closed by late 1781, including the very successful facility at Yellow Springs. Dr. John Cochrane, who had replaced William Shippen upon his resignation in January 1781, had ordered it closed because of scarcity of funds necessary for its maintenance and a perceived need to consolidate operations of taking care of a declining number of sick as the war drew to a close. Most of the remaining patients were transferred to Philadelphia and boarded out in private homes. Although Cochrane's hospitals still suffered from a lack of adequate supplies, at least the mortality rates of the patients were finally declining to a degree. However, he was plagued by the resignations of a number of surgeons and physicians anxious to reestablish their practice back at home.

The story of the Continental medical department and its treatment of soldiers is an embarrassing legacy of bureaucratic incompetence and general malfeasance exacerbated by the dueling egos of the leading medical men of the day such as Morgan, William Shippen, and Rush. Moreover, much of the sickness that befell the soldiers could be traced to their own slovenliness and weak leadership on the part of their officers. Nearly three years into the war and after repeated admonitions provided by him in General Orders, Washington toured the camps at Valley Forge and was shocked by what he saw. Carcasses of dead horses still littered most camps, and offal abounded in the streets between soldiers' huts. He issued General Orders in March 1778 that once again reminded the soldiers of the necessity of keeping their camps and huts clean in order to preserve their health. However, the arrival of Baron Friedrich Wilhelm von Steuben greatly helped Washington with his efforts to properly get the men to police their own living spaces. During the Valley Forge winter of 1778, von Steuben produced a pamphlet titled "Regulations for the Order and Discipline of the Troops of the United States." He was adamant that officers must be more diligent in inspecting the health and cleanliness of their men and that "the captains also must never suffer a man who has any infectious disorder to remain in the company, but send him immediately to the hospital." He went so far as to specifically lay out how the camp latrines should be constructed and that they "must be located three hundred feet to the front and rear of the two tent lines. The quarter-master must be answerable . . . that the sinks are filled up, and new ones dug every four days, and oftener in warm weather."[54]

While former Continental army doctor James Thacher estimated in 1823 that nine out of every ten deaths during the Revolution was attributable to disease, a lack of discipline and a general disinterestedness on the part of Congress relating to the medical department certainly contributed to the number of casualties. Although dysentery (the bloody flux) was the most common ailment of a hospitalized soldier, typhus (putrid fever) carried off most of the men. Earlier in the war, before mass inoculations took place, smallpox was the great killer of soldiers in camp. Death was an ever-present companion in most army camps and hospitals, and no one, including the progressive and enlightened Rush, really had an adequate solution for it. The English philosopher Thomas Hobbes may have been right about the lives of most men of the era, and this seemed to be especially true of eighteenth-century soldiers, whose prospects appeared to be nasty and brutish.

NOTES

1. Robert Morris to George Washington, January 1, 1777, quoted in David Hackett Fischer, *Washington's Crossing* (New York: Oxford University Press, 2004), 363.

2. Captain John Chester to Colonel Samuel B. Webb, in Worthington C. Ford, ed., *Correspondence & Journals of Samuel Blachley Webb, 1772–1777, Vol. 1* (New York, 1893), 182–4.

3. John Adams to William Heath, August 3, 1776, in Richard D. Brown, ed., *Major Problems in the Era of the American Revolution, 1760–1791* (Lexington, MA: D. C. Heath Company, 1992), 191.

4. Josiah Burr, quoted in Howard Applegate, "Constitutions Like Iron: The Life of American Revolutionary War Soldiers in the Middle Department, 1775–1783" (PhD diss., Syracuse University, 1966), 15–22.

5. Charles Patrick Neimeyer, *America Goes to War: A Social History of the Continental Army* (New York: New York University Press, 1996), 117–8.

6. James Sullivan to John Adams and Elbridge Gerry, October 11, 1776, in Robert J. Taylor, ed., *Papers of John Adams*, vol. 5 (Cambridge, MA: Harvard University Press, 1979), 50–52; Neimeyer, *America Goes to War*, 118–9.

7. John Taylor, quoted in James Kirby Martin and Mark E. Lender, *A Respectable Army: The Military Origins of the Republic, 1763–1789*. 2nd ed. (Wheeling, IL: Harlan Davidson, 2006), 77–78.

8. Alexander Graydon, *Memoirs of His Own Time* (New York: New York Times & Arno Press, 1969), 133–6.

9. George Washington, "Recruiting Instructions," January 13, 1777, in John C. Fitzpatrick, ed., *The Writings of George Washington*, vol. 7 (Washington, DC: U.S. Government Printing Office, 1925), 7–8.

10. Joseph Plumb Martin, quoted in James Kirby Martin, ed., *Ordinary Courage: The Revolutionary War Adventures of Joseph Plumb Martin*. 2nd ed. (St. James, NY: Brandywine Press, 1999), 37–38.

11. Ibid., 38–39.

12. Neimeyer, *America Goes to War*, 52; Melodie Andrews, "Myrmidons from Abroad: The Role of the German Mercenary in the Coming of American Independence," (PhD diss., University of Houston, 1986), 286: *Journals of the Continental Congress*, Vol. 5, 653–5.

13. Neimeyer, *America Goes to War*, 61; Edward J. Lowell, *The Hessians and the Other German Auxiliaries of Great Britain in the Revolutionary War* (Williamstown, MA: Corner House Publishers, 1975), 288.

14. Neimeyer, *America Goes to War*, 35.

15. Ibid., 36.

16. Peter Force, *American Archives*, 4th ser., 2:762, 3:1385; quoted in W. B. Hargrove, "The Negro in the American Revolution," *Journal of Negro History*, no. 1 (1916): 126.

17. Neimeyer, *America Goes to War*, 83.

18. Robert K. Wright Jr., *The Continental Army* (Washington, DC: Center of Military History, 1986), 145; Neimeyer, *America Goes to War*, 83.

19. Neimeyer, *America Goes to War*, 74–75; Lorenzo Greene, "Some Observations on the Black Regiment of Rhode Island in the American Revolution," *Journal of Negro History* 37, no. 2 (1952): 88, 171.

20. Neimeyer, *America Goes to War*, 76.

21. Samuel Parsons to George Washington, March 6, 1777, in Ford, *Correspondence & Journals of Samuel Blachley Webb, 1772–1777, Vol. 1*, 189–91.

22. Samuel Parsons to George Washington, May 15, 1777, in Ford, *Correspondence & Journals of Samuel Blachley Webb, 1772–1777, Vol. 1*, 210.

23. Charles Henry Metzger, *The Prisoner in the American Revolution* (Chicago, IL: Loyola University Press, 1962), ix–x.

24. Joseph Rundel, in John C. Dann, ed., *The Revolution Remembered: Eyewitness Accounts of the War for Independence* (Chicago, IL: University of Chicago Press, 1980), 67.

25. John Blatchford, *The Narrative of John Blatchford* (New York: New York Times & Arno Press, 1971), 9–24.

26. Blatchford, *The Narrative of John Blatchford*, 28–31.

27. George Washington to Lord Richard Howe, January 13, 1777, in Fitzpatrick, *The Writings of Washington*, vol. 7, 3–4.

28. Jabez Fitch, *The New-York Diary of Lieutenant Jabez Fitch* (New York: New York Times & Arno Press, 1971), 34–35.

29. William McPherson, quoted in Fitch, *The New-York Diary of Lieutenant Jabez Fitch*, 71.

30. Jonathan Gillet, quoted in Fitch, *The New-York Diary of Lieutenant Jabez Fitch*, 78–79.

31. Captain Thomas Dring, in Albert Greene, ed., *Recollections of the Jersey Prison Ship* (Bedford, MA: Applewood Books, 1829), xiv, 5–7.

32. Ibid., 26–27.

33. Thomas Andros, *The Old Jersey Captive* (Boston, MA: William Peirce, 1833), 9, 13, 15, 17.

34. Dring, in Albert Greene, *Recollections of the Jersey Prison Ship*, 38–42.

35. Ibid., 58–63.

36. Patrick Hughes, quoted in Metzger, *The Prisoner in the American Revolution*, 201.

37. Metzger, *The Prisoner in the American Revolution*, 209–10.

38. Elias Boudinot, "Colonel Elias Boudinot in New York City, February, 1778" in *Pennsylvania Magazine of History and Biography*, 24 (1900–1901): 454.

39. Ibid., 455.

40. E. Wayne Carp, *To Starve the Army at Pleasure: Continental Army Administration and American Political Culture, 1775–1783* (Chapel Hill, NC: University of North Carolina Press, 1984), 26.

41. Richard L. Blanco, "American Army Hospitals in Pennsylvania During the Revolutionary War," *Pennsylvania History* 48, no. 4 (1981): 347–8.

42. Samuel B. Webb, July 14, 1777, in Ford, *Correspondence & Journals of Samuel Blachley Webb, 1772–1777, Vol. 1*, 243.

43. Mary C. Gillett, *The Army Medical Department, 1775–1818* (Washington, DC: The Center of Military History, 1981), 11, 13–14.

44. Richard Blanco, "Continental Army Hospitals and American Society, 1775–1781," in *Adapting to Conditions: War and Society in the Eighteenth Century*, ed. Maarten Ultee (Tuscaloosa, AL: University of Alabama Press, 1986), 153.

45. Gillett, *The Army Medical Department, 1775–1818*, 17.

46. James Fergus, in Dann, *The Revolution Remembered*, 184.

47. Nathanael Greene, in James E. Gibson, *Dr. Bodo Otto and the Medical Background of the American Revolution* (Springfield, IL: Charles C. Thomas, 1937), 121–2.

48. George Washington, quoted in Whitfield J. Bell Jr., *John Morgan—Continental Doctor* (Philadelphia, PA: University of Pennsylvania Press, 1965), 196.

49. Gillett, *The Army Medical Department, 1775–1818*, 31; John Morgan, quoted in Bell, *John Morgan*, 192.

50. Blanco, "Continental Army Hospitals and American Society, 1775–1781," 160.

51. Nancy Shippen, quoted in Blanco, "American Army Hospitals in Pennsylvania During the Revolutionary War," 353.

52. Blanco, "American Army Hospitals in Pennsylvania During the Revolutionary War," 359, 362.

53. Benjamin Rush to William Duer, December 13, 1777, Benjamin Rush to George Washington, December 26, 1777, and Benjamin Rush to Nathanael Greene, February 1, 1778, in L. H. Butterfield, ed., *Letters of Benjamin Rush. Vol. 1, 1761–1792* (Princeton, NJ: Princeton University Press, 1951), 175, 180–1.

54. Stanhope Bayne-Jones, *The Evolution of Preventive Medicine in the United States Army, 1607–1939* (Washington, DC: Office of the Surgeon General, Department of the Army, 1968), 35, 44.

4 "THE YEAR OF THE HANGMAN": 1777 AND CONTINENTAL ARMY COMMUNITIES

As the campaign season of 1777 opened—the year of the hangman, as some called it—George Washington was apprehensive about his new model army. He believed that despite the effort to recruit longer-termed troops, the patriot war effort still too heavily relied on militia to support his Continental army. Writing in late 1776, he noted that:

> To place any dependence upon Militia, is, assuredly, resting upon a broken Staff. Men just dragged from the tender Scenes of domestick life; unaccustomed to the din of Arms: totally unacquainted with every kind of Military skill, when opposed by Troops regularly train'd, disciplined and Appointed, make them timid and ready to fly at their own shadows. Besides, the sudden change in their manner of living, (particularly lodging) brings on sickness in many. . . . To bring Men to a proper degree of Subordination, is not the work of a day, a Month or even a year; and unhappily for us and the cause we are Engaged in, the little discipline I have been laboring to establish in the Army . . . is in a manner done away with by such a mixture of Troops as have been called together within these few months.[1]

Yet throughout the war, Washington could hardly afford to do without the militia. A full two-thirds of the force he had gathered near Morristown, New Jersey, in the spring of 1777 were short-termed militia. One reason for Washington's reticence to rely upon them had to do with individual state's policies of unit rotation. This system moved state militia units in and out of service with the main army or "Flying Camps" (a strategic reserve of militia paid by Congress and gathered near the army to be called upon by the commander in chief in case of emergencies) after service of only a few months. This meant that as soon as the regular drill and discipline of the main army or Flying Camp service began to have an effect on a particular unit, the men were marched for home to be replaced by another "green" militia command that needed similar training.

Although this system was certainly abhorrent to Washington and his generals, it did have one particularly positive effect. Many of the returning short-termed "veterans" became exceptionally effective in tamping down any local loyalist sentiment that might arise in their local neighborhoods. Militia service also served, as historian John Shy noted, as an excellent loyalty test. Local patriot political leaders were quick to notice who showed up for muster and who did not. And if one did not have a legitimate excuse for not attending militia formations with the main army or at local drills, then the militia might one fine day show up with torches and tar at the recalcitrant citizen's house and threaten him and his family with property damage or bodily harm. Thus, it really did not matter how much loyalist sentiment was latently resident in a particular locale. The fact that the patriot militia were constantly drilling, active, and more than willing to use force against loyalists made them particularly effective as a tool of local authority and control. The loyalists could rarely muster similar forces that acted and openly drilled in the manner of the patriot militia even in the south where loyalist sentiment in the backcountry was thought to be especially high.

The Congressionally mandated eighty-eight-battalion Continental army force never fully materialized for Washington. By late spring 1777, Washington had about "forty-three [understrength] regiments of about 200 men" each in central New Jersey. But on the bright side, secret supplies from the French were starting to arrive, to include twenty thousand new Charleville muskets, barrels of precious powder and flints, food, clothing, and blankets. However, for the coming campaign season, Washington would have far fewer than the twenty thousand effectives he had in 1776 to defend New York City, and the British, during this same time, had substantially increased the number of troops they had sent to North America. But the army Washington did have (about nine thousand men) were considered long-termed "regulars," and at least in his mind these men were probably worth more than double the same amount of short-termed militia who were, as he had earlier complained to Congress, in the field on one day and gone the next.[2]

WOMEN AND THE ARMY

There was one significant component of the army that has, until very recently, been neglected by historians, and that was the large number of women who followed and supported army operations, even at times as regular musket-wielding or cannon-firing combat soldiers.

During the eighteenth century, women were an integral and accepted part of regular army regimental establishments. This system was practiced by nearly all European armies of the time, and thus it was copied by the Continental army as well. These "women of the army" were usually the wives of noncommissioned officers (NCOs) and were accorded an official "half-ration" for subsistence. The standard number on the roles of each company was usually around four or five. However, in reality, there were many more. Further, controlling the number of women who followed their husbands, brothers, sons, or lovers into the field and who were found around camp doing various chores was very difficult for most eighteenth-century commanding generals. On being informed by "friends to the government" that the rebel army around White Plains, New York, was about fourteen thousand men, one British intelligence report stated that this number should not be worrisome since "women and Waggoners make up near half the army." A 1778 personnel return from Valley Forge noted more than four hundred women drawing rations. Toward the end of the war, a return from West Point, New York, and New Windsor, Connecticut, listed 405 women and 302 children as receiving rations.[3]

And by all accounts, there were a lot of women with the army. Writing frequently about this subject in General Orders, Washington himself seemed quite exasperated with the number of women in and around his army. On August 4, 1777, he complained that "the multitude of women in particular, especially those who are pregnant, or have children, are a clog upon every movement." Just three weeks later on August 27, he warned that "women are especially forbid any longer, under any license at all, to ride in the waggons, and the officers earnestly called upon to permit no more than are absolutely necessary, and such as are actually useful, to follow the army." And by follow, he meant just that and wanted them to tag along behind the wagon train that trailed behind each brigade. However, Washington was never able to successfully control the number of women associated in various ways with the army, and they usually walked among the men in the ranks (or rode in the wagons if Washington and his officers were not especially vigilant) and set up camp where they pleased.[4]

It is important to note that Revolutionary era camp followers were not prostitutes. This unfortunate connotation developed later during the American Civil War. Although prostitution certainly was present in and around nearly all eighteenth-century army camps, most women camp followers fulfilled a logistics and/or support role of some sort. Moreover, the normally penniless soldiery had little to offer these women in return; thus, most prostitutes operated in and around major cities such as New York's infamous "Holy Ground" and generally avoided the less lucrative army camps. To make extra money, many "women of the army" took in laundry, cooked food for various soldier messes, and sewed and repaired clothing. They quickly became a part of army life in camp, on the march, and even on the battlefield. These same women were often the only ones to assist the wounded after a battle, forward the rations for the men on the march, and, at times, fill in for men cut down in the heat of combat.

During the Revolution, there were several celebrated cases of women acting as combat soldiers. One of the most famous was that of Deborah Sampson Gannett. Masquerading as a soldier named Robert Shurtliff, Deborah Sampson joined the Continental army late in the war, received a bounty for enlisting, and was later selected as a member of the "light infantry" in the Massachusetts line. She saw combat near Tarrytown, New York, was wounded, and ended up serving seventeen months in the line before she was "discovered" after apparently undergoing a violent fever in camp near Philadelphia, Pennsylvania.

Historian Alfred Young has recently written a definitive account, *Masquerade*, on the curious case of Deborah Sampson. The question of how she got away with her "masquerade" is important to understand because there were undoubtedly other women "passing" as men in Deborah's same situation. In sum, Young noted that "she hid herself as a woman, paradoxical as it may seem, by standing out as a man." Deborah Sampson as Robert Shurtliff became a model soldier, hence her selection to an elite infantry formation.[5]

There were at least two other recorded cases of women from Massachusetts who tried, though unsuccessfully, to pass as men. One was Ann (or Nancy) Bailey of Boston, who enlisted in 1777 under the name Sam Gay, received a £15, 10 shilling bounty, was promoted to corporal, and was discovered less than three weeks later. Fleeing the camp, she was arrested and charged with "fraudulently intending to cheat & injure the inhabitants of the state" and for "pretending to be a young man." She spent the next two months in jail. Later in the war, Anne Smith tried to enlist as Samuel Smith and was discovered by a mustering officer's examination. Sent to jail, she blithely informed her jailors that the joke was on them as she had allegedly spent the past three months in the ranks as a soldier already.[6]

However, other women soldiers did not get off so lightly. Women discovered as "passing" for men risked being humiliated by their discoverers. During 1778 in New Jersey, one masquerading woman accidentally tipped an officer off when she allegedly curtsied after handing him a tankard of ale. While she pleaded with the officer that she was only in the army to marry a fellow soldier against her father's wishes, he nonetheless "ordered the drums to beat her Threw the town with the whores march." Remarking on the decision of the state of Pennsylvania to award a pension to a woman soldier in 1822, a New York City newspaper mused that "it would be interesting to collect anecdotes of the services rendered by women during the revolutionary war." Clearly, they believed that there were quite a few. And of course, there was the ultimate sacrifice of Sally St. Clair, who dressed as a man was killed in action at the Battle of Savannah and was only "discovered" as she was being prepared for burial.[7]

Deborah Sampson's service should not be confused with what the large majority of women camp followers did during the war, and her record as a musket-wielding infantryman was indeed exemplary. But besides her conduct as a soldier, how did Deborah Sampson make it seventeen months without being discovered? The answer to this question lies in the everyday routine of a Revolutionary War soldier. First, the army uniforms were made of loose fitting wool. Therefore, a woman could easily disguise her female form. Many women "passing as men" used bandages wound around their chests to suppress any possible evidence of their breasts. When soldiers had to use the latrine or "sinks," as they were called in camp, they could do so at various times by going off into the woods alone or at night when everyone was asleep. Soldiers did not wear undergarments but rather simply unbuttoned a flap on their breeches and pulled up the tails of their long shirts to relieve themselves. Since male soldiers typically urinated in the bushes or trees standing up and squatted to defecate, Deborah Sampson could have possibly gotten away with squatting to relieve herself when other soldiers assumed she may have been in the act of defecating and thus would have never raised an eyebrow. No one assumed then or now that a soldier's life is refined. Further, Revolutionary War soldiers seldom took any occasion to bathe or change their clothes. Therefore, there was little risk of discovery on these counts. A soldier often went weeks without any occasion to take his uniform off. Finally, as a light infantryman, Deborah Sampson would have operated more independently of the main army and would have been on her own and away from large numbers of her comrades for extended periods of time.[8]

One other category of female soldier that needs to be discussed is that of the camp follower who filled in for dead or wounded comrades—usually during the heat of battle. One such person was the legendary Molly Pitcher. Historians now believe that Molly Pitcher was an amalgam of a number of women camp followers who filled in for fallen comrades during combat. As a sort of "G.I. Jane" of her era, the original Molly Pitcher can be traced either to Margaret Corbin or Mary Ludwig Hays—both camp followers with husbands in the artillery. Historian Linda Grant De Pauw believes that Molly Pitcher may even have been a complete postwar fabrication. However, numerous witnesses observed during the siege of Fort Washington Margaret Corbin taking her mate's place at the cannon's mouth, after he was killed. Like hundreds of other women, Margaret had followed her man into the army. When fired, the cannon needs to be sponged out to prevent the burning remains of the previous shot from igniting the next charge prematurely. Woman camp followers often ran buckets of freshwater from the

Molly Pitcher firing canon at the Battle of Monmouth. (*Courtesy of the Library of Congress*)

rear to the artillery line for this purpose. This is what Margaret was doing when she spontaneously took her husband John's place. She was severely wounded and nearly had an arm torn off by British grapeshot. Living as a disabled veteran until about 1800 outside the West Point army post in the village of Highland Falls, she became known as "Captain Molly" and had a reputation for being quite irascible.

The story of Mary Ludwig Hays was slightly different. She became famous because of her actions during the battle of Monmouth in 1778. Mary was identified as serving as a cannoneer after her husband had been wounded at his gun. However, one eyewitness to the battle observed Mary and her husband working the cannon together. In something of a stretch, although possible, this witness also noted that Mary narrowly avoided being wounded when a cannonball allegedly passed completely through her skirts and legs (as they were extended apart as she served the cannon) without her suffering a scratch. If true, this was an incredible stroke of luck but was also just the sort of whimsy later Victorian writers might imagine for Revolutionary-era heroines. We know that Mary did serve and that the Pennsylvania legislature gave her a pension in 1822, but she did not become known as Molly Pitcher until 1876 when a marker was created for her grave in Carlisle, Pennsylvania.[9]

Thanks in large part to the large number of women and other retainers present in camp, Revolutionary-era historian Holly Mayer has described camp life as a virtual "Continental Community," a sort of roving society in miniature held together by rough military justice and a mutual desire for survival. This military tradition of accepting large numbers of camp followers in and around armies was of long and accepted standing.

Indeed, they could be found nearly everywhere. The wife of Private Warner accompanied him on the horrifically difficult expedition of Benedict Arnold and his men through the swamp and bog-ridden Maine wilderness during the early winter of 1775. With famine and extreme privation prevalent throughout most of the journey, Mrs. Warner dutifully stayed behind the line of march to attend to her dying husband, even though by doing so, many contemporary witnesses believed, she was condemning herself to a similar death by starvation. Nonetheless, they were astounded when six weeks later, after she had covered her husband's grave with leaves and sticks (so weak was her condition), this intrepid woman caught up with the rest of expedition and was alive and well when so many of the men on the expedition had succumbed.[10]

Another group of women frequently seen in and around the army were officers' wives. The more senior an officer, the more likely at some point during the year (usually when the army was in winter garrison) his wife and sometimes even his children would join him in camp. Washington's wife, Martha, made frequent and extended visits to camp. This was probably due to the fact that in his eight years as commander in chief, Washington only visited his home at Mount Vernon once for a period of just two weeks. These particular women did not operate under the same rules that applied to the general class of camp followers, who were often subject to orders from officers and summary punishment just like a private soldier in the ranks. Instead, these particular women were treated like the visitors that they were and socialized with each other according to the hierarchy of the day.

Many women also served as nurses. However, this did not become prevalent until 1777. For example, while the teenaged soldier Joseph Plumb Martin was hired as a nurse at the end of the 1776 campaign and his first enlistment, as the Continental army manpower crisis deepened, fewer able-bodied men were offered this opportunity. Instead, this role fell increasingly to female camp followers. In early 1777, Washington asked his commanding officers to "assist Regimental Surgeons in procuring as many Women of the Army as can be prevailed on to serve as Nurses to them who will be paid the usual Price." Later, after the 1777 reorganization of the Continental army medical staff, one hospital matron and ten nurses were allocated for every hundred sick and wounded men. Nurses were to receive 0.24 cents a day plus a full food ration. The matrons, being in a more supervisory position, got more than twice that rate at 0.50 cents a day plus the full ration, which was incidentally nearly double what a line army sergeant made each day. Even with the inducements, there never seemed to be enough women available or willing to perform hospital duty. This was perhaps understandable since Continental hospitals had a great reputation for mortality not only for admitted patients but for the caregivers as well. Most women preferred to take their chances away from such places.[11]

More women were employed as washerwomen than as nurses or cooks. Often, officers were required to certify a particular woman's official status as washerwomen before she was allowed to draw a ration. In fact, there was an army-wide problem with fraud concerning the number of washerwomen allocated to each company and regiment. The rule of thumb was one woman to wash for every ten soldiers or about four to a company. By all accounts, these women did fairly well financially, although there were times when the men complained of price gouging. Colonel Walter Stewart of the Pennsylvania line warned the camp followers that if he found them overcharging for wash above the rates set by the army he would have them drummed out of camp. Orders were later issued that denied rations to those laundresses who violated the established rates. However, inflation toward the end of the war was so pernicious that many officers and men found it more convenient to hire a woman as a permanent member of the regiment in order to avoid ruinous laundry bills.[12]

Occasionally, women not directly "of the army" played a different sort of revolutionary role, that of price enforcer for recalcitrant storekeepers. In 1777, in East Hartford, Connecticut, a group of approximately twenty women "marched about one mile, in martial array and excellent order . . . there attacked and carried away without opposition from powder, law or conscience, Mr. Perkin's store in which was lodged a quantity of sugar designed for the army of which they plundered and bord away in triumph 218lb." During the same timeframe, Abigail Adams recorded that in Boston more than one hundred women marched to a warehouse where a merchant, whom she specially noted was a bachelor, had stored a large quantity of coffee. Demanding the keys, the women were refused by the merchant, whereupon one of their number seized him by the neck and abruptly tossed him headfirst into a nearby cart. He thereupon thought better of his situation and quickly surrendered the warehouse keys. The women loaded the coffee into the cart and drove off. All the other merchants in Boston got the message.[13]

One other category of women who clearly made a contribution to the war effort but, again, not necessarily as recognized soldiers or militia were those who defended their own scattered and isolated frontier settlements from attack, especially from Indians and loyalist militia. Frontier defensive stands by women were both numerous and legendary. For example, in rural Georgia, a six-foot-tall warrior named Nancy Morgan Hart was credited with capturing dozens of Tories during the course of the war. The most famous incident involved her wading the Broad River and personally taking three Tories prisoner. While many of these frontier stories should be taken with a grain of salt, Nancy Hart was indeed a real person and the number of witnesses to her exploits is too numerous to ignore. Moreover, these stories about her did not spring up in the later nineteenth century, like the Betsy Ross and Molly Pitcher legends. Rather, Nancy Hart stories were being told while she was still alive. In fact, by the 1820s, one Georgia congressman wanted to immortalize Nancy's exploits by commissioning a painting of her capture of the three Tories at the Broad River and having it placed in the U.S. Capitol. Later, during the Civil War, Georgia women formed mutual protection societies called "the Nancy Harts." Nancy Hart died in Kentucky in the 1820s, but Hart County, Georgia, was named as a memorial to her revolutionary exploits.[14]

We may never know the exact number of women who served in and around the Continental army. The lax rules regarding the wide variety of roles performed by women for the army make this nearly impossible to estimate.[15] Although most of that service was in the role of camp follower, perhaps at least several dozen served openly as female warriors like Nancy Hart or "passed" as male soldiers like Deborah Sampson. Their contribution to the war effort was certainly not inconsequential.

WARFARE ON THE FRONTIER

Throughout the Revolution, fighting in the American backcountry was constant and exceptionally brutal. Most of the job of defense fell upon local militia bands or even individual families themselves, such as that of Nancy Hart of Georgia. Most often, prisoners were not taken and there were allegations of atrocities, massacres, and scalp bounties being perpetuated by both sides. British Territorial Governor Henry Hamilton, who was known to his American opponents as "the hair-buyer," testified that he had witnessed the Virginian Commander George Rogers Clark personally order sixteen captured Indians be "serially tomahawked to death" by his men. Nonetheless, at the same time, Henry Hamilton noted that Shawnee Indians had recently captured seventy-three American prisoners from various settlements in Kentucky, including the famous frontiersman Daniel Boone, and had brought in 129 scalps to Fort Detroit.[16]

During the war, various Native American tribes allied themselves with the British or American causes. However, owing to the expansionist policies of individual American states both before and during the war, most tribes with a few notable exceptions allied themselves with the Crown. Although initially the Americans hoped that the western border tribes would remain neutral during the conflict, it quickly became evident that this sort of thinking was overly optimistic. Washington himself noted that, "in my opinion, it will be impossible to keep them in a state of neutrality; they must, and no doubt will, take an active part either for or against us."[17]

An Indian warrior with a scalp. (*Courtesy of the Library of Congress*)

By the latter part of the eighteenth century, the native tribes had become dependent on western technology and trade, especially gunpowder, muskets, steel hatchets, and other implements for war and defense. They needed steady access to this technology or they quickly became vulnerable to rival tribes or marauding white settlers. Thus, early in the war, both sides sent various commissioners into the backcountry and attempted to sway the tribes one way or the other, usually through the promise of increased trade or access to such goods. In this regard, the British were much better suited to supply the Indians than the Americans. For example, as early as 1775, the British had at least fifty officers courting the Iroquois nation alone. Dozens of other agents traveled throughout the backcountry visiting and working deals with one tribe or another. One of those agents, John Butler, ridiculed Iroquois sachems for even entertaining the thought of an alliance with the American side:

> Your resolutions are very surprising; where is any one body of men to be compared to the King? As for Genl Schuyler (and other Commisrs) of whom you boast so much, what is he? . . . He has no men, guns, cannon and ammunition and should he survive the summer he must perish by the cold next winter for want of blankets. But the King wants [lacks] neither men nor numbers.[18]

However, few tribes served formally as Continental soldiers or as part of the regular British military establishment. One exceptional case was the Stockbridge tribe of Massachusetts. The Stockbridge enlisted numbers of their warriors directly into the Continental army. Unfortunately, many of these men were killed in a battle near White Plains, New York, in late 1776, where they lost at least thirty-seven of their men in this one single action. Instead, most Native American warriors who became involved in the Revolutionary War served as auxiliaries and as scouts. Operating as independent bands throughout the frontier region, and often led and supplied by British officers posted at Forts Detroit or Niagara, they wreaked havoc on American homesteaders and militia formations in western New York, northern Pennsylvania, the Ohio country, and Kentucky.

During 1776, the southern Cherokee tribe believed that the time was right to take advantage of the American occupation with fighting the British. Supplemented by 1500 pounds of newly arrived British gunpowder, the Cherokee attacked a number of frontier settlements in western Virginia, eastern Tennessee, and North and South Carolina. In response, militia expeditions went after them, but the Cherokee generally avoided engaging them in a set-piece battle and melted back into the forests. Instead, the militia contented themselves with burning Cherokee towns and food supplies after they had been abandoned. This had the strategic effect of convincing the Cherokee to mostly avoid renewing conflict with the "Virginians" (as they called all frontier settlers) for most of the war. Nonetheless, the frontier settlements remained highly vulnerable to raids and depredations on an annual basis.

Typically, the defense of the American backcountry relied on a robust militia or ranger formations that operated out of and between fortified homesteads, blockhouses, and hastily erected wooden stockade-style forts. These forts would be liberally spread throughout the backcountry, and most militia commanders situated them so that they could be mutually supporting. Being totally on the defensive, these fortifications were anything but pleasant. One settler near Harrodsburg, Kentucky, complained that the water around there was full of "the whole dirt and filth of the fort, putrified flesh, dead dogs, horse, cow and hog excrements."[19] Typhoid fever and dysentery were common problems, and it was not uncommon for ambushes and murders to take place at the very doorsteps of a fortified settlement or blockhouse.

The militia would be on occasion—and when the threat seemed likely to overwhelm the backcountry defenders—supplemented by regular soldiers detached for special expeditionary duty from Washington's or Philip Schuyler's Continental regiments.

However, for many militiamen on the western frontier, going off after the Indians presented them with a Hobbesian choice. Colonel William Preston wrote to fellow militia Colonel William Fleming on May 10, 1778, after the murder of a family in western Virginia that he:

> was really at a loss what to do. To leave my Property as an Individual, & my Duty as an Officer in the Militia, is very Disagreeable to me; to continue, thus exposed & Defenceless, an easy Prey to a small Party of Savages, and run the Risque of having my Wife & numerous helpless Family Sacrificed at some unhappy and Unguarded moment looks like madness or Stupidity.

Preston prevailed upon his neighbors to ask Virginia state Governor Patrick Henry for orders that would enable him to leave a guard for the families in the region. Preston noted that if the Governor did not quickly accede to his request, he would "Pay and maintain any Number, to a Sergeants Command . . . at my own private Expence until I got an Answer; & then I shall take the most prudent steps in my Power for the safety of my Family & will, I think, be highly Justifiable in doing so."[20]

Owing to the vagaries of warfare on the western frontier, desertion remained a pernicious problem. General Edward Hand, sent to Fort Pitt by Washington in an attempt to create some semblance of military order on the frontier, wrote to Horatio Gates on April 28, 1778, that he had to send a party of forty soldiers after fourteen deserters. The deserters were ultimately recaptured but not without a fight with their pursuers. One of the deserters was killed outright, and after a quick general court-martial, some of the ringleaders were hanged by General Hand. Hand gave $200 to the party that had recaptured the men.

The Difficulties of Defending Settlers and Territories

Continued attacks on the frontier, mass evacuations of various remote valleys by frightened settlers, ambushes, and desertions by the militia convinced Timothy Pickering to write to Washington in May 1778. He believed that:

> to repel the incursions of the Indians, & reduce the disaffected to obedience, nothing, in my opinion, will be effectual but a regular force, under the direction of good officers. The inhabitants appear, many of them, to be a wild ungovernable race, little less savage than their tawny neighbors; and by similar barbarities have in fact provoked them to revenge.[21]

Eventually, Washington detached the 13th Virginia and 8th Pennsylvania regiments for frontier duty.

One barely literate soldier from the 8th Pennsylvania wrote to his brother in 1779 and described what it was like for him in the ranks on the frontier:

> I got to the Block House A Bout the Midle Of the After Noon whare I had to Stay all Night And got in the Next Day in time to Draw my Cloathing But had Almost been to Late. . . . Duty is Hard & [unreadable] is Very Particular for if a man Dus any thing Amiss Into the gard house with him & he Must Either List [Dur]ing the War or Receive thirty Nine on his back.

This same soldier referred to the frontier Fort Laurens as "fort Noncence" and was not altogether happy about being stationed out west.[22]

In 1778, British officers and the highly capable Iroquois leader, Joseph Brant, led a massive raid of British regulars and Iroquois warriors into the Wyoming valley of Pennsylvania near present-day Wilkes-Barre. In what was described as the "Great Runaway" by many settlers, William McClay, a citizen of the frontier town of Sunbury and, after the war, a leading senator from Pennsylvania, described the situation for the state executive council:

> I never in my life saw such scenes of distress. The river and roads leading down were covered with men, women and children, fleeing for their lives, many without any property at all, and none who had not left the greater part behind. In short, Northumberland county is broken up. Colonel Hunter alone remained using his utmost endeavors to rally some of the inhabitants, and to make a stand, however short, against the enemy. . . . Wyoming is totally abandoned. Scarce a family remained between that place and Sunbury, when I came away. . . . For God's sake, for the sake of the county, let Colonel Hunter be reinforced at Sunbury. Send him but a single company, if you cannot send more . . . [23]

Such pleading compelled Congress and Washington to authorize an expedition against Brant's men in northern Pennsylvania and western New York in early 1779. Led by Major General John Sullivan, Continental regulars chased the Iroquois without really being able to close with them. With the exception of a sharp-pitched battle around present-day Elmira, New York, Sullivan's men largely faced a retreating enemy and had to content themselves with burning Iroquois corn fields and their abandoned and defenseless settlements. Not strong enough to take out Fort Niagara, much of Sullivan's force was eventually discharged at Easton, Pennsylvania, in late 1779 and not replaced. Although Sullivan's short-lived offensive enabled many backcountry farmers to return to the region, ambushes and murders of settlers and small detachments of militia and even regulars continued unabated for the rest of the war. In Special Orders sent by Washington "congratulating" Sullivan on the success of his expedition, the commander in chief noted that:

> Forty of their Towns have been reduced to Ashes—some of them large & commodious that of Chenisee [Genesee] alone contain one hundred twenty-eight Houses, their Crops of Corn have been entirely destroyed which by Estimation it is said would have produced one hundred & Sixty thousand Bushels besides large Quantities of Vegitables of various Kinds, their whole Country has been overrun & laid waste & they themselves compelled to place their own Security in a precipitate Flight to the British Fortress at Niagra. . . . [24]

Nonetheless, regular expeditions against the Indians on the frontier were few and far between. Moreover, the problem of supply and keeping regulars in the region made it difficult for the Americans to follow-up on their success against the Iroquois.

However, during 1778 in the Ohio country, the Americans did meet with more tangible results. William Rogers Clark led a small force of French and American frontier volunteers through to Ohio country and ultimately attacked British outposts at Vincennes and Kaskaskia (in present-day Indiana). The actual purpose of his expedition against the British in the Illinois country remains unclear since real British power in the Northwest continued to emanate from Fort Detroit and Clark's military objectives lay in the opposite direction. Nonetheless, both Vincennes and Kaskaskia fell to Clark's force and did serve to partially relieve military pressure against the Kentucky settlements. Moreover, a relief expedition led by British Territorial Governor Henry Hamilton was defeated and captured in the Wabash country by Clark after a horrendous march with 180 ragged and starved soldiers. The British commander at Fort Michilimackinac noted that "Mr. Hamilton's defeat has cooled the Indians in General." Again, Clark's meager force could do little more than maintain what they had gained. A planned expedition to rid the region of the pernicious problem of the British at Fort Detroit had to be called off because of a lack of men and provisions, and a sixty-man resupply force coming up river from New Orleans to Fort Pitt was ambushed and nearly wiped out by a band of 130 Indians.[25] By 1780, the frontier militia was once again totally on the defensive.

The British campaign to subdue the southern states late in the war saw a resurgence of Indian attacks along the southern frontier, particularly against settlements in the Cumberland valley of Tennessee. These same years also saw the northern frontier explode in an orgy of violence and killing as well, with neither side gaining any real advantage. In 1780, for example, Indian warriors captured a militia force at Skenesborough and then assaulted the American settlements in the Schoharie and Mohawk valleys. Scalpings, murders, and ambushes were prevalent, and once again settlers fled eastward in fear and terror. It was reported that the territory of New York north of Schenectady was nearly abandoned, with more than one thousand homes and barns and "60,000 bushels of grain" being taken or destroyed by the raiders. Only ongoing peace negotiations following the American victory at Yorktown brought any respite to the region.[26]

WARFARE IN THE EASTERN UNITED STATES, 1777

Philadelphia

Meanwhile, back east, it was clear to just about everyone in North America that the British were preparing yet another major offensive in the summer of 1777. Washington's spies inside New York eventually led him to believe that their likely target was the rebel capital of Philadelphia; hence, anticipating an overland move by William Howe from New York City, he continued to rapidly recruit and build his third army in three years in the hills of central New Jersey. To make matters worse, General John Burgoyne in Canada was preparing to invade northern New England and New York, while a smaller force under Colonel Barry St. Leger came eastward via the Mohawk valley. Their obvious objective was a juncture at Albany, New York. With New York City already in British hands, all they would then have to do would be to join the two forces in the New York Highlands and thereby cut off New England from the rest of the states to the south.

Howe's decision to move his army against Philadelphia is one of the more curious choices made by any general during the course of the war on *either* side. Knowing full well of St. Leger's and Burgoyne's forces moving east and south, respectively, toward Albany, his decision to seize the rebel capital appears even more strange. Yet Howe's plan to take Philadelphia was reluctantly approved by the American Secretary Lord George Germain. Perhaps the ease with which the British had heretofore bested Washington and his army at New York made them disdainful of any possible defense the patriots might offer in either theater. Or possibly Howe saw Burgoyne as a potential rival for the glory of crushing the American rebellion and was content to let him hack

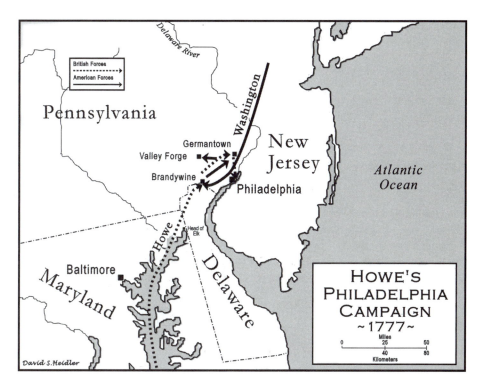

Howe's Philadelphia Campaign

his way south through thick wilderness beset by marauding patriot militia bands such as the Green Mountain Boys, who inhabited and virtually ruled upstate New York. Or, once having taken Philadelphia (since failure against Washington never truly occurred to him), he may have thought that he would have plenty of time to detach adequate forces to link up with Burgoyne. In the end, all this conjecture did not matter as Howe's subsequent decision to take a water route to Philadelphia vice fighting his way past Washington's prepared defenses around Middlebrook, New Jersey, made any cooperation between the two British generals nearly impossible. Moreover, owing to contrary winds and bad weather, Howe was unable to land his troops at Head of Elk, Maryland (about fifty miles southwest of Philadelphia), until nearly the end of August, thereby losing a precious full month of good campaigning weather. Meanwhile, Burgoyne, with a rather cumbersome baggage train and a large number of Hessians and Indian auxiliaries, slowly made his way through the Lake Champlain region toward Albany. Nevertheless, to Washington's dismay, by early July, Burgoyne was as far south as Ticonderoga, having taken the fort when the Americans under Garrison Commander Arthur St. Clair rather precipitously abandoned the place without firing a shot or losing a man. It was potentially only a matter of time before Albany, too, fell to the British.

Washington, feeling compelled by Congress to at least contest the city of Philadelphia, rushed the majority of his Continental army southward, fortified Chadd's Ford on the Pennsylvania–Delaware border, and awaited the British attack that he knew was coming. Watching the army pass through the capital for more than two hours, John Adams noted to his wife Abigail with some admiration that "we now have an Army, well appointed between Us and Mr. Howe . . . " However, something about the Continental army was just not quite right to John Adams:

> I find [the army] to be extreamly well armed, pretty well clothed, and tolerably disci-
> plined. . . . Much remains yet to be done. Our soldiers have not yet, quite the Air of
> Soldiers. They don't hold up their Heads, quite erect, nor turn out their Toes, so exactly
> as they ought. They don't all of them cock their Hats—and such as do, don't all wear
> them the same way.[27]

The September 11, 1777 Battle of Brandywine and the several engagements that immediately followed it were nearly a reprise of previous year's American debacle on Long Island and Manhattan, New York. Howe demonstrated in front of Washington's main line at Chadd's Ford and once again sent an unseen heavy flanking column this time around to the right of Washington's line. Late in the afternoon, Howe finally sent his forces crashing into Washington's flank. With their bayonets leveled and the fifes and drums playing the *British Grenadier*, Washington was once again forced to retreat before his British adversaries. For all intents and purposes, following Brandywine, the loss of Philadelphia was nearly a foregone conclusion and Congress itself quickly relocated to York, Pennsylvania.

However, despite Washington's resolve to continue to oppose Howe's march into the capital, just ten days later the normally competent Anthony Wayne allowed himself and his Pennsylvania division of around three thousand men to be suddenly attacked beginning around midnight and lasting through the early morning hours of September 21, 1777. The engagement was later known as the Paoli Massacre because of fairly credible post-battle testimony that many of the attacking British, and especially their light infantry, assaulted Wayne's hastily prepared forces with cries of "no quarter." Although the British did in fact take some prisoners, there were many dead later recovered from the battlefield

Battle of Brandywine. (*Courtesy of the Library of Congress*)

with multiple—sometimes more than a dozen—bayonet wounds and other live wounded coming in with stories that they had been deliberately and repeatedly bayoneted by the British after they had tried to surrender. With Wayne's normally reliable division scattered over the Pennsylvania countryside, Washington's luck continued to decline as the British were also able to easily brush aside General William Smallwood's Maryland militia of more than one thousand men, who had unfortunately arrived just as Wayne and his men were being driven from their camps. Smallwood himself narrowly escaped being shot by nervous American soldiers, who fired a volley at him. The rider next to Smallwood was killed. Jumping from his horse, Smallwood shouted in anger that "he shou'd have been glad to have seen them as ready to fire on the Enemy as they now seemed on their Friends. They knew my voice and ceased."[28]

It was a black day for the American cause. To the joy of all the latent Tories in the city, Howe's army marched triumphantly into Philadelphia on September 26, 1777. Washington and the army retired twenty-five miles away to Skippack, Pennsylvania. However, he was not ready to concede the area to the British and attempted to surprise a British nine thousand-man outpost at Germantown, Pennsylvania, just a few weeks later. Despite some initial success, Washington was once again forced to concede the field to the tactically superior British.

Meanwhile, with part of the main army still far to the north of Philadelphia guarding northern New Jersey against any possible raids conducted by the British garrison still in New York City, Connecticut soldier Martin once again found himself in the thick of things. Having enlisted that spring for three years or the "duration," Martin had been inoculated for smallpox before coming on to join the main army later that summer. During his time of convalescence, Martin took it upon himself to rob his nurse's kettle pot then simmering with stewed peas with a piece of pork thrown in. He stated that he gorged himself until he was chased off by the pot's owners. Soon after his recovery, however, he was afflicted with boils all over his body. Comparing himself to the biblical Job, Martin blamed his condition on "not having been properly physicked after the small pox."[29]

By mid-August 1777, while Howe's army was still floundering around at sea, Martin was ordered to Peekskill, New York. He described his duty there as hard and fatiguing. And while there, he met with an accident that caused him "much trouble and pain." Being ordered into rowboats for another trip across the Hudson, Martin carelessly leaped in without seeing an oar in the way and promptly broke his ankle. The next morning, Martin's captain decided to try and set it himself, which, according to him, put his ankle "in the same direction" as it was when he first injured it. However, his broken ankle likely kept Martin away from the army long enough for him to miss the Battle of Brandywine. However, having been sent to Bethlehem, Pennsylvania, with the army baggage in the company of officers and men unknown to him, Martin preferred to hobble his way back to his unit in time to take part in the battle of Germantown in October 1777. He blithely noted that "soldiers always like to be under command of their own officers; they are generally bad enough, but strangers are worse."[30]

The Battle of Saratoga

If there is one clearly identifiable tipping point for the entire war, it was the Battle of Saratoga. During the summer of 1777, Burgoyne had driven the Americans back toward Albany. Considering that just the previous year the Americans were in and around Montréal, this was certainly a serious turn of events for the patriot cause.

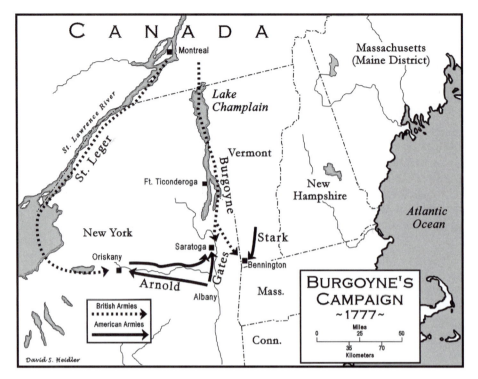

Burgoyne's Campaign

Following the loss of Ticonderoga and the ease with which Burgoyne had thus far been able to move down Lake Champlain, John Adams, for one, advocated a get tough policy in the Northern Department, not necessarily against the British but against his own generals. He bluntly stated that he thought:

> we shall never defend a post until we shoot a general. After that, we shall defend posts, and this event, in my opinion is not far off. No other fort will ever be evacuated without an inquiry, nor any officer come off without a court-martial. We must trifle no more.

Congress immediately sent the scheming former British army quartermaster Gates to take command from Schuyler.[31]

Before Gates arrived to take command of the northern army, several ominous signs occurred that should have alerted Burgoyne that his campaign to take Albany was running out of steam. First and foremost, he had decided that the best way to approach Albany from the Fort Edward/Fort Ticonderoga area was for his engineers to cut a road through the wilderness. For once, Schuyler was active in sabotaging the efforts of Burgoyne's artificers by felling trees along the road they had so recently struggled to cut. Thus, Burgoyne's forward progress was substantially slowed. As a result, his Indian auxiliaries became restless and began plundering the local farmsteads giving fresh incentive for the patriot militia to not only turn out but fight for their very survival. Atrocity stories that particularly featured the butchery of a beautiful twenty-three-year-old woman named Jane McCrea quickly spread throughout the region. Ironically, McCrea was the fiancée of a Tory officer then traveling with Burgoyne. Next, on August 16, 1777, near present-day Bennington, Vermont, a detachment of six hundred Hessians under the command of Lieutenant Colonel Friedrich Baum got themselves severely mauled by the New

Death of Jane McCrea. (*Courtesy of the Library of Congress*)

Hampshire militia under the command of Brigadier General John Stark. The hard-bitten Stark, who had earlier resigned from the Continental army over a promotional dispute, accepted his position as commander only as long as it was recognized that he and his men were independent of the Schuyler's northern army and Congress. Summoning Seth Warner's Green Mountain Boys to join him, Stark's victory at Bennington brought the first bit of good news that the Americans had after a long summer of reverses.

Now, thanks to the slowness of his march to Albany and the excesses committed by his Indian allies, Burgoyne finally began to worry:

> The great bulk of the country is undoubtedly with the Congress, in Principle and in zeal; and their measures are executed with a secrecy and dispatch that are not to be equaled. Wherever the King's forces point, militia to the amount of three or four thousand assemble in twenty-four hours; they bring with them their subsistence, etc., and the alarm over, they return to their farms. The Hampshire Grants in particular . . . abounds in the most active and rebellious race of the continent, and hangs like a gathering storm upon my left.[32]

In more bad news for Burgoyne, St. Leger's force that had been proceeding down the Mohawk valley toward Albany also ran into trouble. And that trouble came in the form of the New York state militia. After fighting an inconclusive but exceptionally bloody battle with the militia at a place called Oriskany Creek, St. Leger, in order to avoid the approach of a force of New England continentals under the command of the redoubtable Benedict Arnold, was forced to unceremoniously leave his supplies and equipment behind and flee back toward Canada. After much tough talk about what he was going to do to the rebels and having to default on his promise to his Indian allies of all the easy war booty waiting for them at Albany, St. Leger's abrupt departure from the theater of war in upstate New York had now left Burgoyne and his army alone and in serious trouble as Americans closed in on him from each side.

Regardless of his later less-than-stellar postwar reputation, the arrival of Gates in Albany immediately after Stark's victory at Bennington clearly electrified the soldiers of the northern army. Moreover, Gates had been given some rather substantial reinforcements, including Arnold's returning New England contingent and Daniel Morgan's 1200-man Pennsylvania, Virginian, and Maryland rifle companies. However, upon arrival, many of Morgan's men were on the sick list, so that at best he had only 374 effectives. Gates himself was able to count about ten thousand total troops with which to initially oppose Burgoyne, but companies of irate militiamen arrived almost daily. However, Gates was in no hurry to rush out and engage him in battle and instead concentrated on drilling and properly equipping his men in preparation for extended combat operations against Burgoyne. Captain Henry Dearborn, who had accompanied Arnold on his earlier expedition through the Maine wilderness, noted that Gates's presence put "a New face upon our affairs."[33]

Gates had his army in motion by mid-September and quickly occupied Bemis Heights, the most commanding terrain in the region. This placed the American army, for once, on secure high ground and Burgoyne's depleted numbers of redcoats and Hessians at a distinct disadvantage. Running into Morgan's riflemen and Arnold's Continentals at Freeman's Farm on September 19, 1777, Burgoyne's army suffered heavy casualties that he could ill afford to lose, although his men retained the field at the end of the day. For example, after Freeman's Farm, Burgoyne's 62nd Regiment of Foot had fewer than sixty men and only a few officers left. The Americans lost far fewer men.[34]

The American soldiers at Freeman's Farm really showed their mettle that day, and many contemporary British observers, including the baroness von Riedesel, wife of the senior Hessian commander, noted the vast improvement in American battlefield behavior in just the last few months. The reasons for this improvement are varied: the arrival of Gates, who perhaps owing to his quartermaster's background immediately went about satisfying the basic needs of the American army with such things as improved food and better clothing and equipment; the disaffection of Burgoyne's Indian and Canadian allies, who left him in the lurch at the worst possible moment; or perhaps the stories of Indian and Tory atrocities such as the widely recounted murder of McCrea caused the militia to turn out in large numbers. In the end, however, Dearborn probably placed his finger on the real reason when he noted that "we . . . had Something more at Stake than fighting for six Pence Pr Day." However, not everything was smooth with the American side. A deep rift soon developed between Gates and Arnold. Arnold was greatly upset that Gates had pointedly made no mention in official reports of his action at Freeman's Farm, and he let him know about it in no uncertain terms. In response, Gates and some of his sycophant subordinates immediately embarked on a character assassination program against the deserving Arnold and schemed to get him removed from exercising any further command over Northern Department troops.[35]

All this made no difference to Burgoyne's rapidly deteriorating situation. He was also running out of food and supplies. Gates anticipated that Burgoyne would make one more last ditch attempt to get out of his situation, and he was right. More than two weeks had passed since the first battle of Freeman's Farm, and Gates and his men sensed the declining strength of their British and Hessian adversaries. On October 7, 1777, Burgoyne attempted to find a way past Gates. This anticipated reconnaissance in force precipitated a general battle near the site of the first battle of Freeman's Farm. And like the first battle, Arnold's presence was again conspicuous. He was seen personally leading a charge against von Riedesel's Hessians in a fortification called Breymann's Redoubt. Interestingly, Arnold led these charges without being in actual command of any troops since Gates and his allies had earlier successfully maneuvered him out of a combat assignment following the first battle of Freeman's Farm.

As more and more American troops arrived at the scene of fighting, Burgoyne was soon in serious trouble and completely on the defensive. Arnold was instrumental in organizing a final direct assault just as daylight was fading out on the Hessians in Breymann's Redoubt. Finally, they broke for the rear, but unfortunately Arnold received a severe wound to his leg—the same one he was wounded in during his assault on the walls of Québec. Musket balls killed his horse from under him, and the animal crashed down on his already damaged leg, fracturing it in multiple places. Arnold's pain must have been horrific. However, he remained conscious and urged Morgan's men to continue the pursuit of the fleeing Hessians.

After suffering another round of heavy casualties in the second battle of Freeman's Farm, Burgoyne knew that the jig was about up. The Americans claimed to have lost only thirty men killed, and the British lost—killed, wounded, or captured—631 men, including 31 officers. The Hessians lost a further 270 total casualties. This meant that more than one-half of Burgoyne's 1700-man reconnaissance in force became casualties. Instead of moving past Gates, he now decided to retreat. Now nearly out of food and ammunition and closely pressed by Gates's men, he decided, rather than risk annihilation, to surrender on October 17, 1777, one of the two standing British field armies in North America.[36]

Burgoyne's surrender at Saratoga was a momentous event for the American war effort. Coming so soon after the loss of the rebel capital of Philadelphia, the results of the battle and the loss of so many valuable veterans, especially the expensive Hessians, created shock waves at Whitehall in Great Britain. King George III himself was alleged to have fallen "into agonies" when he heard the news. But the best news was that, thanks in large part to this particular victory, American diplomats in Paris were able to arrange a Franco-American defense treaty that brought the French openly into the war on the side of the patriots. Suddenly with a stroke of a pen, the war had gone from checkers to chess. The fighting could no longer be confined solely to North America. Moreover, the alliance now caused the British to have strategic concerns over their far more valuable colonies in India and the Caribbean. Finally, the alliance gave the Americans something they did not have—a Navy with which to challenge the heretofore absolute British dominance of the sea lanes and intercoastal waterways.

Burgoyne's surrender at Saratoga. (*Courtesy of the Library of Congress*)

The Delaware River Forts

Meanwhile, back in camp with Washington's main army, the soldiers were informed of the victory to the north. Many units celebrated it with a "feu de joie" (organized musket volleys). This was a common and authorized army tradition for celebrating momentous victories or anniversaries. Rhode Islander Jeremiah Greenman's unit, however, did something slightly different; rather than muskets, they fired thirteen booming cannon shots in succession. It was a day of celebration.

While Washington remained with his army on the outskirts of Philadelphia, Howe seemed to be in no particular hurry to come out of the city. Allegedly, he was more than distracted by his blond mistress, Mrs. Elizabeth Loring, wife of Commissary of Prisoners Joshua Loring. Or perhaps with the approach of winter, Howe believed that he only had to wait for warm weather to return in order to wrap things up in Pennsylvania and with Washington's army. Accordingly, to deny the British use of the port of Philadelphia, Washington used Howe's inactivity to his best advantage by garrisoning several Delaware River fortifications below the city.

The soldier Martin's Connecticut regiment was one of those ordered to reinforce the garrison at Fort Mifflin—occasionally referred to by the soldiers as the Mud Fort since it was situated on a mud flat in the middle of the Delaware River next to a place called Mud Island. Pointed and staked obstructions called "chevaux-de-fries" had been sunk in the river channel to make the passage of ships even more difficult. In combination with the obstructions and the cannon in Fort Mifflin and Fort Mercer on the opposite New Jersey shore at Red Bank, it was thought that it would be nearly impossible for the British to make use of the river. As long as the Americans denied them use of its port facilities, Philadelphia, in reality, would be of very little value to its British occupiers.

By mid-October, with the British feverishly constructing a series of land batteries at a place called "Hospital Point" on the Pennsylvania shore directly across from Fort Mifflin and Mud Island and with winter approaching, Howe began to become concerned about his food and supplies. He decided that the answer to his dilemma was to directly reduce the American river forts. Ordering a tough Hessian force under the command of Colonel Emil Ulrich von Donop to cross over the river and attack Fort Mercer, Howe simultaneously prepared to take Fort Mifflin using his superior naval power in the river. Moreover, von Donop was not leading just any force but the German equivalent of the elite British grenadiers. He had about 1200 men under his command, called the Von Mirbach regiment, and von Donop and his men were outside the walls of Fort Mercer by noon on October 22, 1777.

Washington anticipated that Howe will try to take Fort Mercer and had recently ordered James Varnum's Rhode Island Continentals to reinforce the fort. Later, he added George Weedon's 6th Virginia Regiment as well. Hoping perhaps to repeat the ease with which they had seized other American fortifications in the past, such as Forts Washington and Lee during the New York campaign, von Donop sent officers forward under a flag of truce to demand the immediate surrender of the fort and threatened, as was their tradition, that no quarter would be shown to the Americans if they had to take the place by storm. However, what had so consistently worked for them in the past was now categorically rejected by Colonel Jeremiah Olney. Taking it upon himself to answer for the fort's commander, Colonel William Greene, Olney allegedly replied, "We'll see King George damned first—we want no quarter."[37]

By 4:00 P.M., von Donop began a furious cannonade on the fort, and almost from the start things began to go badly for him. In his rush to take the position, he arrogantly had not reconnoitered the various defenses his troops would face in a direct assault. This mistake proved to be his undoing, and he and his men were quickly chopped to pieces by American artillery firing grapeshot directly into his storming columns and by intense musket fire as his men struggled through various prepared obstacles, abatis, and ditches that created a virtual kill zone for the American defenders. At the large ditch in front of the fort's main wall, von Donop himself was shot down, allegedly hit by no less than thirteen musket balls, and the attack quickly died out. The Hessians had lost about half their men and were forced to retreat back across the Delaware. The American losses were minimal, with only fourteen men killed in action.

To make matters worse for Howe, things were not going very well at Fort Mifflin either. Hoping to take advantage of possible American preoccupation with von Donop's assault on Fort Mercer, Howe's plan for Mifflin was to simultaneously pound its walls and batteries from ships in the river long enough to land a landing force of about two hundred men to take the fort by storm. However, owing to poor nautical charts, the narrow Delaware channel, and contrary winds, the British quickly found that the eighteen-gun sloop *Merlin* and the larger and more valuable HMS *Augusta*, a sixty-four-gun ship of the line, had run aground on the mud flats. The *Augusta* was soon set on fire by American artillery firing heated shot from their batteries in the fort. Late in the afternoon of October 23, 1777, when the fire reached its powder magazines, the *Augusta* blew up in a tremendous explosion. In order to keep the *Merlin* from falling into American hands, this ship was burned as well.

Owing to his failure to take the forts by assault, Howe decided to place his hopes on his engineers, who, to him, were taking an inordinate amount of time getting the shore batteries ready for use. Now, they were his only hope, and he believed that he had enough superior artillery that he could at least pound Fort Mifflin into submission.

Connecticut soldier Martin described his time in the mud fort as the very worst experience that he had to endure during the entire war. At this time, he also observed that the Continental army supply system, shaky even under the best conditions, was clearly starting to break down. He and his unit often went several days without having anything to eat, and they were forced to endure constant shelling from British ships in the river and from their batteries on the Pennsylvania shore. Martin wrote that:

> it was utterly impossible to lie down to get any rest or sleep on account of the mud, if the enemy's shot would have suffered us to do so. Sometimes some of the men, when overcome with fatigue and want of sleep, would slip away into the barracks to catch a nap of sleep, but it seldom happened that they all came out again alive.

Soon, in order to further harass the poor suffering mud-bound soldiers, the British fired grapeshot from mortars so that even the palisades of the fort walls provided them with little protection. Martin recalled that after awhile, the men grew apathetic about their possible fate (as combat soldiers often do during extended sieges). For example, Fort Mifflin had a thirty-two-pound cannon, but it was virtually useless since the men did not possess a single cannonball that could be fired from it. But the British had one that fired intermittently on the fort's main parade ground from their battery at Hospital Point. Once Martin's officers offered a gill of rum to any soldier who could recover a thirty-two-pound ball, he noted that he had:

> seen from 20 to 50 men standing on the parade waiting with impatience the coming of the shot, which would often be seized before its motion had fully ceased and conveyed off to our gun to be sent back to its former owners. When the lucky fellow who had caught it had swallowed his rum, he would return to wait for another, exulting that he had been more lucky or more dexterous than his fellows.[38]

But to Martin, the siege was not all fun and games. The shelling from the British increased daily and especially from a large number of British naval vessels brought up the river for this purpose. Martin wrote that "the enemy's shot cut us up: I saw five artillerists belonging to one gun cut down by a single shot, and I saw men who were stooping to be protected by the works, but not stooping low enough, split like fish to be broiled." Soon, the British had disabled every gun in the fort, and Martin's unit was mercifully ordered to burn what remained of the place and retreat to the Jersey shore.[39]

The Valley Forge Encampment

Much has been written about the epic encampment of Washington's long-suffering Continentals at Valley Forge. However, despite the postwar hyperbole about this encampment being the place of greatest privation for the soldiers, later trials such as the long winter at Morristown in 1779 would be far worse.

One reason Valley Forge likely stood out as a particular trial for the soldiers was that after several months of hard campaigning in and around Philadelphia, the Continental army commissary and quartermaster departments had largely collapsed. Further, the city of Philadelphia was not only the center of government for the patriot cause but also a central clearing house for army support. As one of the largest cities in the entire British empire in 1777, it was connected by all major colonial roads. Moreover, with the British also in control of New York City, supplies coming to the army had to be shipped over rough, circuitous backcountry roads from Baltimore, Maryland, in the south and Boston and New England in the north.

Martin's Connecticut unit arrived in camp about a week before Christmas. When he got there, it was dark. He was hungry and especially thirsty. He stumbled around a bit in the gloom looking for a stream or nearby brook, but he could find nothing to drink. No supplies had been prepositioned, and the soldiers were virtually on their own. In his emergency, Martin paid two passing soldiers three pence—all the money he had in the world at the time—for a drink from their canteen. He stated that "he felt at that instant as if [he] would have taken victuals or drink from the best friend [he] had on earth by force." The only food Martin had been able to scrounge up for two days was a piece of pumpkin that he cooked on a heated rock. Further, he observed that many of the soldiers arriving in camp were clothed in rags and without shoes.[40]

Just days before Christmas and well into the cold weather season, Washington ordered the soldiers to build winter huts. And he was quite specific about their dimensions and how he wanted them constructed. He even offered prizes for the first and best huts produced by the men. Rhode Island Chaplain Ebenezer Denny described them:

> The Huts are to be 14 feet by 16—in hight 6½—twelve Soldiers to a hut—each mess builds their own—Those in each Regiment who build the best are to have 12 Dollars Premium—They are now laying out the ground—tomorrow I expect to take to the ax. . . . After Huts are provided we may send out *large* Scouts to check small parties—For our whole Force to be exposed for the winter as they have been we should have no Army in the Spring—Had we retired to any of the towns we should have Found them crowded with Refugees—May kind heaven render the next Campaign prosperous & put speedy issue to this contest—we ruin the Country for miles round wherever we lay.[41]

Living in these huts must have been trying under the best of conditions. Most squads dug down two feet into the earth in order to save themselves time and labor in cutting down logs. However, this had the subsequent effect of keeping them cold and damp throughout the winter. Most of the huts also had internal mud and stick chimneys. However, these were anything but efficient, and along with the habit of soldiers burning green wood the huts were perpetually smoky as well. The cleanliness of their quarters was also a constant problem for Washington and his officers. Frequently, the men simply threw their trash, bones from their meals, and other offal into the corners of each cabin. Many of these huts had no windows, and the only ventilation was the door itself. All in all, however, one soldier noted: "we have got our Hutts to be very comfortable, and feel ourselves quite happy in them."[42]

Although Prussian volunteer Baron Johann DeKalb was not especially impressed with the army's choice of winter quarters when he wrote that it was chosen "at the instance of a speculator or on the advice of a traitor or by a council or ignoramuses," with the exception of butting up against the Schuylkill River, the camp's approximately two thousand acres possessed everything an army could desire, including being supplied with freshwater (despite Martin's initial difficulties in finding some), having plenty of woods nearby, and, most importantly, being relatively dry. It was also close enough to Philadelphia to threaten Howe but far enough away from the British to prevent them from launching surprise attacks.[43]

After the soldiers were placed into the huts, Washington immediately put them into establishing lines of defense—an outer and inner line with four supporting redoubts. A star-shaped fort was established to defend the wooden bridge that crossed the nearby Schuylkill River. However, as would be the case for most of the winter, his most pressing need was food and forage for his army, and Washington frequently had to send out parties of armed men into the Pennsylvania countryside to impress what he needed.

Being told by his lone commissary officer in camp that the entire initial food supply of the army was a mere twenty-five barrels of flour, Washington wrote to Congress that "unless some great and capital change suddenly takes place ... this Army must inevitably be reduced to one or other of these three things. Starve, dissolve, or disperse, in order to obtain assistance in the best manner they can. . . ." It was as close to despair as Washington would ever get during the entire course of the war.[44]

Moreover, the lack of food in particular caused growing discontent in the ranks. On December 21, 1777, Dr. Albigence Waldo of Connecticut noticed one ominous incident when after not having been fed for several days soldiers began hooting like owls and cawing like crows. This was picked up by unit after unit and echoed throughout the camp. Soon they added the chant, "No meat! No meat!" and were loud enough that even Washington likely heard it in his marquee. After also hearing this soldier's chorus, Waldo rhetorically asked himself in his journal: "What have you for Dinner Boys? Nothing but Fire Cake [raw dough baked in the ashes of a soldier's campfire] & Water, Sir." Waldo sarcastically added that the men had the same response for their supper as well. He stated that he himself was tempted to "steal Fowls if [he] could find them, or even a whole Hog, for [he felt] as if he could eat one." He closed his entry with the warning to "ye who Eat Pumkin Pie and Roast Turkies, and yet Curse fortune for using you ill, Curse her no more, least she reduce your Allowance of her favors to a bit of Fire Cake & a draught of Cold Water, & in Cold Weather too."[45]

As previously noted, part of the reason for the discontent of the soldiery could be laid directly at the feet of the army's commissary and quartermaster departments. Major General Thomas Mifflin had long been ambivalent about his duties as Quartermaster General, and for many months prior to Valley Forge he had all but stopped performing this job for the army and resigned in October 1777. However, it was not until March 1778 that Congress appointed a very reluctant Nathanael Greene as his successor. Likewise, although Commissary General Joseph Trumbull was clearly more efficient and able than Mifflin, he had been ill at home in Connecticut for a number of months prior to the Valley Forge encampment and so he too was not effectively leading his department.

But in reality, the real reason for the suffering of the army at Valley Forge had to do with the sheer magnitude of scale that staff departments faced in keeping an army in the field adequately clothed and fed. Of the problems of the quartermaster department alone, Pickering wrote late in the war:

> If, indeed, the business of the quartermaster general were confined to a few objects, and those only with the army, as in some foreign services; if the supplies of all things necessary in the department were complete; if the various kinds of water craft; if materials for building and other uses; if artificers; if the numerous teams with their conductors and drivers; if forage, straw, fuel, camp equipage, and all the variety of stores required in the American army were provided and brought to his hand, with scarcely a thought of his about them;—the burthens of his office would be essentially lessened and perhaps be equal to only to those of three or four general officers.[46]

The magnitude of the supply problems at Valley Forge are revealed in just what the departments did manage to provide the army from December 1777 to February 1778. During this time, the soldiers consumed "2,200,000 pounds of beef, 2,297,000 pounds of flour, and 500,000 gills of rum and whiskey." At the same time, the quartermaster department was "expected to have on hand more than 240 different items" ranging from "ship's stores to iron mongery."[47] Although there were certainly periods of bureaucratic ineptitude where the men did not get much to eat, especially in February 1778, there was usually a minimal supply on hand. The problem was not consistent deprivation. Rather it was keeping a steady supply of food—especially meat—on hand. While Washington hesitated to impress what he needed from local farmers, in an emergency he had no qualms about doing so.

The sheer task of simply getting these supplies to the army was often overwhelming to even the most demanding and efficient commissary and supply officers. The army was encamped away from navigable waterways, as was the case at Valley Forge, and all materials had to be brought overland via horse- or mule-drawn wagons or ox carts. This traffic depended on unreliable roads, irregular ferry service, and the vagaries of weather, all the while avoiding British and Tory dragoons in the countryside on the lookout for such supplies. The delivery of these supplies also depended on farmers willing to sell their goods at the rapidly depreciating Continental currency rates. However, as was often the case, the problem of food and supply at Valley Forge was largely not related to any actual material shortages. The farmers had grown plenty of food that year. The problem resided in getting it to the soldiers.

Further, there were never enough drivers to be had, and keeping them in service was as difficult as getting soldiers to reenlist for the duration of the war. Even Nathanael Greene was heard to remark after he became quartermaster general "that the Duty is disagreeable in itself." One eighteen-year-old wagon driver from Connecticut named Joseph Joslin described what his life was like carrying barrels of flour and other army supplies on spine-jarring, heavily rutted, backcountry roads. He stated that it was not unusual for him to drive for thirteen or fourteen hours a day in all kinds of weather, having nothing to eat "but Dry Bisket and So it goes." He also resented the fact that all officers he came into contact with took it upon themselves to upbraid him for *their* situation, as if he had something directly to do with. This apparently had quite an effect on young Joslin because in little more than a year he quit the wagon service and wrote in his journal, "I Don't Intend to Drive a team for my Continent anymore . . . good-bye."[48]

Another problem nearly as great as food was getting the men adequately clothed. After campaigning nearly steadily from August to December, the men's clothes and shoes were in tatters. Washington wrote on December 23, 1777, that "few men have more than one Shirt." However, the army did get some relief on New Year's Day when Smallwood's Marylanders were able to capture HMS *Symmetry* loaded with military stores and especially "Scarlett, Blue, & Buff Cloth, sufficient to Cloath all the Officers of the Army & Hats, Shirts, Stockings, Shoes, Boots, Spurs, &c. to furnish compleat Suits for all." Although this fortuitous prize set off intense squabbling over its disposition, at least the army was finally getting what it needed for clothing and shoes. Further, Washington made direct appeals to the state governors for clothing, with some eventual success, and by spring, the clothing situation had been largely remedied.[49]

However, before this clothing was brought to camp, the sight of the Continental army at Valley Forge must have been a shocking one to an outsider coming to camp for the first time. During February, the Baron Friedrich Wilhelm von Steuben arrived at Valley Forge, and he was stunned by what he initially saw:

> The men were literally naked, some of them in the fullest extent of the word. The officers who had coats had them of every color and make. I saw officers at a grand parade at Valley Forge mounting guard in a sort of dressing gown made of an old blanket or woolen bed cover.[50]

At Valley Forge, Washington was able to somewhat reduce the number of men he had to cloth and feed by parceling out units on detached duty such as Smallwood's

Marylanders near Wilmington, Delaware, and another significant detachment at Trenton, New Jersey. Others could be sent out into countryside, as was the case with Martin on a semipermanent detached duty foraging for the army. In fact, for once and ironically during Valley Forge, Martin actually lived fairly well away from the main army as a forager. However, there were seventy-three Continental regiments of varying sizes in camp at Valley Forge, not counting the artificers (engineers) and the artillery brigade. Their total end strength was just below twelve thousand men. Of this number, approximately one-fourth would succumb to various camp diseases before the encampment ended. One reason for this high death rate was likely related to the perpetually unhealthy conditions in the soldier huts, combined with a nonnutritious and inconsistent diet.[51]

One other major issue surrounding the legend that became Valley Forge had to do with the weather. Even today, a favorite contemporary painting of Valley Forge is the image of Washington kneeling and praying in heavy snow beside his white charger. While there is absolutely no evidence that this particular event ever took place, the ice, snow, and the emaciated and ragged soldiery standing guard in horrible weather all make up the iconography that surrounds this particular Continental army encampment. From extant records, we know that the camp received its first substantial snow on Christmas Day. This was followed by another snowfall four days later, so that about six inches remained on the ground by New Year's Day. However, warmer weather set in and all this snow turned the camp into a temporary quagmire until a mid-January storm deposited another foot on the ground. By January 20, 1778, this snow also had melted and the camp was relatively free of snow until February 7. In sum, "of the eighty-eight

A winter scene at the Continental army encampment at Valley Forge; wagon of wood with supplies struggling through snow and mud, and soldiers warming themselves at a fire. (*Courtesy of the Library of Congress*)

days for which weather records are available," snowfall for the winter of 1777–1778 was not particularly heavy nor were the temperatures overly cold. But make no mistake, it was cold at Valley Forge as it is there every winter. It was just not the arctic-like conditions that many of us have been conditioned to believe today. In fact, between December 19, 1777, and March 31, 1778, it even rained for seven of those days. Snow was recorded as "falling or on the ground" for only twenty-nine days that winter. That makes it a bit colder but not overly so than today's era of global warming. Moreover, the Revolution is remembered also as having taken place during what meteorologists today have called the Little Ice Age. Exceptional cold and heavy snow was the norm for those days. Nonetheless, even the less than totally frigid conditions faced by the Valley Forge soldiers on a daily basis would still have been a trial for anyone who did not have the proper clothing, footwear, or food. For example, it was not unusual for officers inspecting guards on duty to find them standing on their hats or stuffing leaves or straw into bundles of rags they had tied around their feet to keep them from freezing. Being outdoors and especially standing a stationary guard post is always a trying time for soldiers in any era. One Connecticut sergeant eloquently summed up the situation quite nicely: "It is trublesum times for us all, but wors for the Solders."[52]

Von Steuben's Contributions to the Army

One of the greatest additions to the Continental army during its entire eight years of existence was the arrival of Baron Friedrich Wilhelm von Steuben. Von Steuben had been recruited by the wily Benjamin Franklin while he was at the Court of Versailles, and Franklin apparently saw some promise in him and believed he could be useful to Washington. However, in order to make his candidacy for high rank in the Continental army more palatable to Congress, Franklin provided him with a letter of introduction that stated that von Steuben was a "baron" of royal personage and also a former lieutenant general in Frederick the Great's Prussian army. Of course he was neither, although he had served Frederick as a captain. Moreover, by 1777, Congress and the army were exceptionally leery of European "volunteer" officers, many of whom turned out to be incompetent adventurers and/or charlatans seeking and gaining high rank and pay in the American army. Their appointments had heretofore served to only cause discontent among the native-born American officer corps. Knowing this, Franklin instructed von Steuben on how to approach Congress and how to behave once he got to the main army at Valley Forge. In following Franklin's instructions to the letter, von Steuben was eventually appreciated by Congress and especially Washington for his service. To further improve his standing with the Americans, von Steuben stated that after he was appointed, he would take no pay from Congress until he had proven his worth to them. The only immediate issue with him was that although he obviously spoke German and was also fluent in French, he could speak hardly a word of English.

Washington believed that von Steuben would be most useful as the army's inspector general (IG). However, during December 1777, Congress had appointed General Thomas Conway, an Irish-born French military officer, as the army IG. To make matters worse, Conway had been recently embroiled in a failed "cabal" to replace Washington as commander in chief and get Horatio Gates appointed as the new commanding general of the army. With the politics of the intrigue still fresh in everyone's mind, Washington was hesitant to advocate von Steuben's appointment as army IG to Congress. However, when von Steuben arrived, Conway was fortuitously away on

Baron von Steuben at Valley Forge. (*Courtesy of Brian Hunt and the Pennsylvania Capitol Preservation Society*)

assignment in the Northern Department; hence, Washington saw an opportunity to appoint him "acting" IG. Moreover, with von Steuben in camp, Washington felt free to ignore the person Congress originally appointed to the position. Conway eventually admitted defeat and resigned.

There is no doubt that during the long miserable months the army remained in camp at Valley Forge, von Steuben performed a tremendous service for the United States. However, as historian Wayne Bodle has pointed out, the army at Valley Forge was especially "fraught with rancor, disgruntlement, and frustration." Although clearly von Steuben did well in getting the IG's department to help improve the army in the areas of drill, discipline, and especially battlefield maneuver, it was not an army "sullenly waiting its 'Prussianization' at the hands of Friedrich Steuben." If discipline and morale solely depended upon von Steuben alone, then the army would have "starved, dissolved or dispersed" long before he arrived in camp. The soldiers at Valley Forge were a contentious lot "but by no evidence a mutinous one" at this point.[53]

Von Steuben began his duties in earnest in early March 1778. At the time, there were few drill and tactics manuals extant in North America; hence, von Steuben created his own and got it approved by Washington. One of the first things von Steuben noticed about how the American army did business was that they had literally copied the British style of allowing NCOs to conduct all drill sessions without many officers normally in attendance. Instead, like their British counterparts, the officers remained aloof and thought that their only real duties were to lead men in battle and maintain discipline in camp. Few of them, especially at the company officer level, knew how to fully drill and maneuver their men and left the details of this particular function to the NCOs, whose own faulty knowledge was soon revealed. From the start, von Steuben saw that this policy was one reason why the Americans had heretofore done so poorly on most battlefields against their British adversaries.

Samuel Ward of Rhode Island, whose combat skills were to later stand out during the Battle of Rhode Island in August 1778, described a "specimen" day in camp at least for officers like him. While he may have been trying to be sarcastic, Ward made it sound fairly relaxing:

> I rise with the sun, after adjusting my Dress, we begin our exercises at 6 O'Clock which last till 8—then we breakfast upon Tea or Coffee—and then I write, read, ride or play, till Dinner time when we get a piece of good Beef or Pork tho' generally of both—and have as good Bread as I ever eat—the afternoon is also ours till 5 O'Clock when we begin our exercises and leave off with the setting sun . . . so that we live uncommonly well for Camp.[54]

Von Steuben's methodology to correct the army's deficiency in drill was as simple as it was effective. He chose a company from Washington's elite—"Life Guard"—to act as a sort of "honor company." After training these men and their officers, they would then spread out to other companies and regiments and do the same. Working through his military secretary, Pierre Duponceau, who spoke fairly good English, von Steuben could also communicate directly with Washington's aides, Alexander Hamilton and John Laurens, in French. His idea was to train the Life Guards and some other picked men, and he even demonstrated the rifle manual of arms to the incredulous soldiers himself. He was such an enigmatic spectacle on the drill field with his booming Prussian voice that these daily drill sessions were watched even by the "women of the army," who usually had much better things to do with their time. Cutting down and simplifying the manual motions to ten, he also shortened the pace of the men on the march to account for the more broken terrain the soldiers usually operated upon in North America. He taught them to wheel into line from a platoon column formation—which made it easier and quicker to form a line of battle—and he took special pains to teach them to use their bayonets. And most important, he impressed upon the officers the importance of attending drill sessions and being knowledgeable about how to maneuver forces on an eighteenth-century battlefield.

On such battlefields, it was bayonets and soldiers who knew how to use them that carried the day. The maximum effective range of the French Charleville smoothbore musket or British "Brown Bess" was, at most, fifty yards. Typically, lines of battle approached each other at this range and delivered one or two volleys and then charged with the bayonet. The other side either stood up to this fire and method of attack or broke and fled. This is what usually happened in the past to American units in places like Brooklyn Heights and Brandywine. This is not to say that the entire American army was loath to use and stand up to a bayonet charge. Rather, most of the units just had not been consistently trained in the use of the bayonet and how to receive a charge or deliver one. Von Steuben's training changed all that. Most important, von Steuben urged the officers from field grade to company command to pay more attention to the details of how to maneuver their troops, soldiers' equipment and cleanliness, and the importance of submitting regular accounts of the number of men they had present and fit for duty in camp. The change in army demeanor had an immediate effect with the men and inspired them with greater battlefield confidence. But soldiers being who they are remain gifted complainers, from Bunker Hill in 1775 to Baghdad in 2006.[55]

Von Steuben stated that it was a little strange to be exerting himself as a lieutenant after all his years in the military service. But his example certainly paid off, and his performance was noted by all who came out to the drill field. John Laurens wrote to his father Henry Laurens, then President of Congress: "It would enchant you to see the enlivened scene of our Campus Martius." Ward noted that von Steuben has "obligingly undertaken to discipline the army and is very indefatigable in his charge." Another officer was amazed that by April 1778, the camp prison was virtually empty. He was worried that, for Valley Forge, this was "a Little unusual but I hope 'tis growing out of fashion as arrests are considered in a more serious Light than heretofore."[56]

By spring 1778, the army was slowly recovering from its administrative meltdown of the Valley Forge encampment. Clothing and adequate food were finally reaching the army, and Washington even had von Steuben organize a sham battle to test his newly reorganized regimental structure. On May 5, 1778, the army received the announcement of formal French recognition of the United States. In celebration, Washington ordered a general review of the entire army. Toasts were drunk and musket volleys fired. The commander in chief inspected the entire army and was satisfied it was ready for action.

NOTES

1. George Washington to Congress, in John C. Fitzpatrick, ed., *The Writings of George Washington*, vol. 6 (Washington, DC: U.S. Government Printing Office, 1925), 110–11.

2. John S. Pancake, *1777: The Year of the Hangman* (Tuscaloosa, AL: University of Alabama Press, 1977), 78–79, 82.

3. British Intelligence Report, August 11, 1778, Continental army personnel returns, quoted in Holly A. Mayer, *Belonging to the Army: Camp Followers and Community during the American Revolution* (Columbia, SC: University of South Carolina Press, 1996), 1, 133.

4. George Washington, General Orders, quoted in Elizabeth Evans, *Weathering the Storm: Women of the American Revolution* (New York: Charles Scribner's Sons, 1975), 12.

5. Alfred F. Young, *Masquerade: The Life and Times of Deborah Sampson, Continental Soldier* (New York: A. A. Knopf, 2004), 94.

6. Ibid., 7.

7. Ibid.

8. Ibid., 104–5.

9. Linda Grant De Pauw, *Founding Mothers: Women of America in the Revolutionary Era* (Boston, MA: Houghton-Mifflin Company, 1975), 190–1.

10. Thomas A. Desjardin, *Through a Howling Wilderness: Benedict Arnold's March to Quebec, 1775* (New York: St. Martin's Press, 2006), 153.

11. George Washington, General Orders, quoted in Sally Smith Booth, *The Women of '76* (New York: Hastings House Publishers, 1973), 171; Linda Grant De Pauw, "Women in Combat: The Revolutionary War Experience," *Armed Forces & Society* 7, no. 2 (1981): 209–26.

12. Mayer, *Belonging to the Army*, 141–2.

13. De Pauw, *Founding Mothers*, 177–8.

14. Booth, *The Women of '76*, 205–6.

15. De Pauw, "Women in Combat," 210. De Pauw has estimated that nearly 20 percent of the total force of the army was female. Most historians believe that this estimate is too high. However, owing to the fact that many women served informally and in auxiliary roles that are difficult to quantify, an estimate of at least 10 percent seems reasonable.

16. Charles Patrick Neimeyer, *America Goes to War: A Social History of the Continental Army* (New York: New York University Press, 1996), 99.

17. George Washington to the President of Congress, April 19, 1776, in *Papers of the Continental Congress* (PCC), reel 186, item 169, 1:291–6.

18. Barbara Graymont, *The Iroquois in the American Revolution* (Syracuse, NY: Syracuse University Press, 1978), 95–98; Neimeyer, *America Goes to War*, 94.

19. Meriwether Peirce to John Fox, May 30, 1779, quoted in Jack M. Sosin, *The Revolutionary Frontier, 1763–1783* (New York: Holt, Rinehart, and Winston, 1967), 106–7.

20. Colonel William Preston to Colonel William Fleming, May 10, 1778, in Louise Phelps Kellogg, ed., *Frontier Advance on the Upper Ohio, 1778–1779* (Madison, WI: The Society, 1916), 47.

21. Timothy Pickering to George Washington, May 21, 1778, in Kellogg, *Frontier Advance on the Upper Ohio, 1778–1779*, 57.

22. James Littell to William Littell, January 29, 1779, in Edward G. Williams, ed., "A Revolutionary Journal and Orderly Book of General Lachlan McIntosh's Expedition, 1778," *Western Pennsylvania Historical Magazine* 43, (1960): 162.

23.   William McClay to the Pennsylvania State Executive Council, in *Pennsylvania Archives*, vol. 6, 634, quoted in Lewis S. Shimmell, *Border Warfare in Pennsylvania during the Revolution* (Harrisburg, PA: R. L. Myers, 1901), 98.

24.   George Washington's Special Order Commending Sullivan's Army, October 17, 1779, in R. W. G. Vail, ed., *The Revolutionary Diary of Lieutenant Obadiah Gore, Jr.* (New York: New York Public Library, 1929) 31.

25.   Captain Arent Depeyster to Frederic Haldimand, June 1, 1779, quoted in Sosin, *The Revolutionary Frontier, 1763–1783*, 119.

26.   Sosin, *The Revolutionary Frontier, 1763–1783*, 134.

27.   John Adams to Abigail Adams, August 24, 1777, in Paul H. Smith, ed., *Letters of the Delegates to Congress, 1774–1789, Vol. 7* (Washington, DC: Library of Congress, 1981), 538–9; Thomas J. McGuire, *Battle of Paoli* (Mechanicsburg, PA: Stackpole Books, 2000), 10.

28.   William Smallwood, quoted in McGuire, *Battle of Paoli*, 122.

29.   Joseph Plumb Martin, in James Kirby Martin, ed., *Ordinary Courage: The Revolutionary War Adventures of Joseph Plumb Martin*. 2nd ed. (St. James, NY: Brandywine Press, 1999), 42–45.

30.   Martin, *Ordinary Courage*, 42–45.

31.   John Adams to Abigail Adams, August 19, 1777, quoted in George F. Scheer and Hugh F. Rankin, *Rebels & Redcoats: The American Revolution Through the Eyes of Those Who Fought and Lived It* (New York: Da Capo Press, 1957), 257.

32.   John Burgoyne to George Germain, August 20, 1777, quoted in Scheer and Rankin, *Rebels & Redcoats*, 266.

33.   Henry Dearborn, quoted in Richard M. Ketchum, *Saratoga: Turning Point of America's Revolutionary War* (New York: Henry Holt and Company, 1997), 346–7.

34.   Ketchum, *Saratoga*, 369.

35.   Henry Dearborn, quoted in Ketchum, *Saratoga*, 369.

36.   Ketchum, *Saratoga*, 405.

37.   Joseph Olney, quoted in David G. Martin, *The Philadelphia Campaign, June 1777–July 1778* (Conshohocken, PA: Combined Books, 1993), 130–1.

38.   Martin, *Ordinary Courage*, 55–56.

39.   Ibid., 57.

40.   Ibid., 63.

41.   Ebenezer Denny, Letter XIX, December 22, 1777, in Jeannette D. Black and William Greene Roelker, eds., *A Rhode Island Chaplain in the Revolution: Letters of Ebenezer David to Nicholas Brown, 1775–1778* (Port Washington, NY: Kennikat Press, 1949), 73.

42.   Martin, *The Philadelphia Campaign, June 1777–July 1778*, 172.

43.   Ibid., 169.

44.   George Washington to Congress, December 23, 1777, quoted in Douglas Southall Freeman, *George Washington: A Biography*, vol. 4 (New York: Charles Scribner's Sons, 1951), 568.

45.   Albigence Waldo, December 21, 1777, in Hugh F. Rankin, ed., *Narratives of the American Revolution* (Chicago, IL: R.R. Donnelley & Sons, 1976), 185–8.

46.   Timothy Pickering to the president of Congress, December 4, 1782, quoted in E. Wayne Carp, *To Starve the Army at Pleasure: Continental Army Administration and American Political Culture, 1775–1783* (Chapel Hill, NC: University of North Carolina Press, 1984), 53.

47.   Carp, *To Starve the Army at Pleasure*, 55.

48.   Nathanael Greene and Joseph Joslin, quoted in Carp, *To Starve the Army at Pleasure*, 61.

49.   John B. B. Trussell Jr., *Birthplace of an Army: A Study of the Valley Forge Encampment* (Harrisburg, PA: Pennsylvania Historical and Museum Commission, 1976), 28.

50.   Friedrich Wilhelm von Steuben, quoted in Joseph B. Doyle, *Frederick William von Steuben and the American Revolution* (New Haven, CT: Yale University Press, 1970), 84.

51.   Trussell, *Birthplace of an Army*, 53.

52.   Trussell, *Birthplace of an Army*, 38; Icabod Ward to Abraham Pierson, January 19, 1778, quoted in Wayne Bodle, *The Valley Forge Winter: Civilians and Soldiers in War* (University Park, PA: Pennsylvania State University Press, 2002), 129.

53.   Bodle, *The Valley Forge Winter*, 130.

54.   Samuel Ward to Phoebe Ward, May 5, 1778, quoted in Bodle, *The Valley Forge Winter*, 225.

55.   Trussell, *Birthplace of an Army*, 58–61.

56.   John Laurens to Henry Laurens, quoted in Bodle, *The Valley Forge Winter*, 201.

5   DAILY LIFE IN CAMP

The soldiers who emerged from the winter of privation at Valley Forge were far different than their predecessors of the previous two years of war. By 1778, the Continental army was now largely made up of long-termed soldiers, who were to be supported during emergencies by state militia. As mentioned in the previous chapter, these soldiers were schooled in Major General Baron Friedrich Wilhelm von Steuben's new, simplified manual of arms and drill methodology. Further, greater military professionalism was also demanded of the Continental officer corps. Gone were the days when officers neglected drill or filled out sloppy unit returns. There were still exceptions to this rule, of course; but it was clear, as the army prepared to break camp in the late spring of 1778, that it was a more professionalized standing force in nearly all respects.

ARMY CAMP LIFE

So how did this professionalism come about? What was it like to be soldier in the ranks preparing for an active campaign season? How did they live in camp and on the march? What did they do all day?

Living Quarters

A typical day for a Continental army soldier always started at dawn. As previously noted, the men were usually billeted during winter months in crudely built huts as they were at Valley Forge. On the march, they found shelter where they could or simply slept out in the open under their blankets, usually sharing them with another soldier. Two men would place one blanket on the ground and the other over themselves and thereby stayed relatively warm. Or if there was time, they were placed "under canvas" or tents that were erected to keep the weather off them during the night, usually only during the warmer months of the year. More often than not, as Joseph Plumb Martin noted, they lodged "under the canopy of heaven for our tent."[1]

The common canvas tent of a soldier usually held about six men and would appear to the modern eye to be similar to a large "pup" tent—large enough that the shorter soldiers could nearly stand up in (the average height of a Continental soldier was only around 5 ft. 6 in.). However, two of these tents could be lashed together to make up a common "wall tent" shelter for around eighteen men. But if it rained or snowed heavily, no amount of canvas was likely to keep most soldiers very dry. Officers were provided with roomier wall tents, and colonels and above (including George Washington for a short period of time at Valley Forge) would use something called a marquee. A marquee looked like a much smaller version of a modern circus tent. This shelter would be large enough for the officer to have personal furniture inside, such as a field desk, a chair, a table, and a cot. During the first two years of the war, and anytime the army was in or near large towns or cities, the soldiers were usually placed in abandoned Tory houses as they were at Cambridge where they slept on their blankets on just about any open space on the floor or were housed in larger groups in warehouses, sugar houses, rope walks, and specially built barracks, nonactive churches, and public buildings, and so on. The principal object was to get them out of the weather in order to cut down on sickness and to provide a modicum of comfort for the soldiers in the ranks. Frequently, the men did considerable damage to their temporary lodgings, outbuildings, and surrounding gardens.

Another methodology of camping was described by Martin, who noted that at Basking Ridge, New Jersey, after marching all day through the snow, he and some of his squad mates pitched three or four tents facing each other, "and then join[ed] in making a fire in the center." Thus, the four groups of men saved on the fatigue of finding enough wood for four separate campfires and could combine their labor into finding wood for one large fire that did duty for four tents. "Sometimes," Martin wrote, "we could procure an armful of buckwheat straw to lie upon, which was deemed a luxury. Provisions, as usual, took up but a small part of our time, though much of our thoughts." At one other time on the march, Martin stated that rather than pitch a tent and trying to find firewood, he simply laid down in a newly ploughed field after an exhausting march "between two furrows and slept as sweet as though I had laid upon a bed of down."[2]

Uniforms

Once awake, the soldiers would quickly dress or simply roll up their blanket and put on their shoes if they slept in their clothes, as they frequently did. The Continental army had a clothier general, and his mission was to provide an annual suit of clothes to each soldier and to replace clearly worn out articles as necessary. However, as was the case with most Continental army logistical departments, the office of clothier general was a troubled one from nearly the beginning of the war—its first director, James Mease resigning around the same time as the quartermaster general and the commissary general left their offices.

Owing to the hodgepodge nature of how the Continental army was formed, getting the army to wear adequate and recognizable uniforms was a constant problem throughout the war. One solution that Washington believed would solve the problem of the army appearing in a wide variety of dress was for the men to possess a hunting shirt of fringed buckskin, linen, or wool. Perhaps remembering his own experience with Virginia provincial troops, in General Orders, on July 24, 1776, he wrote of his preference for the hunting shirt:

> No dress can be cheaper, nor more convenient, as the wearer may be cool in warm weather and warm in cool weather by pulling on undercloaths which will not change the

outward dress, Winter or Summer—Besides which it is a dress justly supposed to carry no small terror to the enemy, who think every such person is a complete marksman.[3]

Although the deerskin shirt lasted longer, it was slightly more difficult to come by unless you hailed from the frontier; hence, many men opted for the linen or wool varieties. The shirt itself was loose and roomy so that the men could achieve the practical layering effect that Washington had recommended. All its edges were usually ornamentally fringed. The men also would sew on two fringed collars; a small one about two inches wide was worn immediately about their necks and would be placed over a larger one of about eight inches. This second collar draped nearly across their entire shoulders. These collars had practical value as well, and soldiers flipped them up in inclement conditions to keep the rain from running down the back of their necks or tied them to keep out the cold. The men dyed these shirts a variety of colors ranging from brown, white, yellow, blue, to even purple. However, the bleached or off-white color was generally favored by many soldiers.

Washington continually struggled with uniformity for the army throughout the war. This was especially a problem when the army operated in conjunction with large numbers of militia. One Hessian soldier who surrendered to Horatio Gates at Saratoga commented that:

> Not one of them was properly uniformed, but each man had on the clothes in which he goes into the field . . . but they all stood like soldiers, erect . . . so still that we were amazed . . . and were all surprised at the sight of such finely built people. . . . Most of the colonels and other officers were in their ordinary clothes.[4]

By mid-war, the Continental army was a great hodgepodge of uniform colors and styles, and the men wore their uniforms in various styles as well. Style was very important to Washington and his senior commanders. For example, the 7th Virginia Regiment was admonished by General Andrew Lewis to perform daily drills and exercises. He also reminded the officers of the importance of uniformity.

> It is recommended to the Colonels to make their men appear as uniform as possible in their Dress, that their Hatts shall be cut, all cocked in Fashion, that their Hair be likewise cut exactly the same length. When the Regiment are under Arms, the Officers to appear in their Hunting shirts; the Officers as well as the men to die their shirts in an universal manner. These [details] may appear Trivial, but they are in fact of considerable importance, as they tend to give what is call'd Espirit do Corps, without which Regiments never grow to Reputation.[5]

While a plain brown coat had earlier been ordered by Congress to more regularly uniform Continental regiments, individual units—often clothed at the expense of their state or even individuals who helped raise the regiment or company—would arrive in camp wearing a wide variety of uniform coats and colors. By late 1775, Massachusetts had provided at least thirteen thousand various uniforms and articles of wear for its soldiers. Often, the choice of uniform, at least at this point in the war, was left up to individual unit commanders. For example, the Salem Rangers were outfitted with short green coats, while the Boston Independent Company wore black coats faced with red and had buttons that read "Inimica Tyrannis." Connecticut dressed some of its units in, of all colors, red coats. This uniform style was immensely unpopular with the men and was soon changed to a different color. Early in the war, Washington ordered the various coats of these first regiments to be cut short so that they could be worn under the hunting shirt.[6]

The standard army uniform coat was made of wool. This was both good and bad news for the soldiers. Wool was warmer in the winter but hot in the summer. However, wool was a more durable cloth and would stand up better to the vagaries of the weather than any other available fiber. Even wet wool was still better than cotton or linen. It also dried out much quicker. A good example of the durability of wool was the case of a Massachusetts farmer who stripped one of the infamous redcoats off a dead grenadier during their precipitous retreat up the Lexington Road on April 19, 1775. After the war, the farmer used this coat to decorate one of the scarecrows in his fields. The historical records of the area noted that this coat was seen clothing the scarecrow for the next sixty years—a true testament to the durability of these wool coats.

Normally what would constitute the uniform coat's lapels or "facings" were of a different color than the coat itself. For example, Washington's Life Guard regimental colors were dark blue coats with buff facings. While never standardized, buff and blue were eventually considered as close to being the official Continental army uniform colors as anything else, but normally only Continentals from New Jersey and New York and Washington's Life Guard wore this particular color scheme for any extended period of time during the war.

In order to differentiate what part of the country various regiments came from, Washington ordered troops from New England to have white facings, those of the middle states to have red, and the southern states to have light blue. However, he was never consistently successful in getting all of his Continentals to conform to his uniform scheme. The "small clothes" or waistcoats, long sleeve linen undershirts, and breeches were usually all white or off-white. During the summer, a black leather stock was sometimes worn around the neck and under the white shirt (to protect the clothing from dirt and grime on a soldier's neck and to provide some additional protection to this critical area of the body from saber slashes or bayonet thrusts). When a soldier did not have a pair of overalls (pants that went from his waist and tied at the ankles or were looped under the soles of his shoes), they wore thick white or gray wool stockings.

After 1776, most enlistments mandated that soldiers be provided with an annual suit of clothes. Officers were required to outfit themselves at their own expense. As the war went on, both officers and men had great difficulty keeping themselves adequately clothed—for the officers, so much so that it was the reason behind why some of them resigned from service. However, on eighteenth-century battlefields, the need to visually identify one's own officers in the heat and smoke of battle was important. To remedy this situation, Washington prescribed a variety of insignia so that the officers would stand out. First, all field-grade officers (majors and above) usually wore a "cockade" or rosette on the side of their tricornered hats. The rosette was usually black, but the officers sometimes varied this by using a variety of colors. During the New York campaign, Martin vividly recalled how the officers ripped the rosettes from the hats before going into battle at White Plains in order to make themselves less of a target to British marksmen.

After the French arrived as full-fledged allies in 1778 with their white *fleur-de-lis* flags, many officers changed their cockades to black and white to symbolize the new alliance. Officers also wore silk sashes usually across their chests, over their uniform coats, and threaded underneath one of their epaulets (if they had them sewn on). For junior officers like the lowly ensign, the sash was tied around their waists. Since the style of the officers was to wear their coats unbuttoned and open, their sashes were immediately visible to their men (and unfortunately also to enemy marksmen). Washington himself wore a light blue sash. "Major Generals would wear purple; brigadiers, pink; aides-de-camp, green." Many officers also sported a gorget. The gorget was usually a kidney shaped piece of metal that was hung around the neck by a chain or piece of rawhide to the level of the officer's upper chest area and was made of highly polished brass or silver. Its function was entirely ornamental. Officers would also on occasion sport epaulets of "metal thread." Senior officers wore epaulets on both shoulders, captains only on the right shoulder, and lieutenants on the left. But epaulets were apparently never very popular with many of the officers. Noncommissioned officers (NCOs) wore strips of cloth on their shoulders and sometimes a woolen sash around their waists. "Red cloth generally denoted a sergeant; blue or green, a corporal."[7]

One interesting feature of soldiers' uniforms was the wide variety of buttons they created. Some common buttons used by the soldiers were made of bone or wood. However, most were created by pouring liquid pewter into molds. Early in the war, these buttons would be etched with a soldier's regimental numerical identification as a button with the number "2," followed by or placed above an abbreviation "CR" for 2nd Continental Regiment. However, after 1777, the buttons would be stamped with the soldier's state line identifier, such as "MB" for Maryland Brigade or "RIR" for Rhode Island regiment.

As for footwear, mounted officers wore boots with spurs that had fold-over tops that extended to just below the knee. Junior officers and enlisted men wore plain leather brogans of just two pieces of leather. The shoes had flat leather soles and a short heel. The upper part consisted of a "vamp" that came up from the front of the shoe and covered the front part of the foot and ended in a leather tongue that extended up toward a soldier's ankles. The back half wrapped around the heel and was tightly sewn together to the front half. The vamp was fitted through a shoe buckle that held it in place with two sharp prongs. There was no left or right shoe, and both shoes were the same. Often

Shoe. (*Courtesy of National Park Service, Museum Management Program and the Guilford Courthouse National Military Park, GUCO320*)

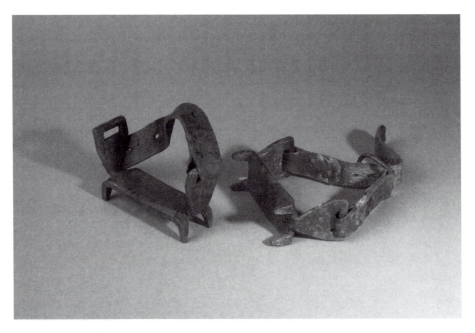

Creepers. (*Courtesy of National Park Service, Museum Management Program and the Valley Forge National Historical Park, VAFO 1313*)

the soldiers would switch them to the opposite side to improve on their evenness of wear. In inclement winter weather, these shoes could be fitted with iron pronged "ice-creepers" that tied directly under the soldier's instep.[8]

By 1779, Washington gave up on trying to get the men to conform to some form of Continental uniform regulations and recommended that Congress require each state clothier to specifically designate the color of their state line uniforms and methodology of wear. He even suggested that Congress provide a pattern to each clothier so that he could be guaranteed some sort of consistency of style. He also desired to have the army do entirely away with the knee-length breeches and go over to clothing the soldiers in overalls. Washington believed that his clothing plan would prevent competition for bolts of cloth of a specific color. His reasoning was that with various colors being used, the competition for specific colors would be reduced and the men would not have to wait for a specific color to be produced. Also on the battlefield, officers could readily identity what state line was in action or motion by the standardized color of their uniforms. Washington did worry that there might not be enough different colors to go around and that there would be stiff competition for colors favored by the soldiery (usually dark blue), so he suggested a lottery to resolve this issue.

However, the Board of War decided to change Washington's proposal in one important respect. Instead of having a variety of colors in the army, a more practical measure was adopted that stated that all coats would be of the dark blue variety with the facings to be colored and represent the various regional groupings. For example, New England troops were ordered to have white facings; those of New York and New Jersey wore buff; Pennsylvania, Delaware, Maryland, and Virginia wore scarlet; and, finally, North Carolina, South Carolina, and Georgia had light blue and their buttonholes edged in white. Artillerymen wore blue coats with scarlet facings, and dragoons wore blue with white facings.[9]

By late 1778, the board had ordered thousands of uniforms from the French. However, most of them did not actually arrive in North America until the early spring of 1781. But the board was following Washington's instructions in one important regard—they were very specific about how they wanted these new uniforms to look and wear on the men:

> The suits to consist of one coat, one waistcoat and one pair of breeches, sized as the French uniform, except that the skirts of the coats are not to reach farther than half way down the thighs. . . . The coats to be made to button as low as the waistband, the lapels loose to button over and the coats not sloped away so as to be incapable of covering the belly in cold or rainy weather, the fashion of Europe be what it may; to have a piece of cloth neatly sewed on each elbow.[10]

In all, the board ordered enough clothing for 98,058 men. However, this order was beyond the power of the American Minister at Versailles to procure and at best he was able to forward about ten thousand uniforms in all. As for shoes, the board complained that those brought in from France did not last a day in the field; hence, they also wrote out specific instructions for more durable soldier footwear. As for hats, this was an issue near and dear to the hearts of the men who liked to wear them folded down over their eyes and necks to give them greater protection from the sun and the rain. The officers were constantly after them to wear them in a more uniform cocked fashion. This issue became so great that it actually precipitated a "hat mutiny" in 1779 with the Rhode

Military cocked hat. (*Courtesy of National Park Service, Museum Management Program and the Morrison National Historical Park, MORR 3884*)

Island troops, who delivered to their commander, Colonel Israel Angell, "a mutinous paper" and indicated that they would wear their hats as they pleased.[11]

Food in Camp

Breakfast in camp was usually done in a haphazard fashion. Usually, a soldier from each squad or "mess" would be appointed the cook. One such man noted in his diary that "Nothing remarkable this day, onely I was chose cook for our room consisting of 12 men, and a hard game too." A common soldier complaint, especially when on the march, was having nothing to cook their provisions in. Elijah Fisher noted that the beef issued to him and his mates was:

> very leen and no salt, nor any way to Cook it but to throw it on the Coles and brile it; and the warter we had to Drink and to mix our flower with was out of a brook that run along by the Camps, and so many a dippin and washin [in] it which maid it very Dirty and muddy.[12]

Getting wood for their campfires was always a trial for most of the soldiers whether in camp or on the march. A common complaint made by local farmers near the army was soldiers stealing their fence rails to use for fuel. Washington himself noted a near riot among adjoining companies who simultaneously laid claim to a stand of locust trees that they wanted "to dress their victuals with." After the first few months of war, Congress declared that the army quartermaster general be required to furnish the troops with fuel and bedding at Continental expense. Thomas Mifflin estimated that each company be allotted an allowance of 1.5 cords of wood per week. In theory, this meant that Washington's army would consume an astounding eight thousand cords of wood in just six months. Sometimes, individuals would be contracted to provide the army with wood. At other times, no one could be found to provide this service. When no wood arrived in camp, the soldiers went off in search of it on their own (or were detailed to do so by their officers). In order to ensure that the army had at least some wood on hand, a party of axmen was usually detailed to travel in advance of the main army and chop up what they could before the men arrived at their daily designated campsites. They carried special quartermaster tools such as cross saws and wedges for splitting wood and were accountable for them. They were also excused from all camp duties. Pilfering and/or loss of these tools became such a problem that Washington directed that each one be inscribed with the mark "CXIII," which was meant to represent "the Continent and the thirteen colonies."[13]

The baking of bread was another problem for the soldiers. Soldiers complained that the bread made in camp or on the march tasted like paste. Indeed, soldiers commonly made "firecakes." As previously noted in the last chapter, these large lumps of hastily prepared dough became a staple of the infantryman's diet, especially on the march when there was not enough time to build actual ovens or for the iron portable ones that followed the army in a wagon to catch-up with the troops. The universal problem with firecakes was their tendency to burn on the outside while remaining uncooked on the inside. This gave them the consistency for which they were infamous, and while they were better than nothing, most soldiers roundly hated them.

More often than not, the flour of a regiment was pooled and men were detailed to bake the bread in nearby houses or in one of the field ovens that followed the army. However, the iron field ovens were so ponderous and heavy that only two could fit into a single large army wagon. During active campaigns and marches, soldiers would be given hard or sea bread to stuff into their shirts and haversacks. During one particular march, Martin had the good fortune during a momentary halt to stop in front of a cask of sea bread and as he stated:

> as very good soldier should upon all important occasions to get as many of the biscuit as I possibly could. . . . I filled my bosom, and took as many as I could hold in my hand, a dozen or more in all, and when we arrived at the ferry-stairs I stowed them away in my knapsack.[14]

The process of baking bread in camp was so haphazard in the early months of the war that Congress moved to appoint German-born Christopher Ludwig as baker-general for the entire army. All army bakers were required to operate under a license, and later a company of bakers were raised to include a director and were paid $50 a month and given a full army ration. Officers were required to inspect the bakeries to ensure that the bakers did their duty and delivered the full ration to the men. Apparently, some of the bakers were in the habit of skimming a small amount of flour allotted to a specific company and then sold it on the side for personal profit. Many believed that this skimming was a perquisite of the baker's trade. However, sixteen men of Captain Job Wright's company complained that the amount skimmed was due them by the baker: "it was a trifle, [but] Every Day it A Mounts [it] will Bee of Value to the Solgers Wich We think is our Just Right." Captain Wright investigated their claims and was told that the profit skimmed by the baker was for "carrying charges."[15]

The only large cooking utensil that the soldiers possibly did have with them in camp was a three-legged or flat-bottomed iron kettle. Each kettle had "a capacity of 9 quarts and weighed from 2 to 3 pounds." The soldiers shared the burden of carrying the pot and lid and sometimes were able to acquire a linen carrying case and slung it across their backs along with the rest of their equipment.

In reality, the Continental army subsisted largely on bread and meat as the main staples. Vegetables were usually hard to come by, and antiscorbutics such as vinegar, beer, and cider, although prescribed in a soldier's ration, were rarely available. As a result, soldiers would frequently forage for additions to their meals. Martin was a renowned forager and did not particularly suffer all that much during the army's legendary winter at Valley Forge. To his good fortune, he had been placed on semipermanent forage duty and had actually gained weight. Having to come camp in the early spring of 1778, his colonel observed that Martin had grown "fat as a pig" and immediately suggested that perhaps he should remain in camp and send another man on forage duty in his stead so that this person "might recruit [rest] himself a little." Martin immediately sensed that his good duty assignment was in peril. He was able to convince the officer that he was only at camp on very "particular" orders and that he and only he must return to his outpost away from the main army. The colonel reluctantly signed Martin's return pass. Sergeant William Young believed that soldiers were natural foragers and "cannot let anything Lay that comes in their way." Other soldiers joked about how they captured a "hissian," which was in reality a goose. An officer named McCumber was tried by courts-martial for plundering. His only defense was that he believed "he had a Right to take anything out side [Continental] lines."[16] But even the best foragers were sometimes confounded by alert sentinels or officers who tried to keep the soldiers from becoming too aggressive in their search for food.

Work at Camp

Once the men had eaten their breakfast, they usually faced one of two prospects for the coming day. First, if especially unlucky, they could be detailed to twenty-four hours of guard duty and they were required to prepare themselves and their uniforms and equipment to be posted by the officer at Guard Mount—usually near sunset in the early evening. Soldiers not assigned to working parties or other details, such as wood cutting, or given the job of "camp colour men"—men whose jobs were to clean up the offal and refuse of the camp—could look forward to several hours of manual of arms exercises and drill that included both a morning and an afternoon session.

Guard duty was especially onerous for most soldiers. Each guard tour usually lasted twenty-four hours, and guards were expected to remain watchful and awake throughout their time on guard regardless of their own personal fatigue or weather. Soldiers who fell asleep on post could and would be severely punished. Martin vividly recalled one particular time during the campaign of 1777 when he was assigned guard duty. The officer of the day with a small escort made his rounds to the sentinel posts during the night and to his chagrin found that the majority of the guards were not doing their duty. One had "stowed himself snugly into an old papermill; another had left his post to procure a draught of milk from the cows in a farmer's yard, and others were found, here and there, neglecting their duty." The officer collected the miscreant guards "to deliver them up to the righteous sentence of a court martial." Martin proudly noted that he was one of the only guards who had dutifully challenged the officer and his party with the countersign. Being placed on guard duty often provided a pretext for men to desert. So many "old countrymen"—recently arrived immigrants from Great Britain—deserted that Washington admonished his colonels to only place trustworthy natives in critical guard positions.[17]

ARMS AND MEN

Throughout the war and especially in camp, soldiers were kept constantly at drill. One major reason for this habit was the exigencies of the eighteenth-century battlefield. The smoke and noise of combat made it almost impossible to hear commands. Thus, the men needed to be able to load and aim their muskets in great rapidity on their own without orders (the best men could perform this action in about fifteen seconds). And most important, they needed to be able to do this under the extreme stress of combat, often having to load in the face of a charging grenadier with a leveled bayonet. Noise was such a factor that the British army—and later the Continental army—habitually fired their muskets in volleys by platoons, the smallest tactical formation on the eighteenth-century battlefield. Occasionally, soldiers fired by companies, battalions, or regiments, but this was very difficult to coordinate especially after the first volley was fired. Firing by platoons in succession was believed to cause a greater distribution of damage to the opposing force. Platoon fire would also ensure that at least some muskets were loaded to repel a charge. The British believed that platoon firing also imbued the men with a sense of patience on the battlefield since they had to carefully listen only to their own officers for orders to load and fire. The one major drawback of the platoon system was that it had a tendency to disrupt the company commander's ability to lead a cohesive unit in battle. Since the armies deployed in multiple compact lines, the units could perform a maneuver called "locking," where the rank of men in the first line kneeled to reload after delivering a volley and the second line of men (and in the British army the third line as well) stepped to the right of the kneeling men and fired over their right shoulder. In the British service, the third rank took a full step to the right and fired past the ear and head of the second-rank man. In ideal situations, once the second and third rank delivered their volleys, the first rank would have reloaded or the entire unit would be given the command to charge the enemy with bayonets.

Muskets, Early Rifles, and Bayonets

As for weapons, most Continental soldiers were armed with a smoothbore musket and a triangular socket bayonet. Early in the war, many colonial Committees of Safety favored a version of the famous and widely produced British "Brown Bess" or "long land" musket with a barrel of forty-seven inches. A later shorter version of forty-two inches was ordered when it was found that there was no loss of accuracy for either type of weapon. The Massachusetts Committee of Safety ordered a number of muskets produced along this same design:

> Resolved, That for every effective and substantial Fire-Arm which shall be manufactured in this Colony with a barrel of three feet and nine inches in length that will carry an ounce ball, a good bayonet with a blade not less than eighteen inches in length, a steel ramrod with a spring to retain the same, two loops for gun strings, and the maker's name stamped or engraved on the lock . . . and resemble in construction, and as nearly as may be, equal in goodness with the King's new arms there shall be allowed . . . the sum of three Pounds.[18]

A Brown Bess produced for the British army would occasionally have a "Tower" or "Dublin Castle" mark to reflect the name of the arsenal where it was stored, but inscribed somewhere on the firelock itself was the royal monogram GR or "Georgius Rex." to denote that it was royal property. However, there is little evidence that the soldiers themselves referred to their weapons as "Brown Bess," and this name is likely a more modern appellation. The Brown Bess musket fired a .75-caliber lead ball. The significance of the smoothbore musket and the heavy lead ball that it fired was found in its "knock down" power. When a soldier was hit by this devastating weapon, it literally knocked him down and even if he was not killed outright he usually stayed down unless some kind soul helped him off the battlefield. Moreover, the large bore of the Brown Bess made it possible to fire ammunition of nearly any caliber found on the North American battlefield. But this advantage also had its drawbacks. The large barrel allowed for rapidity of loading but enabled a significant amount of propellant gas to "blow-by" the round and thus caused the ball to rapidly lose accuracy as it left the barrel. Fired at a relatively low muzzle velocity, the soft lead ball would normally only fly in a straight path for about fifty yards. However, if it hit its target, the tendency of the lead ball upon meeting on object such as a human body would be to flatten out upon impact. The wounds produced by these weapons were horrific. Some Americans were known to cut their musket balls so that the ball would fly in half when fired and also to supplement the musket load with four or five smaller buckshot (sometimes also called small shot) added in to load. Washington believed that in defense all his soldiers should have this sort of load ready to deliver against the attacking British and had "no doubt of their being repulsed" by such firepower.

After the French alliance became a reality, many of the Continental army was armed with the slightly lighter .69-caliber Charleville musket. It is estimated that as early as 1777 over twenty-three thousand Charlevilles had been secretly delivered to the Americans and that these weapons came in more than six variants. The French weapon differed from the heavier Brown Bess in one other respect; its barrel was affixed to the wooden stock by three iron bands. The British weapon attached the barrel of the Brown

Bess with metal pins, which tended to loosen over time. The French firing lock was also slightly superior to that of the British "gooseneck" version. The French used a rein-forced straight "throat-hole" cock which also tended to snap off less frequently than the curved British version. The American army quickly developed a preference for the French musket, and the Committee of Safety weapons rapidly fell out of favor.[19]

One weapon favored by at least a portion of the American army was the rifled mus-ket. Early in the war, the Americans hoped that this weapon will decisively decimate the British before they could get close enough to deliver one of their feared bayonet charges. The major disadvantage of the rifle was its difficulty in reloading since the lands and grooves of the rifled barrel of the weapon and the use of a round musket ball made it a very tough operation to accomplish, especially under fire. The ball had to be tightly fitted or rammed into the barrel and seated home with the use of a greased patch (and often with the aid of a wooden mallet). Thus, the ball had to be physically forced down the barrel by its operator. A musket barrel, on the other hand, was purposely larger than the ball in order to make reloading easier and more rapid. Although the rifle was usually highly accurate from two hundred to three hundred yards, it quickly proved impractical for the style of open warfare practiced by the opposing armies throughout most of the war. A charging musketman with a bayonet could usually close the distance between a rifleman and himself in short order once the rifleman had discharged his piece and was attempting to reload. Moreover, rifles were not fitted with the ability to use a socket bayonet. Instead, most riflemen outfitted themselves with a tomahawk or short hunting sword as a secondary defensive weapon. The tomahawk was seen as a par-ticularly terrifying edged weapon and one that Native American warriors had long used to strike fear in the hearts of their adversaries. It was felt that they would do the same for American riflemen.

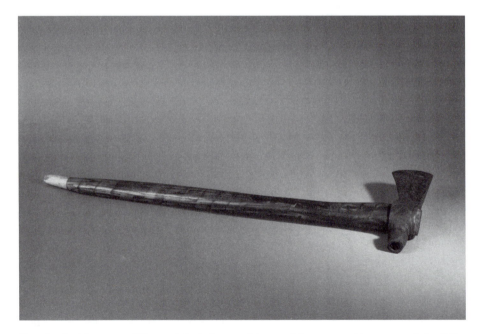

Tomahawk. (*Courtesy of National Park Service, Museum Management Program and the Valley Forge National Historical Park, VAFO 769*)

Despite these drawbacks, a number of hunting-shirt–wearing rifle companies from Pennsylvania, Maryland, and Virginia were raised to supplement the army because it was thought that they would strike terror into the hearts of their British opponents because of their renowned lethality on the battlefield. This early assumption led later historians to wrongly conclude that the rifle and rifle companies had proven to be decisive on many Revolutionary War battlefields. Although it made a good story, in actuality the rifle companies were more often employed on the flanks of the army to harass the enemy or as single marksmen who often climbed high trees to pick off enemy officers at long range. The riflemen were effective but only in a very specific sense as a form of light infantry or sharpshooter. The American riflemen had clear weaknesses, and the British soon discovered it. One British officer wrote in the *Middlesex Journal* in 1776 that:

> About twilight is found the best season for hunting the rebels in the woods, at which time their rifles are of very little use; and they are not so serviceable in a body as musketry, a rest [a place to position the rifle upon] being requisite at all times, and before they are able to make a second discharge, it frequently happens that they find themselves run through the body by the push of a bayonet, as a rifleman is not entitled to any quarter.[20]

There was no standardized army rifle provided to these companies, but the general caliber was around .55 to .60. Many of them were made in Virginia, Maryland, and Pennsylvania, places that had produced them for backwoods hunters for decades. Most of the barrels were octagonal, and the rifle stocks were ornamented with brass fittings. Although the British quickly lost their fear of the vaunted American rifleman, they were still very effective operating as individual marksmen and scouts. Their singular lack of a bayonet and slow reloading time made them less effective when facing troops that had bayonets and could fire at close range nearly three times as fast.

Nearly all of the muskets issued to soldiers on both sides during the Revolution came fixed with a bayonet "locking" lug at the end of the weapon. This lug was a short stub of metal that allowed a "socket" bayonet to be securely fitted over top of the musket barrel via a hollow grooved metal sleeve and locked to the end of the musket. Earlier musket bayonets were of the "plug" variety and were inserted directly into the barrel. Thus, it had to be removed if the infantryman wanted to load and fire his musket. The socket bayonet allowed both musket and bayonet to be wielded simultaneously and represented a quantum leap in technological improvement over the older plug variants. The introduction of the socket bayonet also directly led "to an increase in fire-power and tactical flexibility, as all infantry were now armed with muskets. The change permitted more effective drill, and drill and discipline were essential to fire-power." The bayonet, when used properly by a relatively rapid-firing infantryman, had revolutionized eighteenth-century battlefield tactics, thus the concomitant and necessary emphasis on drill and the manual of arms.[21]

The standard army socket bayonet itself was about twenty-two inches in total length (with about eighteen inches being the blade itself) and included the metal sleeve that fit around the outside of the barrel. When not affixed to the musket, bayonets were kept in a tight leather scabbard or holster that was slung over the shoulder. Sometimes scabbards were in short supply and the soldier would stow his bayonet in his knapsack or haversack. The bayonet did not come with a handle, so it was very unlikely that it would be used in combat by a soldier when not connected to the musket itself. The blade was triangular in shape. This provided for better stability and created a triangular wound on its victims. Such wounds were difficult to stitch together by army surgeons and made secondary infections more likely to occur. It was a particularly vicious sort of weapon. However, when used in conjunction with musket-wielding disciplined infantry, it proved to be decisive on most eighteenth-century battlefields.

All muskets used by the army were fired using flintlock mechanisms. Muskets were of three parts: firing lock, wooden stock, and metal barrel (lock, stock, and barrel). The flintlock required that soldiers maintain working pieces of flint wedged into the firing hammer of the firelock. Most flints only lasted for about eight to ten shots (or less) before needing to be replaced. Thus, in camp and on the march, all soldiers also had to carry a supply of spare flints. When released from the cocked position by pulling on the trigger, this flint would strike a steel piece of the firing lock called a "frizzen" and the sparks that resulted from the friction would (hopefully) ignite loose grains of priming powder previously placed in a firing "pan" on the outside of the barrel and directly beneath the frizzen. This small ignition would then (again hopefully) ignite the larger amount of black powder inside the musket barrel via a touchhole bored into the right side of the barrel itself. The resulting explosion would then propel the .69-caliber round lead ball out of the barrel and toward the enemy. Many soldiers experienced misfires during training and in combat. Typically, a misfire would result from damp powder, improper seating of the powder and cartridge in the barrel, or a "flash in the pan," where the priming pan powder would ignite but not effectively enough for the powder in the barrel to be ignited as well. The only safety mechanism on the firelock was at the half-cocked position. This also enabled the musket man to partially cock the hammer half way to be able to open the frizzen and expose the pan for priming. Occasionally,

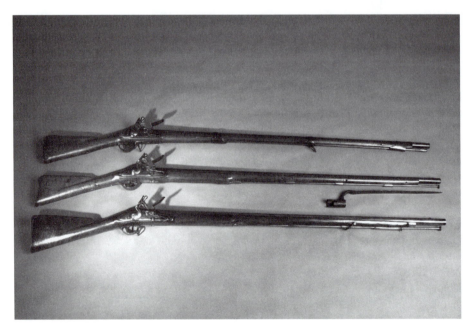

Flintlock musket (top), musket (middle), and socket bayonet (bottom). (*Courtesy of National Park Service, Museum Management Program and the Valley Forge National Historical Park, VAFO 124, 137, 709*)

Gun lock. (*Courtesy of National Park Service, Museum Management Program and the Guilford Courthouse National Military Park, GUCO 13*)

the sear on the hammer would get worn down and fail and cause the weapon to accidentally fire prematurely or go off "half-cocked."

Gunpowder, Cartridges, and Bullets

In order to load their muskets, soldiers usually bit the end off the end of a premeasured paper cartridge and poured the contents of the powder down the barrel. They then rolled the ball down the barrel and tamped the remnants of the paper cartridge on top of the load to hold it relatively securely in place until ready to fire. Some soldiers used a powder horn to scatter the necessary powder grains into the firing pan before firing. Others simply scattered grains into the pan from a cartridge. Soldiers habitually bit the top off of a paper cartridge using their teeth. For this reason, most soldiers in the army had to demonstrate to recruiting officers and army surgeons upon enlistment that they at least had some usable upper and lower teeth before reporting to their regiments. The soldiers kept their muskets relatively free of rust by their liberal application of linseed oil and rubbed their musket barrels with a soft deerskin.

Gunpowder was especially important to the Continental soldier. Early in the war, many militiamen in the Army of Observation showed up at Boston carrying their cartridges in their pockets or loosely arranged in handkerchiefs. This caused a significant

Musket cartridge. (*Courtesy of National Park Service, Museum Management Program and the Valley Forge National Historical Park, VAFO 928*)

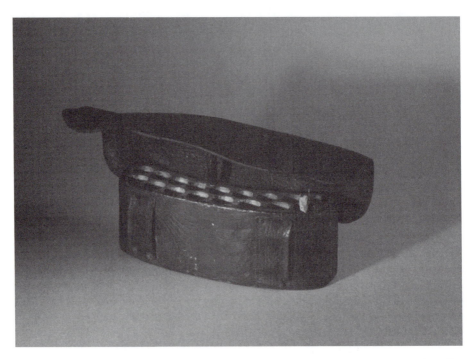

Cartridge box. (*Courtesy of National Park Service, Museum Management Program and the Valley Forge National Historical Park, VAFO 1090*)

amount of the cartridges to fail as they were exposed to the weather and got easily soaked by rain or were jostled about and came apart over time. Thus, it became imperative that each soldier be eventually provided with a cartridge box. The standard army cartridge box was a leather case with a larger flap sewn over the top and affixed with a strap that could be slung over the shoulder of a soldier. The cartridge box hung down low enough, where a soldier could easily flip up the flap on the box and pull out a premade paper cartridge without looking. The large leather flap that covered the outside of the box made the cartridges weather resistant—although they often were not totally effective against especially heavy rain. Better-made cartridge boxes also had a smaller secondary canvas flap sewn inside for further weather protection. Inside the box itself, the soldiers placed a wooden block with cylindrical holes (usually between twenty and thirty holes) cut into it to fit the paper cartridges into place. The tops of the cartridges stuck out of the holes but remained covered by the leather flap when not in use.

All soldiers either carried an iron bullet mold in their haversacks or had immediate access to one. Heated liquid lead would then be poured from a small iron pan into a bullet mold that had an appearance of a modern nut cracker. Once the lead cooled inside the mold, the ball then had to be further cut by a mold cutter to remove any excess lead left (called "sprue"). Once the ball was ready to be placed into a cartridge, the soldier would take a piece of paper and wrap it around a six-inch wooden dowel. The dowel is hollow at one end to allow the ball to rest on top of it. Paper is wrapped around the dowel and twisted at one end to secure the ball, with about an inch of the dowel sticking out of the opposite end. The dowel was then removed and enough powder then poured into the premolded paper cartridge, including some extra powder to prime the pan if the soldier was not using a powder horn. The opposite end of the paper cartridge was now also twisted to secure the powder and then placed inside one of the cylindrical slots carved into the wood block inside the cartridge case itself. This process was repeated until the soldier ran out of ball and powder or all the holes in the box were filled with a premade cartridge. Some soldiers were fortunate enough to have tin canisters instead of the leather-flapped variety. Others wore waist cartridge belts and kept their cartridges inside twelve

Bullet mold. (*Courtesy of National Park Service, Museum Management Program and the Morrison National Historical Park, MORR 1345*)

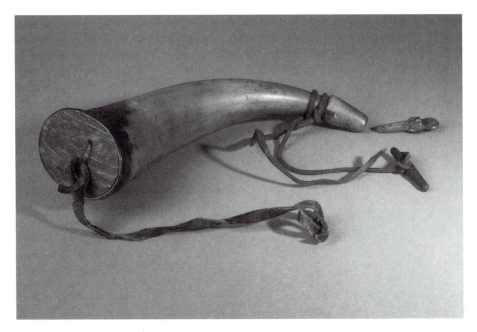

Powder horn. (*Courtesy of National Park Service, Museum Management Program and the Valley Forge National Historical Park, VAFO 1790*)

tin tubes affixed to the belt itself. Such modified boxes were more effective at keeping out the weather, and the tin made them fireproof was well. Sometimes a spark from the flashing pan of a weapon would settle on the top of an open large cartridge box and ignite the remaining cartridges to the eternal regret of its wearer. Moreover, tin canisters, unlike leather carriers which tended to crack, could be painted, which further enhanced their ability to keep out water and errant sparks.[22]

Access to adequate gunpowder was a chronic problem for the Continental forces throughout the war. This issue was so evident that British Governor General Thomas Gage's initial strategy for ending the rebellion revolved around a series of powder raids in and around Boston. Getting a steady supply to soldiers was always on the mind of Washington. As early as the first Christmas of the war, he wrote to Congress and complained that "our want of powder is inconceivable. A daily waste and no supply administers a gloomy prospect." Captured powder and secret supplies sent by the French helped to a degree, but the army never had what it considered enough powder where they felt comfortable with the supply. In fact, at times, powder was so scarce that soldiers would often run up to burning fuses of shells lobbed into their positions by British artillery or naval guns and kicked out the fuses just to get at the powder inside them.[23]

The main ingredient for black powder was saltpeter. This compound was a combination of nitrate salt of potassium, carbon, and sulfur. The carbon was normally provided in the form of charcoal, hence its black-gray color in finished form. Although the patriots had easy access to materials for the gunpowder, it was saltpeter that they needed the most. The largest deposits of this compound were found in India, but that source was entirely dominated by the British. The French had developed a way to manufacture saltpeter from animal waste and even human excrement. Congress quickly authorized a variety of schemes to produce it and released pamphlets and other instructions designed to make, as an enthused John Adams wrote, "Every stable, Dove House, Cellar, Vault, etc.," into a "mine of salt petre." Nonetheless, the amount of domestically produced saltpeter about approximated that smuggled courtesy of the French.[24]

Swords and Spears

Cavalry or dragoons were armed with a variety of shortened muskets (also called "musketoons") and pistols. However, the main battle weapon of a Revolutionary War cavalryman was his sword. These came in two varieties: the saber and the broadsword. They were fairly large weapons and required great dexterity on the part of its user. Some had single edges, while others had double edges. All came with a variety of hilt guards that gave a modicum of protection to its wielder. Most cavalrymen of the war, such as renowned cavalry Colonels "Lighthorse" Harry Lee and William Washington, believed that once cavalrymen are engaged, pistols and musketoons were of little value. Massachusetts cavalry Captain Epaphras Hoyt stated that "nothing decides an engagement sooner than charging briskly with this weapon [swords] in hand. By this mode of attack, a body of cavalry will generally rout one that receives it with pistols ready to fire." Most of the swords were easily three feet long. Officers' swords for the infantry, however, were thinner and designed for stabbing and running their opponents through the body. Occasionally, light infantry and riflemen, lacking a bayonet, would be armed with short straight hunting swords, which resembled very long knives.[25]

Special weapons seen in the ranks and usually wielded by NCOs and, occasionally, junior officers were halberds (for sergeants) and spontoons (for junior officers). These weapons that dated back to medieval times served mostly as a symbol of rank. Measuring approximately seven or eight feet long, these weapons appeared decorative

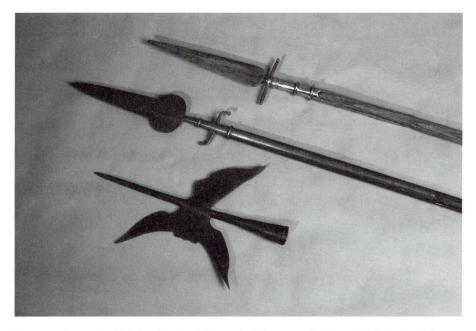

Spontoon (top and middle) and halberd (bottom). (*Courtesy of National Park Service, Museum Management Program and the Valley Forge National Historical Park, VAFO 627, 602, 566*)

and also possessed a functional iron ax or a spear-like weapon on its end that, in practical terms, could keep a charging bayonet-wielding infantryman at bay, prod a cowering or faltering soldier back into ranks, or, if held horizontally to the ground, help a unit to maintain its line formation. The idea of officers being issued spontoons was thought to also relieve them of the problem of reloading their weapons, so that they could pay more attention to action on the battlefield and still have some means of protecting themselves. In his famous and highly successful assault on the British at Stony Point, Major General Anthony Wayne himself carried a spontoon into combat.[26]

But such weapons were not without their drawbacks against a sturdier musket and bayonet. Captain Stephen Olney of Rhode Island found himself in the spectacular night assault on Redoubt Number 10 during the Battle of Yorktown and described what happened to him:

> I have not less than six or eight bayonets pushed against me. I parried as well as I could with my espontoon, but they broke off the blade part, and their bayonets slid along the handle of my espontoon and scaled my fingers: one bayonet pierced my thigh, and another stabbed me in the abdomen just above the hip bone. One fellow fired at me and I thought his ball took effect in my arm; by the light of his gun, I made a thrust with the rest of my espontoon, in order to injure the sight of his eyes; but as it happened, I only made a hard stroke in his forehead.[27]

Early in the war, largely owing to the lack of enough muskets, and especially bayonets, some thought was given to arming the men with pikes and spears. Many of these ancient instruments of war were still in use as late as the battle of White Plains on October 28, 1776. However, Washington himself had to intervene with some specific recommendations on how these spears should be made and in one of his first General Orders to the army noted that:

> the people employed to make spears, are desired by the General to make four dozen of them immediately, thirteen feet in length, and the wood part a good deal more substantial than those already made, particularly in the New Hampshire Lines, are ridiculously short and light, and can answer no sort of purpose, no more are therefore to be made on the same model.[28]

In 1777, Washington informed Daniel Morgan that he had asked for seven-foot spears to be supplied to his riflemen as a substitute for their lack of a bayonet and warned him to avoid contact with the enemy and especially that of their "horse" until he had received them. When the spears finally arrived by late June 1777, Washington was not altogether happy with their particular design either and complained to the Board of War that the thickness of the wood shafts and iron plates that were placed to protect the head of the spear were not adequate to keep them from being cut in two by a saber stroke. Interestingly, the shafts were equipped with an iron hinge in the middle so that the spear could be folded and more easily transported by riflemen on the march. However, Washington was further disappointed that the spears did not originally come with slings for ease of carry. While there is no evidence that these spears were ever issued to Morgan and his men, most of his soldiers, as previously noted, continued to carry a variety of hunting knives and tomahawks as secondary armament.[29]

Artillery Weapons

The army was supplied with a rather astounding variety of artillery weapons. There were so many different sizes and calibers of artillery and mortars in use that it must have been tremendously difficult for the ordnance department to keep the artillery adequately supplied with shot and shell even under the best of conditions. All guns and mortars were of the smoothbore variety and were generally rated by either the diameter of their bores or the weight of the balls and shells that they fired (i.e., thirteen-inch mortars or twenty-four-pound howitzers). The cannons themselves were usually made out of brass, bronze, or iron. The heavier guns (twelve-, twenty-four-, and thirty-two-pounders) were normally used in defense or sieges, whereas lighter guns (three-, four-, or six-pounders) might be parceled out to infantry units and follow directly behind or in support of attacking infantry. Generally speaking, eighteenth-century artillery was not very effective in the offense but could be quite deadly as a defensive weapon, especially when firing grapeshot (clumps of loosely soldered-together iron balls that resembled a clump of grapes). Grapeshot fired from cannon into compact infantry ranks acted as a sort of monster sawed-off shotgun and literally mowed down men in files. Most six-pound guns were effective up to two thousand yards, but more often, because the gunner had to see the strike of his shot in order to correct his aim, they usually did not engage the enemy any farther than five hundred yards. Brass howitzers had shorter barrels than the field guns and could elevate their tubes and thus could lob fused shells over the walls of fortifications and entrenchments, whereas heavy and light mortars were frequently used in siege operations and only fired at high angles.

Equipment

Eating and drinking on a daily basis are a common routine of human existence, and these two activities took up much of a soldier's day in finding and preparing his daily victuals. Revolutionary War soldiers frequently neglected to carry around a canteen. These items were not a standard issue—as they would become in later conflicts—and they were never used with any consistency by the soldiery at large. The most common type found among the men was the wooden "keg" style that looked liked a miniature barrel. The keg staves were held together by wooden or sometimes iron hoops and were equipped with a leather sling. Occasionally, a glass bottle or flask might substitute for a canteen. The British used tin canteens, and a captured one was highly prized by the Americans. As most other times, the men simply carved out a wooden gourd and attached it to their person via a leather thong cut through the handle of the gourd and used it to dip out of brooks and streams as needed, and for the most part, there were plenty of them around on the eastern seaboard. As previously noted, camp followers often carried buckets of water to the men during marches and even during battles. This system worked as long as there were streams around or the men were close enough for the camp followers to get to them. However, the hundreds of cases of heat stroke and heat exhaustion casualties that afflicted the American forces during the excessively hot and humid Battle of Monmouth Courthouse, on June 28, 1778, is a testament to a lack of water discipline on the part of the army in general. Occasionally, however, in an emergency, a soldier in a squad or mess might be provided a single canteen for six or eight men to share. In reality, this meant less than three or four ounces of water per man per canteen.

Two other items of importance to the soldier were knapsacks and haversacks. These items were used to carry around personal items and any spare clothing the men might be fortunate enough to possess. The knapsack was carried on the back by leather straps that looped over the soldier's shoulders, whereas a haversack was slung across the right shoulder—so that it hung down on the left side—by a linen strap. Sometimes, the leather

Canteen. (*Courtesy of National Park Service, Museum Management Program and the Morrison National Historical Park, MORR 2022*)

knapsack would have its top painted to help further weatherproof it. At other times, the hair would be left on the leather hide that made up the outer side of the knapsack itself. Haversacks were usually made of linen and could be washed in streams and the like. Men would stow their army blanket, extra food such as sea bread, and perhaps some rope for stringing up their tents if they had them. Some soldiers who smoked would store a clay pipe and some twist tobacco (so called because soldiers would buy their tobacco in braided lengths). This tobacco was cut in lengths according to how much money the soldier had to spend (which was usually next to nothing). Nearly every soldier owned or tried to acquire a working jack knife of some sort. This item became indispensable, for nearly everyone in camp used it for a wide variety of tasks, from cutting up his ration of beef to perhaps repairing his clothing and equipment. Occasionally, soldiers perhaps owned a two-pronged iron fork (with usually a wood handle) or spoon for eating utensils. They would use the aforementioned gourds or a crudely carved wooden or horn drinking mug for their water or spruce beer—if they were fortunate enough to be issued some. Frequently, the men would be issued a gill of rum for fortification purposes, and they mixed it with their water in canteens or simply drank it straight down (as many preferred) from a horn tumbler. Officers, of course, having greater access to wagons often traveled with a small chest of eating and drinking utensils.

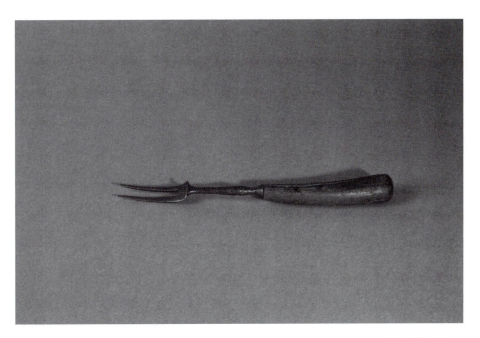

Fork. (*Courtesy of National Park Service, Museum Management Program and the Valley Forge National Historical Park, VAFO 1172*)

ARMY MUSIC

The standard musical unit in the Continental army consisted of fifes and drums. All companies had at least one of each, and some regiments had upwards of twenty musicians, to include a fife major and one for the drums. These men were indispensable to army life and sounded army commands from dawn to dusk. They signaled when meals were to be served and when officers needed to report to their commanders and presided at military punishments. Frequently, a drummer, supervised by a drum major, would be detailed to perform the highly unpopular duty of wielding the lash upon a soldier sentenced for punishment.

Fifes were usually made out of some sort of "closely grained" wood that could be ultimately carved into an instrument. Drums were of two basic types: snare and side drums or bass drums. The bodies of the drums were made of wooden staves and bound tightly together, top and bottom, with wooden hoops. The top hoop would be covered with a tightened smooth animal skin and stretched across the outer edge of the hoop itself. The skin was tightened across the top hoop with strands of rope that connected to the bottom of the drum and allowed the drum skin to maintain adequate tension. The tighter the tension, the sharper the drum beat. The body of the drum would be usually labeled with a unit designator and painted for greater preservation. Bass drums were generally assembled like the smaller snare drum but were larger. They clearly do not resemble the bass drums of the modern era in nearly any way. They were about two feet deep and "were carried horizontally across the chest and beaten with two wooden strikers." Trumpets and horns were also used but mainly in conjunction with cavalry since fifes and drums were impractical for mounted units. Bugle horns, in deference to the hunting horns long used in Europe, became the standard instrument for the more dispersed light infantry. Morgan's rifle companies eschewed all musical instruments. Occasionally, units would form formal army bands for entertainment, and sometimes, musically talented prisoners of war (POWs) (especially Hessians) were offered an opportunity to get out of prison in exchange for playing in one of these bands. These military bands of about nine men were used mainly for the recreational purposes of the officers in camp or, at least in one instance, to get fifers and drummers to reenlist for this softer duty. These bands usually played flutes, clarinets, trombones, trumpets, and something called a hautboy (an oboe-like instrument).[30]

RECREATION

Not all time in camp or on the march was all work and drill. Men did partake in recreation when the occasion called for it, and there were not other duties to attend to. Although Washington took an exceedingly dim view of gambling with dice and cards and tried to suppress these traditional soldier pastimes as much as he could, they were still commonplace in most army camps. The army had traditional days of celebration, such as the 4th of July after 1776, Thanksgiving Day, Christmas, and New Year's Day. They even expropriated the traditional celebration of the King George III's coronation day (September 22) and changed it to the "King's damnation day." His birthday (June 4), heretofore widely celebrated in the colonies, was now totally ignored in the army camps. In deference to the large number of Irish-born soldiers in the ranks, St. Patrick's Day was also a cause for celebration. On such official celebration days, drill was usually suspended, prisoners in the guardhouse not guilty of capital offenses were set free, and gills of rum were liberally distributed to the soldiers. Frequently, a formal feu de joie (or organized musket volleys) would be led by officers or NCOs. Rifle frolics or marksmanship contests were organized. Games such as checkers (draughts) and chess were played. Footraces and wrestling matches were organized by the men. Most officers and soldiers who could write wrote letters home or to friends in other states. Soldiers who had money or good credit could visit nearby sutler's booths and buy pies or other scarce foodstuffs not normally supplied in their regular army ration.[31]

Ensign George Ewing of the 3rd New Jersey Regiment described camp life in some of his letters as fairly convivial—at least for the officers, who frequented each other's tents despite Washington's strict prohibition against such conduct and often played cards with each other late into the evening and engaged each other in games of chance. Ewing noted that soldiers he had been detailed to guard were allowed to play ball as a form of exercise. On some afternoons, he himself played a game called "base," which was an earlier form of baseball. On other occasions, he attended camp theatrical productions.[32]

Practical jokes (sometimes with a deeper message) were common as well. Ensign Ewing observed some of his troops tie burning hay to the tail of their quartermaster's horse. The men believed that the quartermaster was not a very good one and got a laugh at the expense of the officer. Martin wrote about how he and his squad mates decided to play a little game on their officers who had strictly forbidden the men from firing off weapons in camp. They loaded an old musket with powder, cocked it, and placed a slow match in the firing mechanism "so that the old barrel would speak for itself with a voice that would be heard. The officers would then muster out, and some running and scolding would ensue: but none knew who made the noise, or where it came from." After the officers returned empty-handed to their huts, Martin and his friends repeated the same trick several times in the course of the night, but after a while he noted that "the officers [got] tired of running so often to catch Mr. Nobody." Later in the war, Martin thwarted a more serious practical joke that might have had deadly consequences if it had actually been carried out. On this occasion, Martin's unpopular company commander was subject to a "gunpowder plot" by some of the soldiers in his command. They loaded a wooden canteen with three and a half pounds of gunpowder and said that they planned to give their officer "a hoist" and placed the loaded canteen under the officer's bunk. Martin immediately recognized that the loaded canteen would likely kill the captain and talked them out of the scheme. They settled on booby-trapping another musket instead.[33]

RELIGION

Most American regiments, unlike their British and Hessian opponents, were adequately supported by chaplains and had clergy assigned to each regiment. Three chaplains even petitioned Congress to supply the army with thirty thousand bibles. However, Congress declined to produce this amount because of the cost and expense of printing and paper and suggested instead to import twenty thousand bibles from Europe. There is no evidence that this proposal was ever acted upon. Many men in the ranks came to camp with their own personal bibles, and Washington mandated that regular services be held in army camp each Sunday. He firmly believed that regular attendance at divine service by the men would reduce their compulsion toward vice and gambling. While encamped at Valley Forge, Washington also encouraged the men to attend nightly prayer services. Early in the war, chaplains used the pulpit to score political points with the men. Rhode Island Chaplain Ebenezer David preached to six hundred soldiers at New York "that our Land had for a long time groaned under ecclesiastical tyranny &c" in reference to the attempt by the Crown to establish an Anglican bishop in the colonies to be supported by local taxes. He further added that "some of the officers told me [my] Doctrine was sound but would not have gone down 20 years ago."[34]

As a chaplain, David was shocked by the behavior of the men and even other chaplains in camp and wrote to his friend Nicholas Brown from Prospect Hill, Massachusetts, on January 29, 1776:

> What *GOD* is about to bring to pass in the Kingdome of His Providence is known by him alone. It behooves us to view his hand discharge our Duty & Leave the event with Him. . . . There is nothing dispirits me so much as the wickedness of our land—the Prophanety of our Camps is very great—the stupidity of our sick amazing, and I could wish that those of us who officiate as Chaplains were not lacking in Faithfulness. . . . There is a great need of some persons who dare oppose vice & mentain the Doctrine of Dependency upon GOD—I was grieved to hear a preacher mention our connection with the Tories as the great Sin of the day like that of Israels entering into Covenant with the Cannenites &c. I need not tell you that such low turns are popular But I must close.[35]

Despite David's misgivings, many letters from officers and especially those of the New England troops contained substantial evidence of their piety. On the day before the army entered the encampment at Valley Forge, Washington ordered a special service to be held in "Thanksgiving and Praise . . . to God for the manifold blessings he has granted us." He ordered a similar service on May 6, 1778, to commemorate the formal announcement of the alliance with France. Major Albert Chapman of the 5th Connecticut

Regiment summed up the feelings of much of the soldiery in the army camps when he wrote, "may we maintain our Liberties & Rites that God has given us to Inlist ourselves under the banner of Jesus Christ & fight like a good Soldier for him that loved us and gave himself a ransom for our sins."[36]

ONWARD TO MONMOUTH COURT HOUSE

The Continental army that emerged from Valley Forge was hardly healthy. Thousands of soldiers remained in hospitals scattered around the Pennsylvania back-country so that many regiments were mere shadows of what they were during the fall of 1777. For example, in January 1778, Brigadier General Charles Scott's Virginia Brigade had on paper 1,287 men. But in reality, Scott could only muster 473 effectives. At least 253 men could not march because these soldiers lacked shoes and clothes.[37]

However, one significant reinforcement did arrive during the spring of 1778 and that came in the form of repatriated Major General Charles Lee, a heretofore highly regarded former professional British army officer, who had been recently exchanged for twice-captured British Major General Richard Prescott. Charles Lee soon resumed his position as Washington's senior major general with the army and de facto second in command. Charles Lee was a rather odd character in an era of characters. Extremely thin and awkward, he liked to travel with a pack of hounds. He was exceptionally outspoken and did not try to hide his open contempt for Washington and his leadership of the army.

It was clear to even the rank and file that their time in camp was finally coming to an end. Martin wryly commented that since being on detached duty "Dame Fortune had been kind but now 'Miss-Fortune' was coming in for *her* set in the reel." Martin wistfully commented that during the Valley Forge winter he "had enough to eat and been under no restraint; had picked up a few articles of comfortable summer clothing among the inhabitants; [his] lieutenant had never concerned himself about us; we had scarcely seen him during the whole time." Now, however, he and his mates had been ordered back to the army and were "engaged in learning the Baron de Steuben's new Prussian exercise; it was a continual drill." On detached duty, he wrote that "we went when and where we pleased 'and had none to make us afraid'; but now the scene had changed. We must go and come at bidding and suffer hunger besides."[38]

At the same time as the French alliance was announced (May 1778), William Howe was replaced by Henry Clinton. Clinton immediately decided to abandon Philadelphia and return the army to New York City. Placing his sick (and about three thousand loyalists) aboard ships, Clinton and about ten thousand of his men prepared to cross New Jersey. However, it was not likely to be a rapid passage as the British wagon train alone consisted of at least 1500 wagons and stretched across the rough New Jersey roads for at least twelve miles. His army was only able to travel thirty-five miles in six days. But Clinton's glacial pace gave Washington an opportunity to strike while the British were considerably strung out across the state of New Jersey.

Meanwhile, largely thanks to the French alliance, the situation for the Americans had turned remarkably around. Now, member of Congress Elbridge Gerry noted:

> the king of England [was] considered by every whig in the nation as a tyrant, and the King of France applauded by every whig in America as the protector of the rights of man!. . . . Britain at war with America, France in alliance with her! These my friend, are astonishing changes.

But more important, with the French alliance came crucial "sinews of war" in arms, loans, clothing, and equipment. Thousands of muskets, shot, cannons, tents, and, most important, powder now poured into New England ports and were sent by wagon to Washington's and Gates's armies in the New Jersey and New York backcountry. No longer would Washington's men have to kick the fuses out of still sizzling bombshells just to get the powder out of them.[39]

A few days before the battle at Monmouth Court House, Washington had ordered the Marquis de Lafayette forward with about four thousand troops to probe toward the British at Monmouth Court House in New Jersey. Initially, Major General Charles Lee had recommended the young Frenchman for this assignment, but when he found out that the advance force to the given Lafayette amounted to nearly one-half the Continental army, Charles Lee demanded the right to take command and Washington consented.

Even early in the morning of June 28, 1778, the day portended to be excessively hot. Charles Lee had sent his advance elements forward to engage Clinton's rear guard and then ordered Charles Scott's Virginians along with Henry Jackson's brigade and William Maxwell's New Jersey troops and a few other units on a circuitous march to catch Clinton's rear guard in a pincer movement. And it might have worked, too, if Clinton had not decided at that moment to send Lord Cornwallis's entire division of Grenadier Guards back toward the Court House to reinforce his rear guard. Now, instead of being on the defensive, at this point, the British locally outnumbered the Americans.

There is no doubt that the fighting that morning was confusing as both sides were fairly unfamiliar with the ground and the size and disposition of each other's forces. Nonetheless, the pressure on Maxwell and Scott slowly built up. Without receiving orders to move one way or the other (no one seems to have received any sort of orders from Charles Lee that morning), Scott made the decision to retreat with his Virginia brigade when a crucial artillery battery pulled out of the fight. As he passed by General Maxwell, he shouted to him that "we must get out of this place." Since Scott covered Maxwell's right, Maxwell also ordered his men to retreat. Soon Charles Lee's other detachments were also headed rearward, and before he knew it, he had a full-scale retreat on his hands and was closely pressed by Cornwallis. Charles Lee tried to reform his troops near the Court House, but at this point, owing to the confusion in the precipitous retreat of most of his force, he only had about two thousand effectives in line to confront Cornwallis's surging Grenadiers.[40]

It was at this point in the battle that Washington rode up and immediately surveyed the scene. According to legend (most accounts of this fateful meeting on the battlefield between Charles Lee and Washington come from nineteenth-century sources), Washington allegedly become enraged over Charles Lee's conduct of the battle and swore at him. While this would have been very out of character for the usually fully reserved Washington, it was possible that he was frustrated that Charles Lee had let things get out of hand so quickly. Most of the swearing legacy can be attributed to an after-the-war vignette recounted by Scott, who perhaps out of an attempt to preserve his own badly shaken reputation, which by all accounts was certainly in question at Monmouth Court House, stated that on that very hot June day he heard Washington swear "like an angel from heaven." Later local accounts such as Franklin Ellis's history of Monmouth County (1885) had Washington allegedly responding to Charles Lee's excuses over his retreat by shouting "D—n your multiplying eyes, General Lee! Go to the front, or go to hell, I care little which." Other statements had Charles Lee claiming that the Continentals were simply not able to meet British Grenadiers.[41]

Most of these apocryphal stories should perhaps remain in the legend category awaiting further corroboration. However, what *was* obvious that afternoon was that Washington was clearly exasperated with Charles Lee on a number of counts. Tench Tilghman, an aide-de-camp to Washington and one of the few verified contemporary witnesses to the meeting between the commander in chief and Charles Lee, observed Washington intensely questioning Charles Lee as to the situation on the battlefield. Either out of confusion or owing to the intensity of the fighting that morning, Charles Lee could only stammer "Sir! Sir!" to Washington's questions as to why the army was in precipitous retreat. Washington tersely demanded that if Charles Lee had not believed in this operation, "he should never have undertaken it." But there is no mention by Tilghman that Washington actually swore at Charles Lee, although it was clearly apparent that the commander in chief was angry at him and his mumbled excuses about why the army was in retreat. This session, however, was quickly cut short when another aide, Robert Harrison, arrived and informed Washington that the enemy was literally "within 15 minutes march" of their present location. Washington pondered his next move when Tilghman spoke up and stated that a Lieutenant Colonel David Rhea of the 4th New Jersey Regiment was a local native and willing to help the general with placing troops on the battlefield to his best advantage. Washington virtually "leaped" at this news, and Rhea was immediately brought to headquarters to assist in bringing up the rest of the army to repulse Cornwallis's Grenadiers. Posting arriving troops behind a providentially positioned nearby hedgerow, Washington quickly took personal command of the army and began to turn things around. Later, Alexander Hamilton wrote that "I never saw the General to so much advantage. . . . His coolness and firmness were admirable. He instantly took measures for checking the enemy's advance, and giving time for the Army, which was very near, to form and make a proper disposition." Incredibly, Charles Lee shows up as the lines are being formed and Washington left him in charge of the local situation and galloped to the center of his army to organize things there. Fortunately for the Americans, Cornwallis's piecemeal attacks against the reconstituted Continental line failed, and he, in turn, was now required to retreat. Washington attempted to organize a counterattack, but the virtual heat exhaustion experienced by most of his men made this next to impossible. By the next morning, Clinton was now in full retreat toward New York City.[42]

But Charles Lee still remained a problem, and just two days after the end of the only battle thus far, where Washington's army had actually held the field against a British field army, he demanded that Washington explain his dissatisfaction with him:

> From the knowledge I have or your Excellency's character, I must conclude that nothing but misinformation of some very stupid, or misrepresentations of some very wicked person, could have occasioned your making use of such very singular expressions as you did on my coming up to the ground where you had taken post: they implied that I was guilty either of disobedience of orders, of want of conduct, or want of courage.[43]

Outrageously claiming in two highly inflammatory post-battle letters to the commander in chief that any success of the army at Monmouth Court House was entirely due to his conduct and dispositions, Charles Lee demanded and received a court-martial in July. The trial and dispositions lasted into August, but Charles Lee was ultimately found guilty on all three charges that had been preferred against him: his failure to press the attack on the enemy at Monmouth Court House; retreating without orders; and disrespect to Washington as expressed in his two post-battle letters. All the generals involved in the retreat that day, including Scott, Maxwell, and even the highly regarded Wayne, all "gave testimony damaging to Lee." The court ordered him sent home for a year and suspended from duty. However, so great was Charles Lee's bubble military reputation that Congress only narrowly upheld the verdict. But Charles Lee was not one to take anything lying down, and in another insulting letter, this one addressed to Congress, he provided the straw that finally broke the camel's back, and Congress moved to totally dismiss him from any further army service.[44]

Despite the problems with Charles Lee, the fighting at Monmouth Court House was truly a watershed event for the Continental soldiers in the army. Rhode Island soldier Jeremiah Greenman had found himself with Charles Lee's column the morning of the battle and nonchalantly stated that "a number of our men died of the heat a retreating." He also confirmed that many soldiers did not carry canteens and that some of the men had thrown away their packs because of the excessive heat that day. He wrote that "such a Number of Solders that water is almost as scares as Liquor & what is got is very bad indeed."[45]

The ubiquitous soldier Martin noted that the combat élan of the American troops was quite high that day and that "the men did not need much haranguing to raise their courage." The officers even had to order the "sick and lame" to stay behind and asked them to exchange their weapons for any faulty ones being carried by able bodied-soldiers. The men refused and stated that "if their arms went, they would go with them at all events." Martin commented on the extreme heat as well. He was also fortuitously one of the soldiers who observed Washington himself arrive on the battlefield and heard him ask one of the officers "by whose order the troops were retreating?" Martin stated that the general mumbled something that he could not make out, but it was clear to him that "at that instant he seemed to be in a great passion; his looks if not his words seemed to indicate as much." Martin was later in on the counterattack in driving some of the British from an orchard. He mentioned that he fired his musket at a man "he had singled out and took aim directly between his shoulders (they were divested of their packs). He was a good mark, being a broad-shouldered fellow." Martin stated that he did not know whether he hit him or not because of the smoke but hoped that he had not—although he admitted that he "took as deliberate aim at him as ever I did at any game in my life."[46]

While it was clear that the army still had significant command and control problems, its overall performance on the battlefield at Monmouth had to please the commander in chief, despite the early morning reverses experienced by Charles Lee's column. It was also apparent that the "continual drill" led by von Steuben at Valley Forge was starting to pay off. At Monmouth, the army had finally come of age.

NOTES

1. James Kirby Martin, ed., *Ordinary Courage: The Revolutionary War Adventures of Joseph Plumb Martin*. 2nd ed. (St. James, NY: Brandywine Press, 1999), 74.

2. Ibid., 101, 74.

3. GW Quote, July 24, 1776.

4. Hessian soldier, quoted in John K. Mahon, *History of the Militia and the National Guard* (New York: Macmillan Publishing Co., 1983), 39.

5. Charles Campbell, *The Orderly Book of that Portion of the American Army Stationed at or near Williamsburg, Virginia under the Command of General Andrew Lewis, from 18 March 1776 to 20 August 1776* (Richmond, VA: privately printed, 1860), quoted in Michael Cecere, *Captain Thomas Posey and the 7th Virginia Regiment* (Westminster, MD: Heritage Books, 2005).

6. Marko Zlatich and Peter F. Copeland, *General Washington's Army 1: 1775–1778* (Oxford: Osprey Publishing Company, 1994), 5.

7. Dorothy Denneen Volo and James M. Volo, *Daily Life During the American Revolution* (Westport, CT: Greenwood Press, 2003), 193, 195.

8. C. Keith Wilbur, *The Revolutionary Soldier, 1775–1783* (Old Saybrook, CT: The Globe Pequot Press, 1993), 19.

9. Detmar H. Finke and H. Charles McBarren Jr., "Continental Army Uniforms and Specifications, 1779–1781," *Military Collector & Historian* 14 (Summer 1962): 36.

10. Board of War, quoted in Finke and McBarren, "Continental Army Uniforms and Specifications, 1779–1781," 38.

11. Finke and McBarren, "Continental Army Uniforms and Specifications, 1779–1781," 40; Israel Angell, July 25, 1779, in Israel Angell, *Diary of Colonel Israel Angell* (New York: Arno Press, 1971), 67.

12. Lemuel Lyon and Samuel Haws, *Military Journals of Two Private Soldiers, 1758–1775* (Poughkeepsie, NY: A. Tomlinson Publishers, 1855), 79; Elijah Fisher, *Elijah Fisher's Journal While in the War for Independence, and Continued Two Years After He Came to Maine. 1775–1784* (Augusta, ME: Press of Badger and Manley, 1880), 7.

13. Erna Risch, *Supplying Washington's Army* (Washington, DC: Center of Military History, 1981), 142–3.

14. George Scheer, ed., *Private Yankee Doodle: Being a Narrative of Some of the Adventures, Dangers, and Sufferings of a Revolutionary Soldier* (Boston: Little, Brown, 1962), 23.

15. Charles Knowles Bolton, *Private Soldier Under Washington?* (Williamstown, MA: Corner House Publishers, 1976), 86–87; Job Wright's company, quoted in Charles Patrick Neimeyer, *America Goes to War: A Social History of the Continental Army* (New York: New York University Press, 1996), 123, 203.

16. Martin, *Ordinary Courage*, 70; Neimeyer, *America Goes to War*, 136; Louise Rau, ed., "Sergeant John Smith's Diary of 1776," *Mississippi Valley Historical Review* 20 (1933–1934): 252, 256–7; *Papers of the Continental Congress*, reel 71, item 58, 333.

17. Martin, *Ordinary Courage*, 39–40; Bolton, *Private Soldier Under Washington?*, 148.

18. Harold Leslie Peterson, *The Book of the Continental Soldier: Being a Compleat Account of the Uniforms, Weapons, and Equipment with Which He Lived and Fought* (Harrisburg, PA: Stackpole Books, 1968), 31.

19. Ibid., 37–38.

20. Frank Moore, *Diary of the American Revolution*. 2 vols. (New York: Charles Scribner's Sons, 1860), 349–50; Peterson, *The Book of the Continental Soldier*, 43.

21. Jeremy Black, *Warfare in the Eighteenth Century* (London: Cassell Publishers, 1999), 158.

22. Wilbur, *The Revolutionary Soldier, 1775–1783*, 22–24.

23. George Washington to Congress, December 25, 1775, quoted in Volo and Volo, *Daily Life During the American Revolution*, 152.

24. John Adams, quoted in Volo and Volo, *Daily Life During the American Revolution*, 154.

25. Peterson, *The Book of the Continental Soldier*, 89.

26. Ibid., 99–100.

27. Catherine Williams, *Biography of Revolutionary Heroes: Containing the Life of Brigadier Gen. William Barton and also of Captain Stephen Olney* (Providence, RI, 1839), 277; Peterson, *The Book of the Continental Soldier*, 100.

28. "General Orders," July 14, 1775, in John C. Fitzpatrick, ed., *The Writings of George Washington*, vol. 3 (Westport, CT: Greenwood Press), 338.

29. Peterson, *The Book of the Continental Soldier*, 103–4.

30. Ibid., 191–7.

31. Bolton, *Private Soldier Under Washington?*, 164–8; Volo and Volo, *Daily Life During the American Revolution*, 201.

32. John W. Jackson, *Valley Forge: Pinnacle of Courage* (Gettysburg, PA: Thomas Publications, 1992), 179.

33. Martin, *Ordinary Courage*, 92; Scheer, *Private Yankee Doodle*, 263–5.

34. Jackson, *Valley Forge*, 167; Ebenezer David to Nicholas Brown, June 9, 1775, in Jeanette D. Black and William Greene Roelker, eds., *A Rhode Island Chaplain in the Revolution: The Letters of Ebenezer David to Nicholas Brown, 1775–1778* (Port Washington, NY: Kennikat Press, 1949), 3.

35. Ebenezer David to Nicholas Brown, January 29, 1776, in Black and Roelker, *A Rhode Island Chaplain in the Revolution*, 10–11.

36. Major Albert Chapman, quoted in Jackson, *Valley Forge*, 168.

37. Harry M. Ward, *Charles Scott and the "Spirit of '76"* (Charlottesville, VA: University Press of Virginia, 1988), 45.

38. Martin, *Ordinary Courage*, 71.

39. James Kirby Martin and Mark E. Lender, *A Respectable Army: The Military Origins of the Republic, 1763–1789*. 2nd ed. (Wheeling, IL: Harlan Davidson, 2006), 116, 119.

40. David G. Martin, *The Philadelphia Campaign, June 1777–July 1778* (Conshohocken, PA: Combined Books, 1993), 216.

41. Ward, *Charles Scott and the "Spirit of '76,"* 51.

42. Douglas Southall Freeman, *George Washington: A Biography*, vol. 5 (Fairfield, NJ: Augustus M. Kelley Publishers, 1952), 28–30.

43. Charles Lee to George Washington, June 30, 1778, quoted in Freeman, *George Washington*, 34.

44. Ward, *Charles Scott and the "Spirit of '76,"* 51–52.

45. Jeremiah Greenman diary entries June 28–30, 1778, in Robert Bray and Paul Bushnell, *Diary of a Common Soldier in the American Revolution, 1775–1783: An Annotated Edition of the Military Journal of Jeremiah Greenman* (Dekalb, IL: Northern Illinois University Press, 1978), 122.

46. Martin, *Ordinary Courage*, 77.

6 MORRISTOWN AND MUTINY

Seventeen seventy-eight was certainly a turning point in the American war effort and for the soldiers in the ranks. The battle of Monmouth Court House proved that American soldiers could at least stand up to the British on something that approached an equal level. Now, with French assistance openly pouring in, their prospects for the first time since the British had evacuated Boston in 1776 looked brighter. The French alliance had transformed the conflict into a European war, and during the summer, Admiral Count d'Estaing was headed to the American eastern seaboard with a fleet that would finally challenge British sea supremacy—a factor that had heretofore been so detrimental to the American war effort. However, chronic problems of replenishment and supply continued to dog the American army and would do so until nearly the end of the war.

Most of the soldiers in the ranks at Monmouth Court House had enlisted for a term of "three years or the duration of the war." Their organization, disciplinary problems, and other camp issues greatly resembled those of professional British and Hessian opponents. One factor, however, that the American soldier had to deal with that did not commonly affect the redcoats was the issue of their army pay. Since nearly the beginning of the war, every state to include the Continental Congress had emitted reams of paper money so that by mid-war, currency inflation was totally out of control. However, the pay of the soldiers clearly had not kept pace with the rate of inflation. What made things worse was that inflation also rapidly drove up the cost of goods and foodstuffs, so that the monthly wages of the soldiery quickly became valueless. The fact that the army habitually reneged on their established daily ration, the promised annual suit of clothes, and even paying the men on a regular basis and the declining Continental currency made the men in the ranks nearly mutinous to say the least.

BOUNTIES AND PAY

As previously noted, the pay scale of a Continental private was approximately $6.66 per month. This pay at the beginning of the war, when compared with what the average redcoat earned, was considered fairly good compensation. Within months of fighting breaking out, a bounty was commonly added as a further inducement toward enlistment. This bounty varied from state to state and locality to locality. Often, men like Joseph Plumb Martin offered themselves up in a bidding war so that they could get "as much for [their] skin as [they] could" before agreeing to enlist as a substitute for a militiaman who may have been drafted by his town in order to fulfill the state's Continental quota. Later, offers of one hundred acres of land were added in. Where this land was located was not exactly specified.

Cash bounties always seemed more popular with the men than land bounties. The reasons for this are varied but predominately centered on the fact that soldiers preferred to have hard cash in their hands right away vice the *hope* that after the war, in some distant wilderness, they could get clear title to a parcel of land. Further, the issue of which state controlled these lands was still being debated and would not be fully settled until the United States adopted a national constitution in 1787. At the end of 1776, Congress was very hopeful, as the terms of enlistment expired for most of the army, that the offer of a land bounty would have "salutary" consequences. Nonetheless, the offer was largely ineffective. One possible reason for this result was that the original land offer by Congress was "non-transferable," meaning the soldiers could not dispose of them during the war. Thus, with William Howe chasing George Washington across the Delaware River during the "times that tried men's souls," the land bounties were largely meaningless to men in a beaten and retreating army.

By 1780, Major General Alexander MacDougall, who would later become a central actor in the 1783 Newburgh conspiracy of disgruntled army officers, convinced Congress to allocate large tracts of land to the Continental army officer corps. Major generals, for example, were to receive 1100 acres, and even lowly surgeon's mates received a minimum of four hundred acres. Notably, no offer was made to compensate the commander in chief. Washington likely made it clear through back channels that this might be seen as inappropriate and not virtuous of a republican commanding general.

The state of Maryland led five other "landlocked" states in getting the larger states with western claims to relinquish them and in fact resisted signing the Articles of Confederation until they did. The Marylanders were especially concerned that the states holding western claims would simply sell their rights back to the national government and thereby retire their own war debt, whereas the landless states would not have this opportunity and would be impoverished trying to retire their own debt through taxes alone and would be only able to pay their soldiers cash bounties. The state of Virginia finally led the way toward creating a public domain, and the issuance of land bounties could proceed toward the end of the war. In all, it has been estimated that the government ultimately issued 16,683 land bounties to veterans of the Revolution, who technically had claim over 2,666,080 acres of land.[1]

While offers of land bounties were not as attractive as many thought they would be, on other occasions, men could be tricked into signing the enlistment papers as a "liquor enlistee." These were gullible young men who would be plied with liquor by recruiting officers until they could be convinced to sign the enlistment papers. Such tactics were a traditional staple of the recruiting trade. One such unfortunate who was tricked by a recruiter was Joseph Doble of Pennsylvania. Doble found himself drawn to a local tavern when a recruiting party happened to be in the area. This was always a time of great activity, with local wags boasting and laughing amid recruiters trying to beguile the young men into signing the terms of enlistment. On this particular day, Doble, no doubt encouraged by several rum toddies and in the presence of his friends, loudly proclaimed to one and all that he "would take money from any body that would bestow it on [him] but not with any design for being a soldier." When Thomas Jenny, the recruiting officer at the tavern, heard this boast, he quietly slipped the bounty money into Doble's pocket without his knowledge and then immediately announced to those milling about that Doble had accepted the Continental bounty and "had enlisted" for the war. Horrified, Doble took the money out of this pocket and tried to give it back to Jenny, who refused to take it. He then threw the money at Jenny and ran out of the room to the uproarious laughter of the crowd. Jenny even went as far as to advertise in the local paper that Doble was a deserter. In his defense, Doble ran a counteradvertisement that explained the whole escapade from his point of view.[2]

Inflation and Payment Problems

Most often, when men did enlist after 1776, they would be given cash and a land bounty, an annual suit of clothes, and a clearly defined weekly ration as part of their enlistment contract. Later, as more pernicious inflation set in, bounties of $200, $500, and, in some cases, even $1000 were offered as an inducement for service. To make matters worse, in 1777, the government estimated that a soldier's ration was worth about 0.11 cents a day. When the rations failed to arrive or were not provided in the quantity specified, the soldiers either had to forage (steal) for what they needed or had to use their paltry army pay that was rapidly growing worthless at sutler's booths (civilian entrepreneurs who followed the army and sold, for profit, food and drink and other items to the soldiers). For example, Connecticut Sergeant Icabod Ward complained that at Valley Forge, "a pound of butter cost one-sixth of an entire month's wages and a small bread pie nearly half."[3]

In an attempt to correct the issue of pay, Congress established a new pay scale on May 27, 1778. Higher-skilled soldiers such as cavalrymen, artillerymen, farriers, and senior NCOs were now to receive more money. While the poor, suffering infantryman's pay remained at $6.66 a month, "corporals, drummers, and fifers got two-thirds of a dollar more than the infantry." Sergeants and drum majors, for example, got $9. Artillery sergeants got a relatively astounding $10 a month. Even so, by 1778, owing to runaway inflation, most of the men were virtually "soldiering" for free no matter what their salary scale reflected.[4]

A major complaint among the soldiery was the army practice of applying a "stoppage" to their pay for various reasons. A stoppage was a payroll deduction for the cost of replacing damaged or lost arms, uniforms, and equipment, and so on. If a soldier were fined at a court-martial, this also would be deducted as a stoppage from his pay. Thus, a soldier who was generally owed a mere $72 for a year's service rarely ever received this actual amount. Private Elijah Fisher bitterly commented that:

> if I had anone [sic] of [stoppages] before I had Engaged I never would have gone [enlisted] the six months. But jest so they use the sholgers. They promise them so and so and after they have got them to Enlist they are Cheated out of one-half they ought to have by one or another of the officers.[5]

Cash bounty competition between states and localities particularly exasperated Washington and made recruiting long-termed soldiers for the Continental army especially difficult. At one point in the war, the state of Connecticut offered $33⅓ more than that of the Congressional bounty. New Jersey offered $53⅓, while Maryland eschewed offering cash and proposed an additional land bounty instead. This would have been a good deal for Maryland since the land offered would likely be located outside its boundaries and thus incur no expense whatsoever to the state of Maryland. In New England, Massachusetts and New Hampshire offered an additional $86⅔ above what Congress was giving. This spiraling competition caused the men to hold back from enlisting, in hopes that the price would go even higher (as it eventually did).[6]

Early in the war, a paper dollar passed for one Spanish milled dollar (the famous Spanish pieces of eight). As the Continental money printing presses and state emissions flooded the market with rapidly devalued dollars, it became necessary for Congress to establish depreciation tables so that the soldiers might get certificates of depreciation that would make up for the difference in the actual value of their wages. For example, inflation was so bad by 1778 "that it took 600 Pennsylvania paper dollars or 681 Continental paper dollars to buy what was worth 100 silver dollars." Revolutionary era economic historian John J. McCusker observed that just five years after the Battle of Bunker Hill, Congress had to declare that all Continental and old paper currency "would no longer be recognized as legal tender currency" in the United States.[7]

But even "official" depreciation rates were ineffective. Secretary to Congress Charles Thomson noted that while the "official" Congressional rate in the town of Philadelphia was one Spanish milled dollar to 40 Continental paper dollars, the actual black market rate was much higher at 100 to 1. Toward the end of the war, Continental soldier army pay was virtually worthless; thus, the men put great emphasis on the bounty and their ability to sell their certificates of depreciation to speculators. Their thinking was that they needed money *now* vice later. However, many officers, including the commander in chief, believed that soldiers with money were not conducive to good order and discipline in camp and were just as likely to take any money they had and spend it on liquor provided by a conveniently located sutler or gamble it away.[8]

Lack of pay was a factor in a 1779 mutiny in the North Carolina Line. Led by a Sergeant Samuel Glover, the North Carolinians were upset over not being paid for the

Continental bills, American currency during the Revolutionary War. (*Courtesy of the North Wind Picture Archives*)

past fifteen months. Glover "demanded their pay," on behalf of "His Brother soldiers," and stated that he would "refuse to obey the Command of his superior Officer and would not march 'till they had justice done them.'" "Unfortunately for Glover, the mutiny was suppressed and he was sentenced to death by a court-martial for his role in leading the affair. After the sentence was carried out, his widow, Ann Glover requested that the state of North Carolina grant her and her children a pension. Although she was sorry her husband led the mutiny, she stated the reasons for her request: "Ask you what must the Feeling of the Man be who fought at Brandywine, at Germantown, and at Stony Point and did his duty, and when on another March in defence of his Country, with Poverty staring him full in the face, he was denied his Pay?" Soldiers' families really suffered as the war ground on, so that by 1780 numbers of them were being forced to beg for food, door to door in their hometowns.[9]

Seventeen eighty seemed to be the worst for soldiers' pay as Congress essentially surrendered responsibility to pay the army back upon the individual states. Most states solved the issue of paying their troops by issuing depreciation certificates—redeemable after the war. In essence, the soldiers were not actually paid, but if they waited until the war was over, they could receive the full amount plus interest on the certificates. This really amounted to an involuntary loan by the soldiers to their states—something that the soldiers clearly could not afford. As a result, many sold them to speculators at a fraction of their face value. In one of the more tragic ironies of the war, former Massachusetts soldiers were required to pay taxes to "redeem those certificates for the speculators, thereby paying twice for the privilege of receiving a small part of their army pay in cash."[10]

Inflated money also seriously handicapped the army's ability to pay for supplies. The expenditures of the commissary and quartermaster departments skyrocketed in just two years. These two departments alone cost the treasury $5,399,219 in 1776 and then the cost expanded to an astounding $37,202,421 by 1778. One congressional committee believed that in 1779, these departments would cost over $200 million that year. This sort of inflation caused the entire country's finances to collapse, to include its ability to support the Continental army. Before 1779 was over, "Congress thrust support of the war on the states by adopting the system of specific supplies." This system was run on a strictly contractual basis, where an army department would estimate what it needed for the soldiers and Congress would then apportion to the states a quota for providing it. This Congressional proclivity for state quotas was rather astounding since heretofore such a system had been singularly unsuccessful in getting the states to man the army. It is inconceivable how they now believed that the states would be able to supply it as well on a quota system. However, as was probably the case, the Congress lacking a national means to compel the states to do much of anything had very little choice in the matter.[11]

William Ellery of Rhode Island wrote that "Congress are at their wit's end," as to how to raise the money to pay for these contracts. So, true to form, Congress levied a quota upon the states to supply the Continental treasury with $15 million a month. However, the states were loath to raise new taxes and then not actually control the money. Thus, the government fell back upon a barter system where "an estimate of needed supplies" was drawn up by the Commissary General and then Congress apportioned what each state needed to supply to the army. For example, in December 1779, Congress requested that "Virginia, Maryland, Delaware and Pennsylvania, New Jersey and Connecticut furnish the Continental army with designated quantities of corn and flour, some supplies to be delivered at once and others by the first of April." Very quickly, Congress made this system applicable to all the states. The major problem with the system of specific supplies was that it did not take into account the amount of supply actually available in each state or the willingness of an individual state to meet its quota. Moreover, the army's method of estimating what it really needed was rudimentary to say the least. Frequent shortages resulted from their chronic underestimation of what the army needed to operate on a month-to-month basis.[12]

Quartermaster Nathanael Greene was especially critical of this system and lashed out:

> The measure seems to be calculated more for the convenience of each State than for the accommodations of the service. The aggregate quantity ordered, tho' far short of the demands of the army, is proportioned on the states in such a manner, that it would be difficult, if not impossible, to draw it into use: and this difficulty will increase as the scene of action may change, from one extreme of the Continent to another.[13]

A good example of how this flawed system directly impacted the army was in the methodology it adopted to obtain its meat supply. In an effort to make their Congressional quota, army commissary agents were contracted by the states to forward a weekly or monthly supply of beef. However, owing to various reasons, they could never perform this function on any consistent basis. Finding cattle and driving them to the marketplace or directly to army camps where they could be slaughtered and immediately consumed or salted and preserved in casks for future use was a time-consuming and inexact process. Further, even when states did supply provisions, breakdowns in the system occurred. For example, when the state of Maryland sent about five hundred cattle to Head of Elk, Maryland, as Washington had requested, there was no one there to receive them. Army officials, lacking specific instructions, refused to receive or pay for the cattle. While there, numbers of them had to be sold off to provide feed for the rest. Meanwhile, the soldiers went without meat since any breakdown in the supply process caused immediate food shortages in the army. President of Pennsylvania Joseph Reed noted to Washington that "the System necessarily implies a Receiver different from the purchaser, the latter delivering on account of the State and the other receiving in behalf of the Continent."[14]

More often than not, the states simply ignored their quota to supply the army, such as when the legislature of the state of Delaware adjourned in November 1780 without furnishing their requested supplies. In any case, this sort of neglect directly impacted the lives of the soldiers in the field. To further complicate matters, the army lacked storage facilities for their supplies. Much flour was wasted because of exposure. Army magazines were improperly supervised, and the tremendous amount of wastage caused further shortages.[15]

THE BATTLE AT NEWPORT, RHODE ISLAND

Not long after the battle for Monmouth Court House was concluded, the French fleet with at least five thousand embarked troops aboard (which included two battalions of the famed Irish "Wild Geese" Brigade) finally arrived near the Delaware Bay capes. Incredibly, the fleet took weeks longer than normal to make the crossing because of the tendency of its commander, Admiral Count d'Estaing, to chase after every merchantman he happened to run across. If he had arrived just ten days earlier, d'Estaing might have caught some of Howe's transports leaving Philadelphia and forced the small British fleet guarding New York to put to sea, leaving the city exposed to a possible American attack. However, when the French fleet and troops finally did arrive in theater in July 1778, d'Estaing's ships and men were in dire need of rest and repair. More ominously, scurvy had broken out among some of the soldiers aboard the ships. To make matters worse, d'Estaing could not find any sign of Washington; hence, he moved his fleet up toward Sandy Hook, New Jersey. Rowing ashore, he walked directly into a Tory community and nearly got himself captured before the alliance even got started. Finally, French-speaking, European-educated John Laurens of Washington's staff was able to row out to meet with the French admiral.

Laurens handed d'Estaing a letter from Washington that urged him to immediately attack Lord Richard Howe's inferior fleet inside the Sandy Hook bar. D'Estaing told Laurens that he was ready to do just that and desired Washington to move his army to threaten New York by land. Unfortunately, d'Estaing could not find any pilots capable or brave enough to get the French fleet past Sandy Hook's treacherous shoals. As a result, Washington now suggested that a combined assault be undertaken against the six thousand-man British and Hessian garrison at Newport, Rhode Island. Meanwhile, Washington detached James Mitchell Varnum's Rhode Islanders and Henry Jackson's Massachusetts troops to Providence, Rhode Island, to join the militia already there under the command of Major General John Sullivan. Unfortunately for the French, Sullivan had the well-earned reputation for being a very difficult person to work with. As a result, allied cooperation in their first operation together was highly strained from start to finish.

While d'Estaing and Sullivan squabbled over just about everything, in early August, Lord Richard Howe arrived off of Narragansett Bay from New York with his fleet to challenge the French. Rather than land his soldiers, d'Estaing decided to put them back to sea and attack the British. However, as he did so, a major storm arose and scattered both fleets and especially damaged much of the French fleet, to include d'Estaing's flagship *Languedoc*, which had been at sea for months. As a result, d'Estaing was forced to put into Boston to effect repairs to his ships, leaving Sullivan and his large force of militia and regulars outside British lines in Newport wondering whether their French allies

The French vessels *Languedoc* and *Marseillais* outfitted with new sails, having rejoined the French fleet under the command of Count d'Estaing. (*Courtesy of the Library of Congress*)

would ever return. Sensing that the momentum had now swung his way, British General Robert Pigot launched a counterattack in late August 1778 that ultimately drove the Americans away from Newport and entirely off Aquidneck Island. If it had not been for the valiant rearguard action of the largely African American 1st Rhode Island regiment, Sullivan's army might have had to surrender to Pigot.

Immediately following the retreat of the Americans off the island, recriminations between Sullivan and Admiral d'Estaing began as to who was to blame for the failure to seize Newport. Sullivan was very direct in asserting that the French Admiral possibly lacked the necessary courage for the entire venture. D'Estaing countered that his damaged ships would have done Sullivan little good until repairs could be effected. The two men were nearly at the point of fighting a duel. Fortunately, a significant amount of diplomacy was expended by Marquis de Lafayette, Laurens, and Washington himself to repair the tears in the new alliance.

But some damage was clearly done. Many in the army were not thrilled with the efforts of their new allies. Writing to his brother, Colonel Benjamin Eyre noted:

> If the French fleet has a right to fight when they please & Run when they please & leave Genl. Sullivan when they please & his Armey on a small island where a brittish fleet can surround it when they please which we may expect every hour I do not understand the Alliance made with france twelve hours of their assistance would have put the Enemy completely in our possession. We are now here & masters of the field. But to morrow we may be a retreating army.[16]

And indeed they were. The French provided Sullivan and company with the perfect excuse for their failure, and in fact they were at least in part responsible. On the other hand, Sullivan had more than enough men on the island to challenge Pigot and possibly seize Newport even without French assistance. His major problem was that the majority of his force was militia. When d'Estaing suddenly sailed off to face Lord Howe, many militia units began to drift away on various missions and pretexts. This number even included the eminent John Hancock, who had come south to Aquidneck Island when the situation looked very bright for an easy American–French victory at Newport. Now, with the French fleet limping into Boston harbor, Hancock had decided that he could be more effective in helping them repair their damaged fleet in Boston in order to speed their return to Narragansett Bay.

Nonetheless, most local observers of the action placed the blame for the retreat on their new erstwhile allies. Other writers caustically referred to the French as "Heroes of Flight." Samuel Barrett sarcastically wrote to General William Heath that "if this is Gallic faith we have formed a sweet and hopeful alliance!" In order to counteract this sudden anti-French upheaval, Lafayette urged Washington himself to come to Rhode Island and assume personal command. Washington declined, but Lafayette noted that he believed that the real reason behind all the angst coming from the Americans was directly related to their pre-battle boasting to their family and friends about how easy it was all going to be and instead had been forced to shamefully retreat once again.[17]

MISERY IN CAMP AT MORRISTOWN

While Henry Clinton sent large numbers of troops southward in 1779 under Lord Charles Cornwallis to invade the southern states, Washington continued to spar with Clinton around New York City. Early in the year, Martin's Connecticut troops were sent into central Connecticut near the Redding–Danbury area. Lack of adequate food, clothing, and pay continued to cause the men severe privation; from 1779 onward, they more frequently began to resort to some sort of collective action (mutinies and acts of individual rebellion) to get what they needed to survive.

Washington occupied the "highlands" of the Hudson River (that area of New York just above the city). This included establishing a strong presence and army depot at West Point, on the west bank of the Hudson River. West Point was strategically important because of the fact that the river turned in a sharp bend at this particular location. Placing cannon on the bluffs above the river and even stretching a large iron-linked chain across the Hudson denied the British the ability to use their naval superiority to interdict supplies and men coming in from New England. In order to draw troops away from defending vulnerable Connecticut, the British launched a series of attacks against the highlands that threatened the American bastion at West Point. They quickly seized a fortification at Verplancks Point, taking a small detachment of North Carolina troops prisoner, and fortified Stony Point, a mere fourteen miles down river from West Point. This activity forced Washington to recall Continental troops back to the highlands. This may have been just what Clinton desired, as he quickly unleashed former Royal Governor William Tryon with a raiding force that nearly leveled the coastal towns of New Haven, Fairfield, and Norwalk, Connecticut. While these raids were underway, Washington sent Major General Anthony Wayne's light infantry corps on a daring night assault to retake Stony Point. Without firing a shot and only using the bayonet, Wayne's men captured over six hundred British prisoners. However, lacking enough men on the west side of the Hudson, Washington was forced to withdraw Wayne's force and the British were ultimately able to reoccupy Stony Point with little trouble.

Later in the fall of 1779, Martin's unit was sent back to Verplancks Point to level the now-abandoned British works, and Martin stated that he and his mates:

> were occupied in this business nearly two weeks, working and starving by day, and at night having to lie in the woods without tents. Some of our men got some peas which had been left behind by the British, but one might as well have boiled gravel stones soft.

Thus, it was clear that the coming winter months portended to be ones of extreme privation.[18]

While not widely acknowledged by historians, the Morristown, New Jersey, winter of 1779–1780 was longer and harsher than anything the army had heretofore experienced, including the legendary Valley Forge encampment. On January 3, 1780, a massive blizzard hit the Morristown camp, dumping snow in places up to six feet deep, which, according to one observer, buried men "like sheep." In sum, the men at Morristown experienced twenty-eight major snow storms between December 1779 and April 1780. These storms made the roads next to impassable and made feeding the army even more difficult.[19]

By December 1779, the army began to build huts along the same lines and dimensions of those they had created at Valley Forge and were finally out of the weather by New Year's Day 1780. Martin described how the huts were arranged:

> Four huts, 2 in front and 2 in the rear, then a space of 6 or 8 feet, when 4 more huts are placed in the same order, and so on to the end of the regiment, with a parade in front and a street through the whole, between the front and rear, the whole length 12 or 15 feet wide. Next in order in the rear of these huts the officers of the companies built theirs with their waiters in the rear of them. Next the field officers in the same order; every two huts, that is one in front and one in the rear, had just their width in front

indefinitely, and no more to procure the materials for building; the officers had all in the rear. No one was allowed to transgress these bounds on any account whatever, either for building or firewood.[20]

Martin remembered his time at Morristown as a "hard winter," with January 1780 being especially cold. In fact, it was so cold that the bay between the Jersey shore and Staten Island had frozen hard enough for Washington to attempt a raid against the British there using sleighs to convey his troops. Unfortunately, the British were prepared for this possibility and had likely been tipped off, according to Martin, "doubtless by some Tory." The ability to cross the frozen waters around New York was so tempting to Washington that he moved many of his troops into the northern suburbs of Westfield, Elizabeth, and Springfield, New Jersey, placing the men in houses with the inhabitants. Martin sarcastically noted that "a fine addition we were, doubtless, to their families, but as we were so plentifully furnished with necessaries, especially in the article of food. We could not be burdensome to them."

Martin described this time as one of being continually on guard duty in extremely cold conditions. He recounted how this worked:

Suppose I went upon the Woodbridge guard, I must march from the parade at 8 o'clock in the morning and go a distance of 10 miles and relieve the guard already there, which would commonly bring it to about 12 o'clock; stay there 2 days and 2 nights, then be relieved and take up the afternoon of that day to reach our quarters at Westfield, where as soon as I could get into my quarters, and generally before I could lay by my arms, warned [ordered] for Elizabethtown the next day. Thus it was the whole time we lay here, which was from the middle of February to the latter part of May [1780] following. It was Woodbridge, and Elizabethtown, Elizabethtown and Woodbridge, alternately, til I was absolutely sick of hearing the names mentioned.[21]

Because Martin's unit was operating in a heavily Tory-leaning neighborhood, his unit was required to move its guard from house to house to keep from being surprised by British raiders. At other times, they needed to keep at least one-half of the entire guard on sentry posts and had to patrol all the roads and farm lanes leading to New York in order to avoid being surprised. During this time, Martin noted that he had many friends killed and/or captured by British raiders from New York City and their local Tory sympathizers. The frozen water was a two-way street. By late May, Martin and his unit returned to their old huts near Morristown. He was thoroughly glad to get back to them.

But it was also tough times for the soldiers in camp back at Morristown. Dr. James Thacher noted during March 1780 in his journal that:

The present winter is the most severe and distressing which we have ever experienced. An immense body of snow remains on the ground. Our soldiers are in a wretched condition for the want of clothes, blankets and shoes; and these calamitous circumstances are accompanied by a want of provisions. It has several times happened that the troops were reduced to one-half, or to one-quarter allowance, and some days have passed without any meat or bread being delivered out. The causes assigned for these extraordinary deficiencies, are the very low state of the public finances, in consequence of the rapid depreciation of the continental currency, and some irregularity in the commissary's department. Our soldiers, in general, support their sufferings with commendable firmness, but it is feared that their patience will be exhausted, and very serious consequences ensue.[22]

Starvation, Plundering, and Lack of Money

It was clear that by January 1780, the army was on the verge of starvation. Earlier, as an emergency measure, Washington had asked Congress to deduct about five thousand barrels of flour that had been gathered in Maryland to support the French troops in Newport. One other reason for a food shortage at Morristown was a drought in the summer of 1779. Low water in the summer followed by frozen streams of a harsh and early winter virtually shut down grist mills up and down the eastern seaboard. Further, the usual lack of adequate army transportation and roads blocked by snow and ice exacerbated the food shortage issue. The situation was so bad that Washington warned the state governors that unless they received adequate supplies in short order, "there is every appearance that the army will infallibly disband in a fortnight." While the commander in chief was clearly playing up the army's extremis for effect upon the governors, it was also very clear that at no other time during the war was the army so dangerously close to starvation and collapse. As at Valley Forge, Washington was forced to consider impressment of supplies from New Jersey farmers around Morristown. More often than not, roving bands of hungry soldiers simply robbed and plundered the surrounding farmsteads on their own in order to keep from starving to death.[23]

Long tired of hearing from "sunshine patriots" that the whole country was behind the army and that aid and succor was on the way, Connecticut Captain Ebenezer Huntington was clearly feeling neglected when he wrote to his politically influential father Jabez Huntington from his camp on December 21, 1778:

> If you mean to do anything, do it soon. Convince us you have not forgotten us, which we have reason to believe. . . . Our Money gone, our friends few, or none who will Lend money. . . . The bare Idea of Fifty Dollars per Month is nothing, and my wages is no More, it will Scarcely support me a Week, in addition to the Ration I draw. Notwithstanding the Money is so Depreciated, almost everyone is Lending a helping hand, while the Loss falls almost Entirely on the Army, who serve at fixt Wages, and who ought not to suffer in the Least by the Depreciation of the Currency.[24]

All issues concerning army supply woes seem to lead directly back to the problem of currency depreciation. Farmers were loath to sell their produce and cattle at the established army rates, knowing full well that the money they received was largely worthless. One commissary agent in New Jersey lamented that, "nothing but force will induce the farmers to thresh; they fear Depreciation & regulation & think themselves most Secure with their property in hand." Yet grain needed to operate alcohol stills were allegedly producing corn liquor in Pennsylvania at record rates. Easier to sell and transport at higher prices than what the government gave them for their threshed wheat and corn, grain alcohol was a sure hedge against runaway inflation.

Even if commissary agents could find adequate supplies, the lack of money to purchase them was profound. Agent Robert Hoops complained to his superiors on Christmas Day 1779 that "Money—Money—Money—for god's sake, without it I can do little—*send me what* Cash you can." Adequate supplies of food were out there; the agents just needed something to buy them with. Agent Isaac Carty stated that he could spend a half million pounds in a few "Weakes" and that "their Shall be Nothing wanting in my part to Compleat the Supplys for the use of the Continantle Army if Suplyed with Cash." Forage was scarce, and wagon drivers could command up to £20 a day in pay not including their ration and meal for their teams. So desperate was the situation

British soldiers quartered in an American colonist's home. (*Courtesy of the North Wind Picture Archives*)

of the army that Washington ordered Indian corn meal ground for his men to eat vice being normally fed to the livestock.[25]

Except for the cold and snow, the camp grounds around Morristown and Jockey Hollow had much to offer from the strategic point of view. From here, Washington could threaten New York City, maintain communications with West Point, and be in a relatively favorable position to move troops south as it was soon readily apparent from information provided by spies in New York and by the increased number of British transports heading south that Clinton was in the process of opening up a new theater of operations—most likely around Charleston, South Carolina. However, owing to the closeness of the British and the continued depreciation of Continental currency, many local New Jersey farmers engaged in what was known as "the London trade." The London trade was essentially farmers secretly selling their goods to the British in exchange for hard currency. Many farmers, near destitute themselves, figured that they either sell for the hard currency that the British offered or risk having their grain and livestock impressed by Washington's men or risk having to accept worthless Continental scrip for them. The hard frozen ground and rivers actually assisted in keeping this trade active since the British formed convoys of sleighs and mounted guards to bring farmers' produce to them in large quantities. Major General Baron Johann DeKalb placed armed men in rowboats in the Rahway River and on Bound Creek near Newark to try and cut down on the London trade, which, he noted, "was mostly carried on at night."[26]

Coupled with the problem of the London trade was substantial amount of partisan or "refugee" activity in and around the Morristown camps. This activity created a virtual mini civil war in northern New Jersey and was a precursor to what was to follow in the southern states for the next three years. Several very active groups of sympathizers were the New York and New Jersey volunteer brigades and especially those of Lieutenant Colonel John Graves Simcoe's Queen's Rangers who were made up predominately of displaced refugees from New Jersey and New York. The British called them "provincial units." And the refugees made life very difficult for Washington's cold and poorly supplied army. One of the most active partisans was a James Moody, who was originally a farmer from Sussex County and had earlier fled to the protection of the British in New York. Traveling in civilian clothes and acting with other refugees, they struck at guard posts and army supply wagons nearly at will. Allegedly, Moody was even able to enter the main camp at Morristown to collect valuable intelligence on American supply problems and he relayed this information directly back to Clinton in New York. Moody even nearly pulled off a plot to kidnap New Jersey Governor William Livingston.[27]

Owing to the continual raiding by both sides and with soldiers plundering and robbing farmsteads in order to survive, the territory between Morristown and Staten Island, New York, became a virtual no-man's-land. For example, it was alleged during the American raid on Staten Island that five hundred sleigh loads of loot were brought back to camp. New Jersey militia Colonel Sylvanus Seely freely admitted that "the inhabitents of the Island are sorely Plundered." The plunder taken by the American army was so outrageous that Major General Lord Stirling and Washington himself appointed the Reverend James Caldwell, a minister in a local Presbyterian church, to act as a recovery agent. The choice of Caldwell was unfortunate in that he was also a part-time quartermaster for the army. Local refugees claimed that Caldwell was "a Retailer of Sedition on Sundays; and Ammunition Shoes and Boots the Week Days; as Store-Keeper for the annoyance of the bodies of the Loyalists, military and civil." Despite having recovered at least some of their property, New Jersey loyalists under the command of Colonel Abraham Buskirk and guided by Cornelius Hetfield Jr. and other members of his family raided Elizabethtown (modern-day Elizabeth, New Jersey). According to Buskirk, "it was impossible to keep the refugees from Burning the Presbyterian Meeting House & Court House, against both which (especially the former) the Refugees had particular Resentment."[28]

And there was much truth in Buskirk's report. The Presbyterian Meeting House at Elizabethtown was where the Reverend James Caldwell preached on Sundays. Caldwell's wife was basely murdered by a soldier during the raid. The court house was torched because it contained the jail cell where Cornelius Hetfield Jr. (sometimes spelled H-a-t-f-i-e-l-d) was incarcerated in 1779 as patriot leaders auctioned off his farm to the highest bidder.

While the Elizabethtown raid was taking place, a second raiding force under Major Charles Lumm attacked Newark. The town was easily approachable once again because of the frozen ground and streams. During both raids, the British and refugees carried off a number of military prisoners, burned buildings and supplies, and took special care to seize "a few Very Obnoxious Men" (civilians), whom they wanted to pay back for their activities either in direct support of the army or in connection to those who were in it. For example, during the Elizabethtown raid, Buskirk took a Mr. Belcher Smith, "son of [ardent Patriot] Mr. Peartree Smith." However, they were especially pleased with the capture of the brother of Major Matthais Williamson. Williamson had been directly involved with the disposition of the Staten Island raid plunder.[29] By 1780, it was clear the war had become a very personal affair, with dozens of patriot and refugee families such as the Hetfields using the violent times and the close proximity of both armies to settle old personal scores.

Other than the cold, the occasional raids, and continued lack of basic supplies, life for the soldiers in the Morristown camp settled into a routine that the army was very familiar with since Valley Forge. Eating, drilling, standing inspections, pulling guard, and fatigue details made up most of the soldiers' day. What was different about Morristown was that all this was done in much colder weather and with less available food. However, lessons learned at Valley Forge paid off at Morristown, and Washington ensured that all company commanders exercised their companies on a daily basis. Washington stated in General Orders that noontime roll calls were to take place and that the men were to be paraded without arms and "their Rolls called." Main camp guard duty was required and needed the largest number of soldiers. At Morristown, about five hundred men were required for every twenty-four-hour guard assignment, and this duty came up for each man about once every two weeks. Usually, the main guard assigned to relieve the old guard would assemble to have their arms and equipment inspected by the appointed commanding officer of the guard in the early evening near sunset. In most cases, this officer was a general. However, at Morristown, so many generals were absent on furlough or away from camp that colonels were also detailed to fulfill this duty. The main guard also provided men to man the camp stockade located in the town court house. Details were assigned to guard commissary detachments and to provide security for the various hospitals scattered across the New Jersey countryside.[30]

Guards were literally posted everywhere, and perhaps they needed to be. Washington arrived at Morristown in December 1779 with 11,538 rank and file present and fit for duty. Even owing for the detachment of the 2500-man Maryland brigade in the late spring of 1780, the June strength returns of Washington's main army listed barely six thousand men present for duty. This was an alarming diminishment of the army that had arrived camp just six months earlier. Some of the fall off in end strength could be attributed to the usual case of men, whose enlistments expired at Morristown, simply marching for home; in other cases it may have been due to increased sickness related to the extreme cold and exceptionally poor diets of the soldiers, but in reality at least some of the army committed the crime of desertion.

CRIME AND PUNISHMENT

All Continental army soldiers since 1775 were forced to swear to conform to specific Articles of War. These articles focused on expected military discipline, and most importantly, they specified a uniform code of military justice concerning typical disciplinary violations such as mutiny, desertion, disrespect, and cowardice in the face of the enemy. The articles prescribed the amount and type of punishment that could be inflicted upon a man to include which ones merited the death penalty. All officers were empowered to enforce the Articles of War, and many violations could be corrected on the spot by officers who could cane or beat the alleged violator for a variety of minor infractions. However, in all cases where the death penalty was a possibility, the men were usually (but not always) afforded the benefit of a court-martial.

Levels of Punishment

The original American Articles of War were considerably milder than what they became later. The British version often prescribed punishments of five hundred lashes or more for even minor offenses, whereas the more pious Americans (especially those in New England) reverted to Mosaic law as their guide and prescribed punishments for similar offenses that did not exceed forty lashes. Interestingly, the state of South Carolina wrote Articles of War for its state provincial troops that allowed sentences that even eclipsed those of the British, although there is no confirmation, for example, of such extraordinary punishments being carried out. There is some evidence that the inordinate fear that South Carolinians had over the possibility of slave insurrection and mutiny carried over to their military institutions, hence the very harsh codes for desertion and mutinous conduct. After the Continental articles were approved, South Carolina moved to conform to the new rules.[31]

Most often, and especially early in the war, shaming was prescribed for such common soldier offenses as theft or drunkenness. In these cases, soldiers might be forced to march around camp with a log tied about their necks or to wear a large board sign that announced their crime, such as "thief." At other times, harsher physical shaming lessons could be ordered, where men were required to sit for hours on a hard, narrow board made up to look like a child's hobby horse where it was thought that they would be the object of derision from other soldiers passing by. Another punishment that was much more severe was being hung up by one hand "on Piquet." This was a post that suspended a man by one arm above the ground. Just a few minutes of this punishment caused severe agony and men frequently had their shoulders separated in the process. At other times, they could be forced to run between two parallel lines of men called the gauntlet. Sometimes a man would be sentenced to run repeatedly through these lines, for days on end. Each

Typical punishments in the Continental army. (From Randy Steffen, *The Horse Soldiers*, Volume 1, 1776–1850, Norman: University of Oklahoma Press, 1977. *Copyright University of Oklahoma Press*)

man in the lines was required to hit the offender with his fist or a stick. At other times, to ensure maximum punishment was inflicted, the offender would have a soldier with a bayonet pointed at his breast walk slowly backward in front of him.

Washington and most of the Continental officer corps believed that the milder original articles were one reason behind the renowned lax discipline of the American army. He implored Congress to provide him with better tools to enforce discipline and asked them to create new articles that would do just that. John Adams suggested that the Americans simply copy verbatim the British Articles of War, but he took a lead role in establishing a newer, Americanized Articles of War. In September 1776, Congress enacted a new set of articles that generally fell between the milder original articles and the much harsher British template. For example, the new articles allowed up to one hundred lashes for many offenses, but Congress was not ready to adopt the British standard of five hundred or more or many similar offenses. Desertion, however, was considered a very serious crime, and the new articles specifically allowed those convicted of such offenses to be given the death penalty. Even as early as 1776, the crime of bounty jumping (enlisting several times under different names in different units) in order to illegally take advantage of the offered bounty money also made the soldier liable to receive the death penalty. John Welch of the New Jersey line allegedly enlisted a number of times in less than a year. In Welch's case, he was never caught. The real trick for these sorts of enterprising men was to avoid being "recognized" in camp by the officer who had originally enlisted them. Most soldiers caught in this activity usually received the death penalty. "One soldier, executed in 1778, was convicted of having enlisted seven separate times."[32]

The Death Penalty

Nonetheless, Washington pushed throughout the entire war for Congress to create a larger gradation of punishments and strongly advocated raising the lash limit to five hundred. His complaint was that because of not having much discretion in the punishments allowed, courts-martial were condemning more men to death. The commander in chief believed that death sentences "were so frequent as to render their execution in most cases inexpedient." Thus, soldiers who received gallows reprieves were fairly high. Revolutionary era historian Allen French noted that out of 225 identified cases where soldiers were sentenced to death, he could find evidence of only forty that were actually carried out. At other times, soldiers avoided the death penalty by agreeing to serve on board a Continental man of war or to serve in the ranks for the duration of the war.[33]

One sensational case of gallows reprieves being handed out occurred at the Morristown encampment on May 26, 1780, where eleven men had been convicted of desertion and were sentenced to death. Eight men were to be hanged and the remainder shot. Dr. James Thacher recorded the dramatic event in his journal. Most executions were days of great gravity and ceremony, with the regiment of the condemned man assembled usually in a U-shaped or square formation around the gallows or place of execution. The condemned men's graves were pre-dug, and they often had a view of their caskets as they proceeded to the place of execution. "At this awful moment," noted the doctor, "while their fervent prayers [were] ascending to Heaven, an officer comes forward and reads a reprieve," by Washington himself for ten of the men. The man not reprieved was Private James Coleman of the 11th Pennsylvania Regiment. Coleman was considered more culpable than the others and had allegedly forged a number of discharges that enabled him and more than one hundred soldiers to leave the army. He was hanged as an example to the rest of the gathered soldiers.[34]

Mutinies

The number of soldiers condemned to die rose as the war deepened. Desertion was the most usual crime for a soldier to garner a death penalty, but increasingly, from 1779 onward, the crime of mutiny was starting to be seen with greater frequency. The day before Coleman was hanged, Martin and his Connecticut brigade returned from outpost duty in northern New Jersey. He noted that they "had entertained some hopes that when we left the lines and joined the main army, we should fare a little better." "Instead," what Martin and his mates received was "a little musty bread and a little beef about every other day, but this lasted only a short time and then we got nothing at all." Out of frustration, Martin and others decided that "they could stand it no longer" and "saw no other alternative but to starve to death, or break up the army, give all up, and go home." Martin observed that the men were walking about the camp "growling like soreheaded dogs." At evening roll call, some men hung around to abuse the adjutant, who had remained behind on the parade after the other officers had gone to their quarters. Suddenly, a man loudly stamped his musket butt on the ground and shouted, "Who will parade with me?" At this, "the regiment immediately fell in and formed." Martin's regiment then marched toward the other two Connecticut units to induce them to join in as well. He noted that they wanted no one to appear to be in charge so that they could not be later singled out at a court-martial.[35]

Hearing the commotion, officers raced ahead of Martin and his fellow mutineers and were able to parade the neighboring regiments "*without* arms" and prevented the mutineers from possibly getting to them. Nonetheless, Colonel Return Meigs of the 6th Connecticut Regiment tried to physically block the men from their weapons and received a "severe wound in his side by a bayonet in the scuffle," which, Martin noted, "cooled his courage at the time. He said he had always considered himself the soldier's friend and thought the soldiers regarded him as such, but had reason now to conclude he might be mistaken." But Martin admitted that he believed that the wound Meigs had received had been entirely accidental owing to the growing darkness and the number of men in the scuffle. But since they were prevented by the quick-thinking officers from getting the entire line to mutiny, the men decided to return to their huts with the officers following behind in the rear. A soldier in the rear of the regiment and closer to the officers called out, "Halt in front." The officer quickly seized him since they supposed he was one of the ringleaders. However, the men wheeled about and pointed their bayonets at the officers who had grabbed the soldier and he was immediately released without further incident. Martin and the rest returned to their huts, and the parade in front of them still milled about "in groups" and as he noted:

> venting our spleen at our country and government, then at our officers, and then at ourselves for our imbecility in staying there and starving in detail for an ungrateful people who did not care what became of us, so they could enjoy themselves while we kept a cruel enemy from them.

Soon the army provided the men with something to eat, and they seemed to calm down. There is no record of any further recriminations on the part of the officers.[36]

Still Martin received scant rations. He vividly recalled a time not long after he had been involved in the short-lived mutiny where he got a cow's liver from some butchers who were in the act of cutting up some meat for the officers. He threw it in his kettle to boil it, but "the more [he] seethed it, the harder it grew." Nevertheless, he ate it all and went to bed. However, he awoke in the middle of the night feeling "dreadfully." Going to sick call as soon as possible in the morning, he was given a "large dose of tartar emetic" by an army surgeon. This purgative was designed exactly for this kind of ailment. It was not long before Martin noted that he was discharging "the hard chunks of liver like grapeshot from a fieldpiece." He observed that "the liver still kept coming, and I looked at every heave for my own liver to come next, but that happened to be too well fastened to part from its moorings." Martin questioned whether his readers would think his recollection of this event to be a "trifling matter," but in his opinion it was "a suffering and not a small one of a Revolutionary soldier."[37]

After the great Connecticut line mutiny of May 1780, others seem to spring up with greater regularity. The largest one to ever take place in the army occurred on New Year's Day 1781. This time the complaint was not over a lack of food. Rather, it was a disagreement between the men in the ranks over their term of enlistment and their officers who stated that they had signed for the duration of the war.

The argument itself was really over semantics. When the Pennsylvanians had originally signed up, they had agreed to the terms of "three years or the duration of the war." To the men, they thought that this meant they would serve a *maximum* of three years or less if the war ended earlier. To the officers, they took it to mean that three years was a *minimum* term and that since the war was still ongoing, they were obliged to continue to serve. Since the army commonly enlisted for calendar years and enlistments traditionally expired on New Year's Day, Wayne was heard to remark in a clear reference to Shakespeare's *Julius Caesar* "that he sincerely wished the Ides of January was come & past." However, the men seemed to have the better point since if the intent of the government was to keep the men in service for the duration, there was no necessity then of establishing the three-year time limit. Most likely, the government chose to interpret these enlistments toward its own benefit since it affected over 1500 men.[38]

So they decided to mutiny in order to get some of their grievances met. In fact, they were well organized and quickly drove or ordered their officers from camp, including a red-faced Wayne, and the appointed sergeant ringleaders had the men fall out under arms. Those who refused to participate were threatened with physical violence. The mutineers clearly recognized that in participating in such activity there was safety in numbers, and no one in the line was allowed to remain neutral. Marching their men to Princeton, New Jersey, which was purposely half way to Congress in Philadelphia and half way to the British in New York, the Pennsylvanians demanded their discharges and to "be paid without fraud," in reference to the long-hated army policy of deducting various "stoppages" from their pay. They also wanted "no aspersions cast against them for participating in the mutiny" after their demands had been met by the government. They were also upset with the army policy of not allowing the men to dispose of their depreciation certificates as they saw fit without having to consult with an officer. Finally, they wanted their legal discharges, and they believed that it was "their right" and they wanted them now.[39]

Fortunately for the men involved, Washington was ill-prepared at that moment to deal with such an uprising because his army was spread out from Philadelphia to West Point. Instead, and without consulting Washington or even Congress, the president of Pennsylvania and former army officer Joseph Reed rode out to the mutineers' camp and began negotiations with the men for the purpose of reaching an equitable settlement with them. When army officers tried to present documentation that the men had enlisted "for the war," they were physically prevented from doing so by the men. So to restore order, Reed agreed to accept a soldier's verbal oath as to what terms he had originally signed up for. As a result, over 1300 men were discharged before Washington or other officers such as Wayne could do anything about it. While Washington vowed to never let another such mutiny occur again, "like the aftershocks of a cataclysmic earthquake," a number of other regiments began to make demands as well. Most notably, the New Jersey line had been kept from joining the Pennsylvanians because their commanding officer, Colonel Francis Barber, had told them that they would get whatever terms were given the Pennsylvanians. Most of the men were placated by this promise, except for a small group camped at Pompton, New Jersey. Hearing this, Washington immediately sent Major General Robert Howe with a group of New England soldiers and he was ordered to immediately put to death the first New Jersey ringleaders he could locate. Surrounding their camp, Howe charged into it in the predawn hours and captured the whole lot without a fight. He quickly identified two sergeants for execution and formed a firing squad. Incredibly, this squad clearly not desiring to kill one of their own purposely missed their targets kneeling bound and gagged in the snow just a few yards away. Howe dismissed them and then ordered a second squad to replace the first. These men finally ended the lives of the two ringleaders in a volley of musket fire.[40]

Following the mutinies of the Pennsylvania and New Jersey lines, Continental officers such as Wayne were very quick to arrest and court-martial soldiers who expressed any disgruntlement or even vaguely mutinous behavior lest these things quickly spread to the other men. For example, not too long after the Pennsylvania mutiny was over, a popular soldier called "Macaroney Jack," who had been very active in the January mutiny, was ordered to be flogged for some trivial offense. Macaroney Jack made the mistake of his life when as he was being trussed up to be whipped he called out, "Dear brother soldiers, won't you help me!" The officers, hearing this, screamed out, "Take him down, take him down," and he was returned to the guard house to be now tried for the more serious crime of inciting a mutiny. This time, poor Macaroney Jack was sentenced to death and was executed by his own comrades by musket fire. Fifer Samuel Dewees later commented that soon after this incident, he avoided officers in camp "lest they might construe my conduct in some way or other into an offense. All disposition of mutiny was entirely put down by these steps of cruelty."[41]

The issue of mutiny even followed the army south. In 1782, the reconstituted Pennsylvania line was ordered south to join Greene's southern command. Greene believed that some of the old mutineers were "spreading Contagion" and that "the seeds of discontent and mutiny" were deeply rooted in the Pennsylvanians. Greene decided to make an example of a Sergeant Gornell, who had been openly grousing and threatening about the lack of food and pay in Greene's army. Greene also noted that Gornell "had been remarkably active in the former mutiny at Morristown." Greene had Gornell executed and sent several others including one of his own waiters to the laboratory—a "place long renowned as an army hell-hole." This, noted Greene, "had a better effect upon the army than their execution—The discontent has disappeared altho the sufferings continue."[42]

At the Morristown encampments, Washington was eventually required to deal with the rampant plundering of the soldiers. While at first he looked the other way out of necessity, by the end of January 1780 he was forced to crack down on such activity. Washington ordered his officers to check on the men in their huts at various hours of the night to make sure that they were there. Washington also observed that "scarcely a night passes without gangs of soldiers going out of camp and committing every species of robbery, depredation, and grossest personal Insults." Washington admonished the men that many of those attacked had heretofore "manifested the warmest attachment to the army by affording it the most generous and plentiful relief." In order to cut down on such conduct, Washington directed that if any man was caught "beyond the chain of sentinels after retreat beating," he was to be given "one hundred lashes on the spot."[43]

Desertion and Drunkenness

Although plundering and mutiny were certainly serious crimes, the most common offense consistently found in all Continental army orderly books was desertion. On average, eighteenth-century armies experienced a desertion rate of around 20 percent, and the Continental army was no different. For example, at Morristown, at least 1,066 soldiers deserted, with an average rate of 152 men per month. The month of February 1780 alone saw 218 men desert.[44]

Interestingly, desertion statistics reveal that if a soldier was inclined to desert, he usually did so within the first six months of his enlistment. After that, the rate of desertion fell remarkably off. For example, in 1777, the desertion rate of New Jersey troops was an astounding 42 percent. The following year it dropped to just 21 percent. Many of the deserters were "old countrymen" (recent immigrants from the British Isles). In other cases, immigrants in the army with little or no attachment to the state or locality who had signed up to serve had a higher tendency to desert. This was so pernicious that Washington desired that none but native-born soldiers be selected as members of his elite Life Guard. Even so, this unit still recorded desertions during the war.[45]

The large number of Irish and German immigrants serving in the ranks made the army, in Washington's opinion, liable to "tampering" by the enemy. Commonly found in colonial newspapers were advertisements with descriptions of recent deserters:

—DESERTED from Captain John McGowan's Company of the Sixth Pennsylvania Regiment the following persons, viz.: JAMES WALLACE, born in Ireland, aged thirty years, five feet six or seven inches high, smooth in complexion, brown hair, usually resides in Derry Township, Lancaster County. Francis McClusky, born in Ireland, about the same age and size, smooth complexion, light brown hair, and worked for some time at Captain William Old's forge.[46]

In fact, a review of the *Maryland Gazette* desertion advertisements revealed that from May 1777 to December 1777, 58 percent of the advertisements mentioned that they were Irish. Although Irish immigrants may have run off in large numbers, there is substantial evidence that the lines of the middle states were replete with men born in Ireland and Germany. However, desertion during the war had a tendency to even itself out. Civilian observer Ebenezer Buck noted that so many men seemed to be deserting both armies that he "believed we [the Continental army] keep about even with them."[47]

Drunkenness has always been the bane of armies, and the Continental soldiers in camp and on the march certainly did their share of drinking. Soldiers found simply drunk normally received fewer lashes. However, most drinking offenses were the root cause of much more serious ones, such as that committed by Private Edmund Burke of the 3rd New York Regiment. Burke, while drunk and disorderly, had been charged with assaulting a fife major with a deadly weapon and disobeying the orders of Ensign Josiah Bagley. Rather than the lash, Burke was sentenced to be shot. He remained under a sentence of death for over two months when Washington decided to pardon him in order to make a point with the rest of the men about the dangers of drinking and drunkenness. Burke had heretofore been a fairly good soldier, and demon rum nearly cost him his life.[48]

THE ECLECTIC ARMY OF 1780

By the summer of 1780, Washington himself seemed to be tiring of the army relearning lessons over and over again. In a letter to his kinsman John Augustine Washington, he lamented:

> We have no system, and seem determined not to profit by experience. We are, during the winter, dreaming of Independence and Peace, without using the means to become so. In the Spring, when our Recruits should be with the army and in training, we have just discovered the necessity of calling for them. And by the Fall, after a distressed, and inglorious campaign for the want of them, we begin to get a few men, which come in just time enough to eat our Provisions, and consume our Stores without rendering any service; thus it is, one year Rolls over another, and with out some change, we are hastening to our ruin.[49]

During the summer of 1780, Martin transferred to a specialized corps of Sappers and Miners, then commanded by Captain David Bushnell, more famously known as the inventor of the first American submarine, the *Turtle*. On a march one day, for various reasons, Martin and a few of his comrades fell behind their unit. Since the Miners were new and very small, no one seemed to know where their camp was located. So they decided to wait for the baggage train to arrive, where the drivers typically had more information on what unit was where. During this waiting period, Martin was able to observe part of the army of 1780 as it marched by. He was amazed at what he saw:

> When that of the middle states passed us, it was truly amusing to see the number and habiliments of those attending it; of all specimens of human beings, this group capped the whole. A caravan of wild beasts could bear no comparison with it.[50]

Martin believed that these men "beggared all description" and that they were speaking in dialects "as confused as their bodily appearance was odd and disgusting. There was the Irish and Scotch brogue, murdered English, flat insipid Dutch, and some lingoes which would puzzle a philosopher to tell whether they belonged to this world or some other undiscovered country."[51] By 1780, the army was clearly a very eclectic body.

NOTES

1. Jean H. Vivian, "Maryland Land Bounties during the Revolutionary and Confederation Periods," *Maryland Historical Magazine* 61 (September 1966): 237–8.

2. Advertisement of Joseph Doble, *Pennsylvania Journal*, April 17, 1776; Charles Patrick Neimeyer, *America Goes to War: A Social History of the Continental Army* (New York: New York University Press, 1996), 114–5.

3. Sergeant Icabod Ward, quoted in Wayne K. Bodle and Jacqueline Thibault, "Valley Forge Historical Report" (Valley Forge Research Project, Valley Forge Historical Park, 1980), 162–3.

4. Neimeyer, *America Goes to War*, 124; John B. B. Trussell Jr., *Birthplace of an Army: A Study of the Valley Forge Encampment* (Harrisburg, PA: Pennsylvania Historical and Museum Commission, 1976), 79.

5. Diary entry, February 10, 1779, in Elijah Fisher, *Elijah Fisher's Journal While in the War for Independence, and Continued Two Years After He Came to Maine. 1775–1784* (Augusta, ME: Press of Badger and Manley, 1880), 14–22.

6. Charles Knowles Bolton, *Private Soldier Under Washington?* (Williamstown, MA: Corner House Publishers, 1976), 50.

7. John J. McCusker, *How Much is That in Real Money? A Historical Commodity Price Index for Use as a Deflator of Money Values in the Economy of the United States* (Worcester, MA: American Antiquarian Society, 1992), 352–3.

8. Neimeyer, *America Goes to War*, 126.

9. Charles Royster, *A Revolutionary People at War: The Continental Arm & American Character, 1775–1783* (Chapel Hill, NC: University of North Carolina Press, 1979), 296–297; petition to the General Assembly from Ann Glover, widow of Samuel Glover, January 10, 1780, in Walter Clark, ed., *The State Records of North Carolina*, vol. XV (New York: AMS Press, 1968–1978), 187–8.

10. Royster, *A Revolutionary People at War*, 298.

11. Erna Risch, *Supplying Washington's Army* (Washington, DC: Center of Military History, 1981), 20.

12. William Ellery to the Governor of Rhode Island, December 21, 1779, in Edmund C. Burnett, *Letters of Members of the Continental Congress: January 1 to December 31, 1778*, vol. 4 (Washington, DC: The Carnegie Institution of Washington, 1921–1936), 545; Risch, *Supplying Washington's Army*, 229–30.

13. Nathanael Greene to George Washington, quoted in Risch, *Supplying Washington's Army*, 232.

14. Joseph Reed to George Washington, August 3, 1780, quoted in Risch, *Supplying Washington's Army*, 239.

15. Risch, *Supplying Washington's Army*, 238–9.

16. Benjamin Eyre to Colonel John Eyre, August 24, 1778, in "Original Letters and Documents," *Pennsylvania Magazine of History and Biography*, V (1881), 477; Paul F. Dearden, *The Rhode Island Campaign of 1778: Inauspicious Dawn of Alliance* (Providence, RI: Rhode Island Bicentennial Foundation, 1980), 106.

17. Dearden, *The Rhode Island Campaign of 1778*, 106–8.

18. James Kirby Martin, ed., *Ordinary Courage: The Revolutionary War Adventures of Joseph Plumb Martin*. 2nd ed. (St. James, NY: Brandywine Press, 1999), 99.

19. Bruce W. Stewart, "Morristown: A Crucible of the American Revolution," in *New Jersey's Revolutionary Experience*, ed. Larry R. Gerlach (Trenton, NJ: New Jersey American Revolution Bicentennial Celebration Commission, 1875), 13.

20. Martin, *Ordinary Courage*, 101.

21. Ibid., 103.

22. Dr. James Thacher's March 1780 Journal entry, James Thacher, *Military Journal of the American Revolution* (New York: New York Times & Arno Press, 1969), 190–1.

23. S. Sydney Bradford, "Hunger Menaces the Revolution, December, 1779–January 1780," *Maryland Historical Magazine* 16 (March, 1966): 5–6; George Washington, Circular Letter to the Governors of the Middle States, December 16, 1779, in John C. Fitzpatrick, ed., *The Writings of George Washington*, vol. 17 (Westport, CT: Greenwood Press), 273–4.

24. Ebenezer Huntington to Jabez Huntington, December 21, 1778, *The American Historical Review*, vols. 1–5, October 1895–July 1900, Reel 2.

25. Robert Hoops to Ephraim Blaine, December 25, 1779, and Isaac Carty to Ephraim Blaine, December 28, 1779, in Bradford, "Hunger Menaces the Revolution," 9–10.

26. Samuel S. Smith, *Winter at Morristown, 1779–1780: The Darkest Hour* (Monmouth Beach, NJ: Philip Freneau Press, 1979), 14.

27. Ibid., 17.

28. Ibid., 24–26.

29. Ibid., 26–27.

30. Ibid., 17–18.

31. Caroline Cox, *A Proper Sense of Honor: Service and Sacrifice in George Washington's Army* (Chapel Hill, NC: University of North Carolina Press, 2004), 97.

32. Neimeyer, *America Goes to War*, 137; James Kirby Martin and Mark E. Lender, *A Respectable Army: The Military Origins of the Republic, 1763–1789* (Wheeling, IL: Harlan Davidson, 1982), 132–3.

33. Neimeyer, *America Goes to War*, 143; Cox, *A Proper Sense of Honor*, 99.

34. Neimeyer, *America Goes to War*, 144; Thacher, *Military Journal of the American Revolution*, 233–4.

35. Martin, *Ordinary Courage*, 109.

36. Ibid., 111.

37. Ibid., 114.

38. Neimeyer, *America Goes to War*, 148.

39. Ibid., 149.

40. Ibid., 151–2.

41. Carl van Doren, *Mutiny in January* (New York: Viking Books, 1943), 253; John Smith Hanna, ed., *A History of the Life and Services of Captain Samuel Dewees* (Baltimore, MD: printed by Robert Neilson, 1844), 228–32; Neimeyer, *America Goes to War*, 153–4.

42. Nathanael Greene to George Washington, May 18, 1782, *Papers of the Continental Congress*, Reel 175, item 155, 2:441; Neimeyer, *America Goes to War*, 155.

43. George J. Svejda, *Quartering, Disciplining, and Supplying the Army at Morristown, 1779–1780* (Washington, DC: U.S. Department of the Interior, 1970), 105.

44. Ibid., 109.

45. Neimeyer, *America Goes to War*, 138.

46. Ibid., 39.

47. Ebenezer Buck to David Kelly, August 24, 1778, *Feinstone Collection*, David Library of the American Revolution, Washington Crossing, PA.

48. Svejda, 116.

49. George Washington to John Augustine Washington, July 6, 1780, in John C. Fitzpatrick, ed., *The Writings of George Washington*, vol. 19 (Westport, CT: Greenwood Press), 136.

50. Martin, *Ordinary Courage*, 117–8.

51. Ibid., 118.

7 THE LAST YEARS OF THE WAR

By late 1780, the problems of army supply continued to multiply. With no money, the administration of the quartermaster and commissary departments was especially difficult. However, significant amounts of French aid were finally arriving in enough quantities to make a difference. The country and especially the army were just getting over the treason of Benedict Arnold, and the potential loss of the American bastion at West Point because of intrigue and espionage had been a near-run thing.

THE REVOLUTIONARY WAR IN THE SOUTH

So far, the war in the south had gone especially bad for the American cause. British forces under Lord Charles Cornwallis had successfully taken Savannah, Georgia, and Charleston, South Carolina, with thousands of prisoners, arms, and equipment. The most significant event of 1780 in the south, however, was the battle of Camden, South Carolina. It was here that the American army under the so-called hero of Saratoga, Horatio Gates, came as close to being annihilated in battle as any army during the course of the entire war. Gates had been ordered south after the Savannah and Charleston debacles, and he was now in command of his second field army, thanks to his supporters in Congress who believed that the victor of Saratoga was capable of pulling off yet another miracle victory.

On the eve of the battle at Camden, Gates had assured his men that "rum and rations" were just a few days away. On August 15, 1780, he ordered a night march to get around the British flank. Before the men left, Gates, true to his word, provided them with "a hasty meal of quick baked bread and fresh beef, with a desert of molasses, mixed with mush or dumplings." According to Gates' adjutant, Colonel Otho Williams, he believed that this meal "operated so cathartically, as to disorder very many of the men." During the march, so many kept falling out to answer the call of nature that by morning they were nearly all exceptionally sick and weak. Gates had decided to send his Virginia brigade forward in the morning to attack the British as they were maneuvering into line. However, they arrived too late and instead of attacking, they were met by "firing and huzzaing" British infantry. The Virginians broke and ran, followed by the North Carolina brigade, who threw down their muskets and ran for their lives. Major General Baron Johann DeKalb and Williams tried to stem the rout by bringing up the elite Maryland brigade that had been held in reserve, but they were also too late. Leading the Marylanders forward, DeKalb was wounded and died three days later. By late afternoon, nearly all the American regiments were fleeing in great disorder. Gates himself literally outdistanced his own army in his flight on a very fast horse and by the next day had made it all the way to Hillsboro, North Carolina (a distance of 120 miles away). The army he had led just two days before simply went home. It was a military disaster of the highest order.[1]

The summer of 1780 in the south saw the war take an especially brutal turn. With both major southern cities now in British hands and with the only organized regular American force for hundreds of miles around now virtually destroyed as the result of the battle of Camden, Cornwallis led his troops into the interior of North and South Carolina and began to wreak havoc. Unleashing an especially aggressive dragoon commander named Banastre Tarleton, Cornwallis and Tarleton quickly developed a reputation for not granting quarter to captured militiamen and partisans. This practice quickly became known as "Tarleton's quarter" (which meant no one would be taken prisoner). In fact, Tarleton became such anathema in the south that later in the surrender accords Cornwallis agreed to at Yorktown the following year, Tarleton was mentioned in the document by name to ensure that he would not be hanged by the victorious Americans and treated as a prisoner of war, something that he refused to do for them.

Very quickly, the fighting in the south took on tones of a full-fledged partisan war. Nathanael Greene, who would later command the reconstituted southern army, described the type of warfare taking place:

> The animosities between the Whigs and the Tories of this state renders their situation truly deplorable. There is not a day passes but there are more or less who fall a sacrifice to their savage disposition. The Whigs seem determined to extirpate the Tories and the Tories the Whigs. Some thousands have fallen in this way in this quarter, and the evil rages with more violence than ever. If a stop cannot be put to these massacres the country will be depopulated in a few months more, and neither Whig nor Tory can live.[2]

Whenever large numbers of British troops were near, but especially in the backcountry, they played a major factor in releasing and supporting Tory sentiment. This was as true in the interior regions of North and South Carolina as it was in the no-man's-land of northern New Jersey. However, once the regular American army had been broken up at Camden, the fighting was led by partisan leaders like Thomas "the Gamecock" Sumter, Andrew Pickens, and Francis Marion (the Swampfox). They led bands of fighters who attacked Cornwallis' supply trains and other Tory units that were bold enough to take on the patriot militias that had heretofore intimidated them.

In South Carolina alone, there were 103 battles and engagements fought mostly during the 1780–1782 timeframe where the South Carolina militia "fought with no one but South Carolinians on *both* sides." For these same two years, the state of Georgia had no patriot government to speak of. Ambushes, midnight hangings, and murders became part and parcel of the southern landscape. The partisan bands (loose groupings of irregular soldiers) represented in many ways the last vestige of patriot control during this particular time.[3]

Clashes at unheard of places like Wahab's Plantation, Hanging Rock, and Fishing Creek, North Carolina, dotted the southern landscape. One particularly vicious fight took place at King's Mountain on the rugged border between North and South Carolina.

For months, Major Patrick Ferguson had been operating with groups of loyalists out of the British outpost at Ninety-Six. During the summer of 1780, they had largely cleared the northwestern part of South Carolina of partisans. However, Ferguson made a major mistake when he threatened to hang patriot leaders and lay waste to the countryside. This caused militia recruiting to skyrocket, and Ferguson and his loyalists soon found themselves surrounded on top of King's Mountain by a particularly rough set of militia, who called themselves the "over the mountain men." The fighting between the forces was from tree to tree. Ferguson himself was soon shot off his horse, and loyalist resistance quickly collapsed. However, that did not necessarily stop the killing. Shouting "Tarleton's Quarter," the "over the mountain men" shot or bayoneted surrendered loyalists and hanged nine others several days later.[4] There is no doubt that King's Mountain was a war atrocity of the first order but no more so than the dozens of no-quarter skirmishes and engagements conducted by both sides throughout the south. Nonetheless, partisan bands forced the British to ultimately abandon northwestern South Carolina and move into North Carolina, where it was hoped that they had stronger loyalist support in the backcountry.

Cornwallis soon lost control over much of South Carolina to the partisan bands. Lieutenant Colonel Nisbet Balfour wrote to Cornwallis about the growing dilemma:

> I must inform Your Excellency that the general state of the country is most distressing [and] that the enemy's parties are everywhere. The communication by land with Savannah no longer exists; Colonel Brown is invested at Augusta, and Colonel Cruger in the most critical Situation at Ninety-Six. Indeed, I should betray the duty I owe Your Excellency did I not represent the *defection of this province* [as] *so Universal that I know of no mode short of depopulation to retain it.*[5]

When Greene arrived in the south to take charge of what was left after the debacle at Camden, he made the bold decision to divide up his forces into three main columns. One column of six hundred men was led by the redoubtable Daniel Morgan. His mission was to continue to put pressure on the British and loyalists in the backcountry near Ninety-Six. The second column was a group of dragoons led by Henry "Light-Horse Harry" Lee. His job was to cooperate with the partisan bands under Sumter and Marion and attack Cornwallis's supply trains and vulnerable guard posts that stretched from the coast to the backcountry. The final column of about one thousand men was led by himself to oppose Cornwallis's main force. Using the Fabian tactics (remaining on the defensive and not allowing his army to be trapped under any circumstances) that he might have picked up from his mentor, George Washington, Greene was careful not to allow himself to get trapped by Cornwallis. Cornwallis, on the other hand, had other ideas and pushed his army toward Greene's column while simultaneously sending Tarleton with about 1100 picked men to bag Morgan's men.[6]

Morgan was very aware of his vulnerability and took immediate steps to meet the British at a place on the South Carolina border known as Hannah's Cowpens. Deftly using the strengths and weaknesses of his militia, he specifically asked them to *not* hold the line (since in his experience he knew they would not in any case). Instead he asked them to deliver two volleys and then retire and reform behind his steady Maryland and Delaware Continentals. Tarleton, long used to seeing the backs of his enemy, noticed the retiring militia and assumed that the American line was once again giving way. He ordered an all-out assault. Unfortunately for Tarleton and his men, they quickly ran head-on into the disciplined regulars that Morgan had kept in reserve on the reverse slope of a hill. To make matters worse for Tarleton, Pickens' militia reformed and also joined in at the exact moment that Morgan sent his own cavalry under Colonel William Washington crashing into his flank. The British broke and ran. In all, only about 140 men (including Tarleton) were able to escape Hannah's Cowpens. In a near reversal of what had taken place at Camden, Tarleton fled back toward Cornwallis's main army. It was a tremendous victory for the Americans and served to make the backcountry even less friendly ground for the British. Moreover, the results of the battle caused Cornwallis to become very concerned about the sudden vulnerability of his outposts in the region, especially that of Ninety-Six. Now with this cavalry nearly decimated and long vulnerable lines of communication between his main army and outposts in the backcountry, Cornwallis was suddenly questioning whether the settlements of northwestern South Carolina were worth it.

Abandoning much of his heavy baggage, Cornwallis chased Morgan and Greene all over the South and North Carolina backcountry, but the more nimble Americans were able to slip away again and again. However, Greene received reinforcements in early March 1781 and decided to take Cornwallis on in a stand-up fight at Guilford Court House, North Carolina.

Deploying his combination of regular and militia force along the lines that had been so successful for Morgan at Hannah's Cowpens, Greene arranged his available troops in depth with his North Carolina militia in front and the cavalry of "Light-Horse Harry" Lee and William Washington on each flank supported by rifle companies. He placed a predominately Virginia militia force in the second line. The third line consisted of his reliable Virginia and Maryland Continental troops. However, rather quickly, Cornwallis's attack struck the first line of North Carolina militia and most ran without firing a single shot. The flight of the North Carolinians seemed to infect other nearby units, and the situation started to look like Camden all over again. Fortunately for Greene, the cavalry and riflemen on his flanks were able to pour in a severe enfilade fire upon Cornwallis's advancing line, and several separate and vicious firefights developed away from the main line, which allowed Greene to prepare his third line of Virginia and Maryland Continentals, the best troops that he had, to receive the attack. Here, success began to swing Greene's way, and they fought the advancing British to a standstill, with Cornwallis making the controversial decision to fire grapeshot into the melee of men in this line, killing both Americans and his own British guards. This action caused both lines to separate, and Greene took the occasion to order a general retreat.

The fight between the 1st Maryland and the British Guards had been especially violent, with neither side giving way. Nathaniel Slade, a North Carolina militiaman, noted that "this conflict between the brigade of guards and the first regiment of Marylanders was most terrific, for they fired at the same instant, and they appeared so near that the blazes from the muzzles of their guns seemed to meet."[7]

Although Cornwallis could claim the field at Guilford Court House, it was certainly a pyrrhic victory since he had lost nearly 25 percent of his men and some of his best troops in the attack against the Marylanders. Moreover, he was forced to abandon the interior of North Carolina and his pursuit of Greene and retreat toward the port of Wilmington, North Carolina. After months of hard campaigning, his army was worn out and he straggled into the North Carolina port with barely 1400 men fit for duty. So while the British held onto the ports of Savannah and Charleston, with just enough men to keep them properly garrisoned, the Americans continued to dominate the interior, and thus, actual control of these states swung back to them. Greene would fight one more major battle in the south at Eutaw Springs, South Carolina, in September 1781. This time, Greene's Continentals appeared to be sweeping the field when many of the men paused to plunder the abandoned British camp and had allegedly uncovered a sizable quantity of rum. During this time, the British were able to reorganize a counterattack and drive Greene's troops once again from the field.

Nonetheless, as historian Robert Middlekauff noted, the British retained many fields during the southern campaign but still lost the Carolinas and Georgia. Cornwallis never received what he believed was adequate support from the purported number of Tories living in the south. "Worse, they did not give him, or his successors, information about his enemy's movements." Instead patriot Carolinians, "ambushed his dispatch riders, attacked his supply trains, and wiped out the Tory forces that dared show themselves." It was true that "the south, like New England and the middle colonies, was enemy country" for the British.[8]

The principal secret of Greene's ultimate success in the south seemed to lie in his strategy to conduct a "fugitive style" of warfare. Deftly utilizing state militia and partisan bands in cooperation and coordination with his very small force of perhaps 1400 regular Continentals, Greene's army could move faster and further than their British opponents. He took special care to use the various grain mills in the Carolina backcountry as locations where he would camp and rendezvous with partisan leaders such as Sumter and Marion. These mills were "associated with county-level structures of command," and

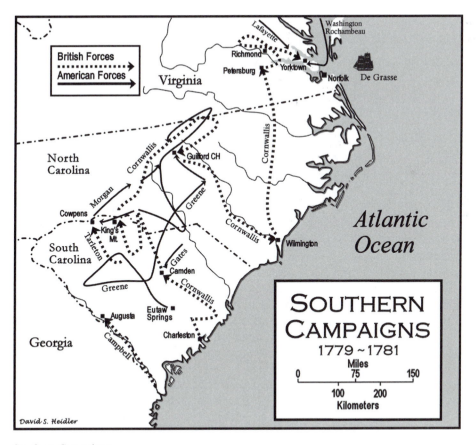

Southern Campaigns

many of their owners held a military rank in the militia. As a result, he could count on the local leadership to help supply his army. Unlike George Washington, whose main army was relatively stationary outside of New York City, Greene's highly mobile force actually had very few soldiers to support and when they needed food and supplies, he usually went to the local militia leaders for help. He also prepositioned supplies and moved his camp frequently to cut down on the amount of local supplies his men consumed. For example, "of the 133 camps [Greene established] between June 1, 1780, and August 30, 1781, only 42, or 31.5 percent lasted more than one night." Greene's experience as former quartermaster general of the army likely helped him here.[9]

Greene was careful never to issue more than three days rations to his men. He knew that the men would likely consume their rations all at once or be forced to carry them on the march. He would instead order the militia to scour the countryside for all available flour and grain to be ground at his strategically located and preselected mill campsites. It was an ingenious methodology that recognized that the army would have to find its own supplies if it were to continue in the field. Moreover, by doing so, they deprived the British of them. This strategy of supply clearly was having an effect on the British. At Eutaw Springs, the battle started when American cavalry ran into a party of British foragers digging yams out of a local farmer's field. They needed the yams as a substitute for bread since Greene has scoured up all that was available and partisans kept resupply wagons from reaching British outposts in the interior.[10]

THE BATTLE OF YORKTOWN

On August 14, 1781, George Washington received intelligence that French Admiral Comte De Grasse was headed toward the Chesapeake capes to challenge the small British fleet there commanded by British Admiral Thomas Graves. However, De Grasse made it clear that he would not stay after October. Moreover, in the late spring of 1781, Cornwallis had decided to abandon the interiors of Georgia and the Carolinas and took his army into tidewater Virginia. Cornwallis's biggest mistake throughout his southern campaign seemed to be his overaggressiveness and thirst for military glory. He never bothered to attempt any sort of pacification program behind the areas where his army traveled. Instead, as payback for their long years of abuse at the hands of the patriot militia bands, he allowed Tory leaders extensive leeway to plunder the homes and farms of their tormentors and even those who had nothing to do with the patriot cause, thereby alienating any possible enclaves of support in the backcountry. As we saw with Ferguson's misplaced aggressiveness with the "over the mountain men," such activity served to magnify patriot and partisan activity instead of reducing it.

During the summer of 1781, with the French in Newport and George Washington's army still on the outskirts of New York City, Henry Clinton was casting about as to what was going to be his next move. As was not unusual in the British high command in America, Clinton was unsure of what to do or even of Cornwallis's actual purpose in southern Virginia. To make matters worse, Cornwallis had no definitive orders from Clinton. So while the command dithered, Clinton ordered Cornwallis to scout out a naval base for future operations in the Chesapeake–Tidewater area of Virginia. After occupying Portsmouth, Virginia, for a short while, Cornwallis ultimately settled on the sleepy river village of Yorktown, also in Virginia.

As long as Cornwallis could count on Graves being in control of the Chesapeake Bay, his base at Yorktown made eminent sense. However, on September 5, Graves ran head-on into the combined fleets of French Admirals De Grasse and Jacques-Melchoir St. Laurent, Comte de Barras and was forced to ultimately withdraw his ships back to New York. The British, for one of the few times in their illustrious naval history, had lost local control of the sea. Now instead of being secure at Yorktown, Cornwallis's force was temporarily bottled up by the French fleet and a small land force led by the Marquis de Lafayette. Lafayette had been sent earlier to Virginia to deal with a raiding force led by the turncoat Arnold. He was now in perfect position to keep Cornwallis exactly where he was until the main army could arrive. To make matters worse for Cornwallis, George Washington and French General Rochambeau had already put their land forces in motion to possibly cooperate with De Grasse two weeks earlier, so the main army was well on its way. By the end of September 1781, American and French forces had hemmed Cornwallis in from the landward side as well and immediately began to conduct siege operations against the British inside Yorktown.

As usual, Joseph Plumb Martin found himself in the thick of things. Having transferred to the Miners, his unit played a central role in the siege operations around Yorktown. His job was fairly strenuous, and true to form, the army was late in getting adequate food distributed to the men. Martin noted that "we were compelled to try our hands at foraging again." Fortunately for Martin and the rest of the Miners, he observed that the woods were full of "shoats," or young hogs:

> fat and plump, weighing, generally 50 to 100 pounds apiece. We soon found some of them and as no owner appeared to be at hand and the hogs not understanding our inquiries (if we made any) sufficiently to inform us to whom they belonged we made free with some of them to satisfy the calls of nature till we could be better supplied.[11]

Martin and his mates helped engineers dig trenches and approaches to the British lines mostly at night when they were relatively safe from sharpshooters and British mortar shells. He and his fellow miners worked on bomb platforms so that by October the Americans and French were raining shells all over the British lines and the town itself. On the night of October 14, Martin noticed several officers affixing bayonets to long staves and rightly figured that an assault was being planned on two redoubts (numbers 9 and 10) that were slightly forward of the main British line. The French were to attack the larger of the two redoubts (number 9) and the Americans, number 10. Martin and his Miners were given axes and were to advance in front of the assault troops and chop through the abatis (entanglements of sharpened tree limbs and branches). The signal to move out was to be three shells fired in quick succession. Martin noted that he had not been long in the trenches before the signal was fired, and the Miners and assault troops rushed toward the abatis. He mistakenly thought that the British were causing many casualties until he later realized that men were falling into shell holes "big enough to bury an ox in" and had not really been hit. He himself fell into one large hole. They finally forced their way through the entanglements and eventually seized the redoubt after some very violent hand-to-hand combat in the trenches.[12]

Cornwallis's Surrender

With the loss of the two redoubts, Yorktown was doomed and Cornwallis was forced to ask for surrender terms. While the details were being worked out, Martin and the Miners:

> were on duty in the trenches 24 hours, and 48 hours in camp. The invalids (sick and wounded) did the camp duty, and we had nothing else to do but to attend morning and

The surrender of Cornwallis at Yorktown. (*Courtesy of the Library of Congress*)

evening roll calls and recreate ourselves as we pleased the rest of the time, till we were called upon to take our turns on duty in the trenches again. The greatest inconvenience we felt was the want of good water, there being none near our camp but nasty frog ponds where all the horses in the neighborhood were watered.[13]

October 19, 1781, was the day selected for the formal surrender of Cornwallis's army. Martin noted the large number of liberated slaves roaming the woods about the camp, many showing signs of being infected with smallpox. He even assisted in the capture of a runaway slave for a Virginia officer and was paid one Continental dollar. (Martin honestly believed that he was being kind by uniting the slave with his former master.) The British marched out to the tune, "the World Turned Upside Down," grounded their arms, and surrendered their colors. The loss of a second British land army in North America was more than the Lord North government could stand, and he resigned his post on March 20, 1782. Soon the new government of Lord Rockingham began peace negotiations with American representatives in Paris.

WINDING DOWN IN THE RANKS

There can be no doubt that the British defeat at Yorktown essentially ended the war effort for the British in North America. But the battle itself was not fully enough to convince the British to cut their losses in North America. They were strongly concerned that the Spanish and French would attack the key British post at Gibraltar. Spanish forces had also recently driven the British out of west Florida. However, the British still held the valuable fur empire in Canada and the sugar islands of the Caribbean firmly in their hands. Moreover, in the spring of 1782, Admiral George Rodney had defeated De Grasse's fleet

"Evacuation Day" and Washington's triumphal entry into New York City, 1783. (*Courtesy of the Library of Congress*)

in the Battle of the Saints and captured De Grasse himself aboard his flagship *Ville de Paris*. Much diplomatic maneuvering would take place between British, French, Spanish, and American commissioners before a peace treaty could be agreed upon.

Nonetheless, Yorktown was still a good reason to celebrate. When word of the victory reached the garrison at Fishkill and West Point, the traditional feu de joie was ordered. So vivid was the memory of the treason of Arnold that many of the men decided to burn effigies of him as an addition to the celebrations. One company with an Arnold effigy remembered that he had been severely wounded in his leg "bravely fighting for America," and they determined "that this particular leg [on the effigy] ought not to be burnt, but amputated; in which the whole company agreed, and this leg was taken off and safely laid by."[14]

Even though Yorktown had largely ended the British threat to the southern states, they still retained sizable garrisons in New York, Charleston, and Savannah. George Washington ordered Rochambeau to remain in Virginia, and he sent the recalcitrant Pennsylvania line to Greene as reinforcement and took the rest of his Continentals back to the New York highlands and northern New Jersey. By July 1782, the British had voluntarily evacuated Savannah and left Charleston by December. Only New York remained in British hands and would continue to do so until November 1783.

Unhappiness over Final Army Compensation

During this time of denouement, the situation in the ranks had fairly stabilized. Lieutenant Benjamin Gilbert was at West Point during the summer of 1782. Writing to his brother-in-law Joseph Dane on July 7, 1782, he stated that "it is a General time of health with our Soldiers. They are weel feed, and as well Clothed as any British troops." However, he noted in a letter to a fellow lieutenant of a mutiny of the Connecticut line due to not being paid since 1781. The reason behind the continued pay issues could once again be laid directly at the feet of the individual states. By this time, Superintendent of Finance Robert Morris determined that if an individual state reneged on paying their required requisition to the national treasury, then that state's officers and men went without pay until they did. But in order to keep supplies flowing to the army, Morris paid civilian commissary and quartermaster agents without fail. This policy was the source of great discontent throughout the army until the very end of the war.[15]

Disgruntlement over compensation was not just confined to the men. At Newburgh, New York, a faction of angry officers was led by Major Generals Alexander MacDougall and Henry Knox. They wanted to be provided half-pay lifetime pensions for their long years of sacrifice in the army. In late 1782, they had sent a strongly worded petition to Congress that declared, "we have borne all that men can bear—our property is expended—our private resources are at an end." They not so subtly threatened that "any further experiments on their patience may have fatal effects."[16] This letter was only the beginning.

In the early spring of 1783, the officers were getting especially restive. One of the ringleaders of this discontent was the near-disgraced Gates. Gates was very active in stirring up officer resentment at Congress not acquiescing to their demands for half-pay pensions for life. Using his personal connections in Congress to get reinstated as George Washington's second in command at Newburgh, he spoke for a group of disgruntled officers known informally as "the nationalists." The nationalists were much more aggressive than even the earlier MacDougall–Knox faction that had sent the intemperate 1782 letter to Congress. These men were determined to emphatically let Congress know that either they received their demanded compensation or they would refuse to disband and possibly seize power themselves. Being informed of what was going on by a loyal Henry Knox, George Washington, in a dramatic moment before his officers, deftly defused the situation by directly reading out loud the more inflammatory parts of the nationalist "Newburgh Address" that had been earlier prepared by Gates' aide Major John Armstrong Jr. Armstrong had written the address, no doubt, at the behest of his chief, Gates. Using his great gravitas and playing on the respect that he had built up among the officers over the past eight years, George Washington was able to shame the officers for even considering such an impolitic document in the first place. In a moment of high drama, he pulled out a pair of eye glasses to read a letter of support from a Congressman. This shocked the gathered officers as they had never seen George Washington wear spectacles before. He noticed their surprise and quietly mentioned that, "gentlemen, you must pardon me. I have grown gray in your service and now find myself growing blind." There was dead silence in the room, and many of the officers wept at George Washington's admission of sacrifice and frailty. But they all got the message. Shamed and regretful, the officers backed down and there was no more mention of a possible coup d'état.[17]

As for the enlisted men, by June 1783, the army ardently wanted to discharge them. However, the Pennsylvania line, recently returned from service near Savannah and Charleston, were informed that they were to receive their back pay in "Morris Notes" for the months of February, March, and April. These notes were essentially a promise made by the government to pay the soldiers at some later day what they were due. However, even this proposal was unsatisfactory since the men had not been paid since December 1782 and there was no mention of notes being issued for the months of January, May, or June. Moreover, once disbanded, the men would have very little power to demand much of anything. Angry soldiers from the Lancaster barracks led by one of their sergeants, Christian Nagle, marched on Philadelphia and gave president of Pennsylvania, John Dickinson, just twenty minutes to respond and informed the legislators that if they did not get their correct back pay, "they would turn…an enraged Soldiery on the Council, who would do themselves Justice, and the Council must abide the consequences." President of Congress Elias Boudinot, who unfortunately happened to be passing by when this commotion was taking place, found himself "grossly insulted and commented that 'to my mortification, not a citizen came to our assistance.'"[18]

Mustering Out of Service

Eventually, the soldiers were able to get their correct pay, at least in the hated Morris notes. And in the end, the soldiers went home. Some left with the next-to-worthless Morris notes and others with very little to show for their long years of service. Martin's final moments in the army seemed to be bittersweet. On the one hand, he noted that some men went right home "the same day as their fetters were knocked off." Others, like Martin himself, stuck around to get their depreciation certificates issued to them so that they could likely sell them for hard cash to speculators waiting to snap them up. Few of the men ever saw their bounty or "Soldier's lands." Martin noted that "no agents were appointed to see that the poor fellows ever got possession of their lands." He fully realized that the average soldier was "ignorant of the ways and means to obtain their bounty lands, and there was no one appointed to inform them." The failure to fairly pay the soldiers as they mustered out of service was the final straw in a long line of abuses suffered by the men at the hands of the government (both national and local). Martin observed that "the country was rigorous in exacting my compliance to *my* engagements to a punctillo, but equally careless in performing her contracts with me."[19]

So Martin eventually mustered out of the army as did thousands of others just like him to return to hometowns and states that had long neglected and forgotten them. Both of Martin's grandparents had died while he was away in the service, and he never returned to his hometown of Milford, Connecticut. One year after the war, he moved to the future state of Maine and took up residence in the village of Prospect (now called Stockton Springs) and remained there for the rest of the sixty-six years of life he had left to him. Martin married Lucy Clewley in 1794, and they had a number of children together. He eventually figured out how to get those "soldier's lands" he lamented about in his journal, for in 1797 he sold his rights to them to a speculator. By 1818, Martin applied for and received an indigent soldier's pension, a sad and unfortunate consequence for one who had served so valiantly and for so long in the cause of liberty.

NOTES

1. Robert Middlekauff, *The Glorious Cause: The American Revolution, 1763–1789* (New York: Oxford University Press, 1982), 454–7.

2. Nathanael Greene, quoted in Kevin Phillips, *The Cousins' Wars: Religion, Politics, & the Triumph of Anglo-America* (New York: Basic Books, 1999), 161.

3. Phillips, *The Cousins' Wars*, 162.

4. Middlekauff, *The Glorious Cause*, 461–2.

5. Lieutenant Colonel Nisbet Balfour to Lord Charles Cornwallis, in Theodore Thayer, *Nathanael Greene: Strategist of the American Revolution* (New York: Twayne Publishers, 1960), 351.

6. James Kirby Martin and Mark E. Lender, *A Respectable Army: The Military Origins of the Republic, 1763–1789*. 2nd ed. (Wheeling, IL: Harlan Davidson, 2006), 168–9.

7. Nathaniel Slade, quoted in Thomas E. Baker, *Another Such Victory* (New York: Eastern Acorn Press, 1992), 65.

8. Middlekauff, *The Glorious Cause*, 495.

9. Lawrence E. Babits, "Greene's Strategy in the Southern Campaign, 1780–1781," in *Adapting to Conditions: War and Society in the Eighteenth Century*, ed. Maarten Ultee (Tuscaloosa, AL: University of Alabama Press, 1986), 139, 141.

10. Ibid., 141–2.

11. James Kirby Martin, ed., *Ordinary Courage: The Revolutionary War Adventures of Joseph Plumb Martin*. 2nd ed. (St. James, NY: Brandywine Press, 1999), 134–5.

12. Ibid., 137–8.

13. Ibid., 139.

14. George F. Scheer and Hugh F. Rankin, *Rebels & Redcoats: The American Revolution Through the Eyes of Those Who Fought and Lived It* (New York: Da Capo Press, 1957), 497.

15. John Shy, ed., *Winding Down: The Revolutionary War Letters of Lieutenant Benjamin Gilbert of Massachusetts, 1780–1783* (Ann Arbor, MI: University of Michigan Press, 1989), 58, 60.

16. Martin and Lender, *A Respectable Army*, 189.

17. Gary B. Nash, *The Unknown American Revolution: The Unruly Birth of Democracy and the Struggle to Create America* (New York: Viking Books, 2005), 372–3.

18. Nash, *The Unknown American Revolution*, 373; Charles Patrick Neimeyer, *America Goes to War: A Social History of the Continental Army* (New York: New York University Press, 1996), 156; Kenneth R. Bowling, "New Light on the Philadelphia Mutiny of 1783: Federal–State Confrontation at the Close of the War for Independence," *Pennsylvania Magazine of History and Biography* 101 (1977): 419–50.

19. Martin, *Ordinary Courage*, 161–2, 164.

BIBLIOGRAPHY

GENERAL REVOLUTIONARY WAR HISTORIES AND REFERENCE WORKS

Alden, John R. *A History of the American Revolution*. New York: A. A. Knopf, 1969.

Anderson, Fred. *Crucible of War: The Seven Years' War and the Fate of the British Empire in North America, 1754–1766*. New York: A. A. Knopf, 2000.

Bailyn, Bernard. *The Ideological Origins of the American Revolution*. Cambridge, MA: Harvard University Press, 1967.

Billias, George A. *The Revolutionary Era: Reinterpretations and Revisions*. New York: The Free Press, 1971.

Black, Jeremy. *Warfare in the Eighteenth Century*. London: Cassell Books, 1999.

Boatner, Mark M. *Encyclopedia of the American Revolution*. Mechanicsburg, PA: Stackpole Books, 1966.

Brown, Richard D., ed. *Major Problems in the Era of the American Revolution, 1760–1791*. Lexington, MA: D.C. Heath and Company, 1992.

Brugger, Robert J. *Maryland: A Middle Temperament, 1634–1980*. Baltimore, MD: Johns Hopkins University Press, 1988.

Carroll, John M., and Colin E. Baxter, eds. *The American Military Tradition: From Colonial Times to the Present*. Wilmington, DE: SR Books, 1993.

Dow, George Francis. *Everyday Life in the Massachusetts Bay Colony*. New York: Dover Publications, 1988.

Eckert, Edward K. *In War and Peace: An American Military History Anthology*. Belmont, CA: Wadsworth Publishing Company, 1990.

Freeman, Douglas Southall. *George Washington*. 8 vols. Fairfield NJ: Augustus M. Kelley Publishers, 1951.

Greenier, John. *The First Way of War: American War Making on the Frontier*. Cambridge, UK: Cambridge University Press, 2005.

Higginbotham, Don. *War and Society in Revolutionary America: The Wider Dimensions of Conflict*. Columbia, SC: University of South Carolina Press, 1988.

Jacobson, David L. *Essays on the American Revolution*. New York: Holt, Rinehart, and Winston, 1970.

Karsten, Peter. *The Military in America: From the Colonial Era to the Present*. Rev. ed. New York: The Free Press, 1986.

McCusker, John J. *How Much is that in Real Money? A Historical Price Index for Use as a Deflator of Money Values in the Economy of the United States*. Worcester, MA: American Antiquarian Society, 1992.

McDowell, Bart. *The Revolutionary War*. Washington, DC: National Geographic Society, 1967.

Middlekauff, Robert. *The Glorious Cause*. New York: Oxford University Press, 1982.

Morgan, Edmund S. *The Birth of the Republic, 1763–1789*. Chicago, IL: University of Chicago Press, 1992.

Morris, Richard B. *The American Revolution: A Short History*. New York: Van Nostrand Press, 1955.

Morris, Richard B., ed. *The American Revolution, 1763–1783*. New York: Harper & Row, 1970.

Nash, Gary. *The Unknown American Revolution: The Unruly Birth of Democracy and the Struggle to Create America*. New York: Viking Books, 2005.

Nash, Gary. *The Urban Crucible: The Northern Seaports and the Origins of the American Revolution*. Cambridge, MA: Harvard University Press, 1986.

Peckham, Howard H., ed. *Sources of American Independence: Selected Manuscripts from the Collections of the William L. Clements Library*. Vols. 1 & 2. Chicago, IL: University of Chicago Press, 1978.

Phillips, Kevin. *The Cousins' Wars: Religion, Politics & the Triumph of Anglo-America*. New York: Basic Books, 1999.

Pole, J. R. *Foundations of American Independence, 1763–1815*. Indianapolis, IN: Bobbs-Merrill Publishers, 1972.

Royster, Charles. *A Revolutionary People at War: The Continental Army and American Character, 1775–1783*. New York: W.W. Norton & Company, 1979.

Shy, John. *A People Numerous and Armed*. Ann Arbor, MI: University of Michigan Press, 1990.

St. George, Robert Blair. *Material Life in America: 1600–1860*. Boston, MA: Northeastern University Press, 1988.

Ultee, Maarten, ed. *Adapting to Conditions: War and Society in the Eighteenth Century*. University, AL: University Press of Alabama, 1986.

Volo, Dorothy Deneen, and James M. Volo. *Daily Life during the American Revolution*. Westport, CT: Greenwood Press, 2003.

Williams, T. Harry. *The History of American Wars, 1745–1918*. New York: A. A. Knopf, 1981.

Wood, Gordon S. *The Radicalism of the American Revolution*. New York: Vintage Books, 1991.

Wright, Robert K., Jr. *The Continental Army*. Washington, DC: Center of Military History, 1983.

Young, Alfred F. *Beyond the American Revolution: Explorations in the History of American Radicalism*. Dekalb, IL: Northern Illinois University Press, 1993.

Young, Alfred F. *The American Revolution: Explorations in the History of American Radicalism*. Dekalb, IL: Northern Illinois University Press, 1976.

AFRICAN AMERICANS IN THE REVOLUTION

Aptheker, Herbert. *The Negro in the American Revolution*. New York: International Publishers, 1940.

Brown, Wallace. "Negroes and the American Revolution." *History Today*, August 1964.

Crow, Jeffrey J. *The Black Experience in Revolutionary North Carolina*. Raleigh, NC: North Carolina Department of Cultural Resources, 1977.

Franklin, John H. *From Slavery to Freedom: A History of African Americans*. 8th ed. New York: A. A. Knopf, 2000.

Frey, Sylvia R. *Water from the Rock: Black Resistance in a Revolutionary Age*. Princeton, NJ: Princeton University Press, 1991.

Greene, Lorenzo J. "Some Observations on the Black Regiment of Rhode Island in the American Revolution." *Journal of Negro History* 37, no. 2 (1952): 142–72.

Hargrove, W. B. "The Negro in the American Revolution." *Journal of Negro History* 1 (1916): 110–37.

Jackson, Luther P. "Virginia Negro Soldiers and Seamen in the American Revolution." *Journal of Negro History* 27, no. 3 (1942): 247–87.

Kaplan, Sidney. *The Black Presence in the Era of the American Revolution*. Rev. ed. Amherst, MA: University of Massachusetts Press, 1989.

Livermore, George. *An Historical Research Respecting the Opinions of the Founders of the Republic on Negroes as Slaves, as Citizens, and as Soldiers*. 4th ed. Boston, MA: A. Williams, 1863.

Maslowski, Peter. "National Policy Toward the Use of Black Troops in the Revolution." *South Carolina Historical Magazine* 73 (1972): 1–17.

Moore, George H. *Historical Notes on the Employment of Negroes in the American Army of the Revolution*. New York: C. T. Evans, 1862.

Nalty, Bernard C. *Strength for the Fight—A History of Black Americans in the Military*. New York: The Free Press, 1986.

Nash, Gary B. *Race and Revolution*. Madison, WI: Madison House Publisher, 1990.

Quarles, Benjamin. "Lord Dunmore as Liberator." *William and Mary Quarterly*, 3d ser., vol. 15 (1958).

Quarles, Benjamin. *The Negro in the American Revolution*. New York: W.W. Norton & Company, 1961.

Tate, Thaddeus. *The Negro in Eighteenth Century Williamsburg*. Charlottesville, VA: University Press of Virginia, 1965.

Wright, Donald R. *African Americans in the Colonial Era*. Arlington Heights, IL: Harlan Davidson, 1990.

THE ARMY OF OBSERVATION AND CANADA

Baldwin, Jeduthan. *The Revolutionary Journal of Jeduthan Baldwin, 1775–1778*. Bangor, ME: The De Bernians, 1906.

Beebe, Lewis. *The Journal of Lewis Beebe*. New York: New York Time & Arno Press, 1971.

Bellesiles, Michael A. *Revolutionary Outlaws: Ethan Allen and the Struggle for Independence on the Early American Frontier*. Charlottesville, VA: University Press of Virginia, 1993.

Bray, Robert, and Paul Bushnell, eds. *Diary of a Common Soldier in the American Revolution, 1775–1783: An Annotated Edition of the Military Journal of Jeremiah Greenman*. Dekalb, IL: Northern Illinois University Press, 1978.

Brooks, Victor. *The Boston Campaign: April 1775–March 1776*. Conshohocken, PA: Combined Publishing, 1999.

Castle, Norman, ed. *The Minute Men: 1775–1975*. Southborough, MA: Yankee Colour, 1977.

Coburn, James W. *The Battle of April 19, 1775*. 2nd ed. Port Washington, NY: Kennikat Press, 1970.

Cress, Lawrence Delbert. *Citizens in Arms*. Chapel Hill, NC: University of North Carolina Press, 1982.

Fenn, Elizabeth A. *Pox Americana: The Great Small Pox Epidemic of 1775–1782*. New York: Hill & Wang, 2001.

Fischer, David Hackett. *Paul Revere's Ride*. New York: Oxford University Press, 1994.

Fisher, Elijah. *Elijah Fisher's Journal*. Augusta, ME: Press of Badger and Manley, 1880.

Galvin, John R. *The Minute Men: The First Fight*. Washington, DC: Brassey's, 1996.

Galvin, John R. *Three Men of Boston: Leadership and Conflict at the Start of the American Revolution*. Washington, DC: Brassey's, 1976.

Gold, Philip. *Evasions: The American Way of Military Service*. New York: Paragon House Publishers, 1985.

Gross, Robert A. *The Minutemen and Their World*. New York: Hill and Wang, 1976.

Heath, William. *Memoirs of William Heath*. Freeport, NY: Books for Libraries Press, 1970.

How, David. *Diary of David How: A Private in Colonel Paul Dudley Sargeant's Regiment of the Massachusetts Line, in the Army of the American Revolution*. Morrisania, NY, 1865.

Huntington, Ebenezer. "Letters of Ebenezer Huntington." *The American Historical Review*, vols. 1–5 (1900).

Ketchum, Richard M. *Decisive Day: The Battle for Bunker Hill*. New York: Henry Holt & Co., 1974.

Martin, James Kirby. *Benedict Arnold: Revolutionary Hero*. New York: New York University Press, 1997.

McCoy, William. "Journal of Sergeant William McCoy of the March from Pennsylvania to Quebec, July 13, 1775 to December 31, 1775." *Pennsylvania Archives*, ser. 2.

Raphael, Ray. *The First American Revolution: Before Lexington and Concord*. New York: The New Press, 2002.

Rau, Louise, ed. "Sergeant John Smith's Diary of 1776." *The Mississippi Valley Historical Review,* vol. XX (June 1933–March 1934).

Roberts, Kenneth, ed. *March to Quebec: Journals of the Members of Arnold's Expedition*. New York: Doubleday, Doran & Company, 1940.

Thacher, James. *Military Journal of the American Revolution*. New York: Arno Press, 1969.

Tomlinson, Abraham, ed. *The Military Journals of Two Private Soldiers, 1758–1775*. New York: Da Capo Press, 1971.

Tourtellot, Arthur B. *Lexington and Concord*. New York: W.W. Norton & Company, 1959.

Wroth, L. Kinvin, ed. *Province in Rebellion: A Documentary History of the Founding of the Commonwealth of Massachusetts, 1774–1775*. Cambridge, MA: Harvard University Press, 1975.

Young, Alfred. *The Shoemaker and the Tea Party*. Boston, MA: Beacon Press, 1999.

THE NEW YORK CAMPAIGN

Bangs, Isaac. *Journal of Lieutenant Isaac Bangs*. New York: New York Time & Arno Press, 1968.

Black, Jeannette D., and William Greene Roelker, eds. *A Rhode Island Chaplain in the Revolution: Letters of Ebenezer David to Nicholas Brown, 1775–1778*. Port Washington, NY: Kennikat Press, 1972.

Countryman, Edward. *A People in Revolution: The American Revolution and Political Society in New York, 1760–1790*. Baltimore, MD: Johns Hopkins University Press, 1981.

Fitch, Jabez. *The New-York Diary of Lieutenant Jabez Fitch*. New York: New York Times & Arno Press, 1971.

Gerlach, Larry R., ed. *New Jersey's Revolutionary Experience*. Trenton, NJ: New Jersey American Revolution Bicentennial Celebration Commission, 1975.

Heller, Charles E., and William A. Stofft, eds. *America's First Battles, 1776–1965*. Lawrence, KS: University Press of Kansas, 1986.

Schecter, Barnet. *The Battle for New York*. New York: Penguin Books, 2002.

AMERICAN SOLDIERS IN THE REVOLUTION

Applegate, Howard. "Constitutions Like Iron: The Life of the American Revolutionary War Soldiers in the Middle Department, 1775–1783." PhD diss., Syracuse University, 1966.

Bolton, Charles Knowles. *The Private Soldier Under Washington*. Williamstown, MA: Corner House Publishers, 1976.

Bradford, S. Sydney. "Hunger Menaces the Revolution, December 1779–January 1780," *Maryland Historical Magazine* 61 (1966): 1–21.

Buck, Ebeneezer. "Letter to David Kelly, 24 August 1778." *Feinstone Collection*. David Library of the American Revolution, Washington Crossing, PA.

Carp, E. Wayne. *To Starve the Army at Pleasure: Continental Army Administration and American Political Culture, 1775–1783*. Chapel Hill, NC: University of North Carolina Press, 1984.

Chambers, John Whiteclay. *To Raise an Army: The Draft Comes to Modern America*. New York: The Free Press, 1987.

Cox, Caroline. *A Proper Sense of Honor: Service and Sacrifice in George Washington's Army*. Chapel Hill, NC: University of North Carolina Press, 2004.

Dann, John C., ed. *The Revolution Remembered*. Chicago, IL: University of Chicago Press, 1980.

Dawson, Henry B. *Gleanings from the Harvest-field of American History*. Morrisania, NY, 1865.

Dwyer, William M. *The Day is Ours*. New York: The Viking Press, 1983.

Eyre, Benjamin. "Original Letters and Documents." *Pennsylvania Magazine of History and Biography*. 1881.

Graydon, Alexander. *Memoirs of His Own Time*. New York: New York Times & Arno Press, 1969.

Hanna, John Smith, ed. *A History of the Life and Services of Captain Samuel Dewees*. Baltimore, MD, 1844.

Harling, Frederick F., and Martin Kaufman, eds. *The Ethnic Contribution to the American Revolution*. Westfield, MA: Westfield Bicentennial Committee, 1976.

Johnson, James M. *Militiamen, Rangers, and Redcoats: The Military in Georgia, 1754–1776*. Macon, GA: Mercer University Press, 1992.

Kajencki, Francis Casimir. *The Pulaski Legion in the American Revolution*. El Paso, TX: Southwest Polonia Press, 2004.

Mahon, John K. *History of the Militia and National Guard*. New York: Macmillan Publishing Company, 1983.

Martin, James Kirby, ed. *Ordinary Courage: The Revolutionary War Adventures of Joseph Plumb Martin*. 2nd ed. St. James, NY: Brandywine Press, 1999.

Martin, James Kirby, and Mark Edward Lender. *A Respectable Army: The Military Origins of the Republic, 1763–1789*. 2nd ed. Arlington Heights, IL: Harlan Davidson, 2006.

Montross, Lynn. *Rag, Tag, and Bobtail: The Story of the Continental Army, 1775–1783*. New York: Harper & Brothers, 1952.

Neimeyer, Charles Patrick. *America Goes to War: A Social History of the Continental Army*. New York: New York University Press, 1996.

Nichols, James R. "The Doughboy of 1780: Pages of a Revolutionary Diary." *The Atlantic Monthly*, July–December 1924.

Palmer, Dave Richard. *The Way of the Fox: American Strategy in the War for America, 1775–1783*. Westport, CT: Greenwood Press, 1975.

Peale, Charles Willson. "Journal of Charles Willson Peale." *Pennsylvania Magazine of History and Biography* 38, 1914.

Rankin, Hugh. *The North Carolina Continentals*. Chapel Hill, NC: University of North Carolina Press, 1976.

Resch, John. *Suffering Soldiers: Revolutionary War Veterans, Moral Sentiment, and Political Culture in the Early Republic*. Amherst, MA: University of Massachusetts Press, 1999.

Risch, Erna. *Supplying Washington's Army*. Washington, DC: Center of Military History, 1981.

Rosswurm, Steven. *Arms, Country, and Class: The Philadelphia Militia and the "Lower Sort" During the American Revolution, 1775–1783*. New Brunswick, NJ: Rutgers University Press, 1987.

Scheer, George F., and Hugh F. Rankin. *Rebels and Redcoats: The American Revolution Through the Eyes of Those Who Fought and Lived It*. New York: Da Capo Press, 1957.

Schultz, A. N., ed. *Illustrated Drill Manual and Regulations for the American Soldier of the Revolutionary War*. Union City, TN: Pioneer Press, 1982.

Sellers, John R. *The Virginia Continental Line*. Williamsburg, VA: Virginia Independence Bicentennial Commission, 1978.

Shy, John., ed. *Winding Down: The Revolutionary War Letters of Lieutenant Benjamin Gilbert of Massachusetts, 1780–1783*. Ann Arbor, MI: University of Michigan Press, 1989.

Trussell, John B. B., Jr., *Birthplace of an Army: A Study of the Valley Forge Encampment*. Harrisburg, PA: Pennsylvania Historical and Museum Commission, 1976.

Walsh, Richard. *Charleston's Sons of Liberty: A Study of the Artisans, 1763–1789*. Columbia, SC: University of South Carolina Press, 1959.

Ward, Harry M. *Charles Scott and the Spirit of '76*. Charlottesville, VA: University Press of Virginia, 1988.

Wheeler, E. Milton. "Development and Organization of the North Carolina Militias." *North Carolina Historical Review* 41 (1964): 307–23.

Wright, John Womack. *Some Notes on the Continental Army: New Windsor Cantonment Publication No. 2*. Vails Gate, NY: National Temple Hill Association, 1963.

TRENTON TO MORRISTOWN

Bodle, Wayne K. *The Valley Forge Winter: Civilians and Soldiers in War*. University Park, PA: Pennsylvania State University Press, 2002.

Bodle, Wayne K., and Jacqueline Thibault. "Valley Forge Historical Report." Valley Forge Research Project, Valley Forge Historical Park, Valley Forge, PA, 1980.

Dearden, Paul F. *The Rhode Island Campaign of 1778: Inauspicious Dawn of Alliance*. Providence, RI: Rhode Island Bicentennial Foundation, 1980.

Doyle, Joseph B. *Frederick William von Steuben and the American Revolution*. New Haven, CT: Yale University Press, 1970.

Fischer, David Hackett. *Washington's Crossing*. New York: Oxford University Press, 2004.

Ketchum, Ralph. *Saratoga: Turning Point of America's Revolutionary War*. New York: Henry Holt & Co., 1997.

Kwansy, Mark. *Washington's Partisan War: 1775–1783*. Kent, OH: Kent State University Press, 1996.

Martin, David G. *The Philadelphia Campaign: June 1777–July 1778*. Conshohocken, PA: Combined Books, 1993.

McCullough, David. *1776*. New York: Simon and Schuster, 2005.

McGuire, Thomas J. *Battle of Paoli*. Mechanicsburg, PA: Stackpole Books, 2000.

Pancake, John S. *1777: The Year of the Hangman*. Tuscaloosa, AL: University of Alabama Press, 1977.

Smith, Samuel S. *Winter at Morristown, 1779–1780: The Darkest Hour*. Monmouth Beach, NJ: Philip Freneau Press, 1979.

Svejda, George J. *Quartering, Disciplining, and Supplying the Army at Morristown, 1779–1780*. Washington, DC: U.S. Department of the Interior, 1970.

Taaffe, Stephen. *The Philadelphia Campaign, 1777–1778*. Lawrence, KS: University Press of Kansas, 2003.

William, Frederick, and Baron von Steuben. *Baron Von Steuben's Revolutionary War Drill Manual: A Facsimile Reprint of the 1794 Edition*. New York: Dover Publications, Inc., 1985.

WOMEN IN THE REVOLUTION

Abrahamson, James L. *The American Home Front*. Washington, DC: National Defense University Press, 1983.

Booth, Sally Smith. *The Women of '76*. New York: Hastings House Publishers, 1973.

De Pauw, Linda Grant. *Founding Mothers: Women of America in the Revolutionary Era*. Boston, MA: Houghton-Mifflin Company, 1975.

Evans, Elizabeth. *Weathering the Storm: Women of the American Revolution*. New York: Charles Scribner's Sons, 1975.

Hoffman, Ronald, and Peter J. Albert. *Women in the Age of the American Revolution*. Charlottesville, VA: University Press of Virginia, 1989.

Mayer, Holly. *Belonging to the Army: Camp Followers and Community during the American Revolution*. Columbia, SC: University of South Carolina Press, 1996.

Young, Alfred. *The Life and Times of Deborah Sampson, Continental Soldier*. New York: A. A. Knopf, 2004.

PRISONERS OF WAR IN THE REVOLUTION

Andros, Thomas. *The Old Jersey Captive*. Boston, MA: William Peirce Publishers, 1833.

Blatchford, John. *The Narrative of John Blatchford*. New York: New York Times & Arno Press, 1971.

Boudinot, Elias. "Colonel Elias Boudinot in New York City, February 1778." *Pennsylvania Magazine of History and Biography*. 24 (1900): 453–66.

Greene, Albert G., ed. *Recollections of the Jersey Prison-Ship*. Providence, RI: H. H. Brown, 1829.

Metzger, Charles H. *The Prisoner in the American Revolution*. Chicago IL: Loyola University Press. 1962.

MEDICINE IN THE REVOLUTION

Bayne-Jones, Stanhope. *The Evolution of Preventative Medicine in the United States Army, 1607–1939*. Washington, DC: Office of the Surgeon General, Department of the Army, 1968.

Bell, Whitfield J. *John Morgan—Continental Doctor*. Philadelphia, PA: University of Pennsylvania Press, 1965.

Blanco, Richard L. "American Army Hospitals in Pennsylvania During the Revolutionary War." *Pennsylvania History* 48, no. 4 (1981): 347–8.

Gibson, James E. *Dr. Bodo Otto and the Medical Background of the American Revolution*. Springfield, IL: Charles C. Thomas Publishers, 1937.

Gillet, Mary C. *The Army Medical Department 1775–1818*. Washington, DC: The Center of Military History, 1981.

HESSIANS, REDCOATS, AND NATIVE AMERICANS

Andrews, Melodie. "'Myrmidons from Abroad': The Role of the German Mercenary in the Coming of American Independence." PhD diss., University of Houston, 1986.

Brumwell, Stephen. *Redcoats: The British Soldier and War in the Americas, 1755–1763*. Cambridge, UK: Cambridge University Press, 2002.

Glatthar, Joseph T., and James Kirby Martin. *Forgotten Allies: The Oneida Indians and the American Revolution*. New York: Hill and Wang, 2006.

Holmes, Richard. *Redcoat: The British Soldier in the Age of Horse and Musket*. New York: W.W. Norton & Company, 2001.

Lowell, Edward J. *The Hessians and Other German Auxiliaries of Great Britain in the Revolutionary War*. Williamstown, MA: Corner House Publishers, 1975.

Schaaf, Gregory. *Wampum Belts: George Morgan, Native Americans and Revolutionary Diplomacy*. Golden, CO: Fulcrum Publishing, 1990.

Trommler, Frank, and Joseph McVeigh. *America and the Germans: An Assessment of a Three-Hundred-Year History*. vol. 1. Philadelphia, PA: University of Pennsylvania Press, 1985.

Weeks, Philip. *The American Indian Experience: A Profile*. Arlington Heights, IL: Harlan Davidson, Inc., 1988.

THE SOUTHERN CAMPAIGN AND THE END OF THE WAR

Baker, Thomas E. *Another Such Victory*. New York: Eastern Acorn Press, 1992.

Bass, Robert D. *Gamecock: The Life and Campaigns of General Thomas Sumter*. New York: Holt, Rinehart & Winston, 1961.

Issac, Rhys. *The Transformation of Virginia, 1740–1790*. Chapel Hill, NC: University of North Carolina Press, 1982.

Lee, Henry. *The American Revolution in the South*. New York: Arno Press, 1969.

Royster, Charles. *Light-Horse Harry Lee and the Legacy of the American Revolution*. Baton Rouge, LA: Louisiana State University Press, 1981.

Selby, John E. *The Revolution in Virginia, 1775–1783*. Williamsburg, VA: The Colonial Williamsburg Foundation, 1988.

Thayer, Theodore. *Nathanael Greene: Strategist of the American Revolution*. New York: Twayne Publishers, 1960.

Van Doren, Carl. *Mutiny in January*. New York: Viking Books. 1943.

Vivian, Jean H. "Maryland Land Bounties During the Revolutionary and Confederation Periods.*" Maryland Historical Magazine* 61 (1966): 231–56.

PAPERS AND WRITINGS

Burnett, Edmund C., ed. *Letters of the Members of the Continental Congress*. Washington, DC: Carnegie Institution, 1921.

Butterfield, L. H., ed. *Letters of Benjamin Rush. Vol. 1, 1761–1792*. Princeton, NJ: Princeton University Press, 1951.

Fitzpatrick, John C., ed. *The Writings of George Washington*. Washington, DC: United States Government Printing Office, 1931.

Ford, Worthington C., ed. *Correspondence & Journals of Samuel Blachley Webb, 1772–1777*. Vol. 1. New York, 1893.

Showman, Richard K., ed. *The Papers of General Nathanael Greene*. Chapel Hill, NC: The University of North Carolina Press, 1983.

Smith, Paul H., ed. *Letters of the Delegates to Congress, 1774–1789*. Washington, DC: Library of Congress, 1981.

Taylor, Robert J., ed. *Papers of John Adams*. Cambridge, MA: Harvard University Press, 1979.

Wilborne, Benjamin B. *The Colonial and State Political History of Hertford County, North Carolina*. Murfreesboro, TN: privately printed, 1906.

GENERAL AMERICAN REVOLUTIONARY WAR WEBSITES

http://www.americanrevolution.com. A general American Revolution website.

http://www.americanrevolution.org. A general American Revolution website.

http://www.americanrevwar.homestead.com/files/valley.htm. Information on Valley Forge.

http://www.archives.gov/education/lessons/revolution-images. Images from the National Archive on the American Revolution and documents related to the Revolution.

http://www.dean.usma.edu/history. United States Military Academy history department site.

http://www.historycentral.com/revolt. Extensive information on American history and world history.

http://www.nps.gov/morr/. National Park Service site on Morristown.

http://www.pbs.org/ktca/liberty. A companion to the television series "Liberty! The American Revolution."

http://www.ushistory.org/march/index.html. A general summary of the American Revolution.

REVOLUTIONARY WAR FILMS AND DOCUMENTARIES

Rebels & Redcoats—How Britain Lost America (2004). PBS series that covers perspective of leaders and soldiers on both sides of the conflict.

The Patriot (2001), starring Mel Gibson and Heath Ledger. A flawed and inaccurate portrayal of the war in the south. Contains good cinematography, however, and is historically accurate relating to weapons and dress of the period.

The Crossing (2000), starring Jeff Daniels. Accurately covers the epic 1776 Delaware River crossing by General Washington (Daniels) and the Continental Army.

"Liberty!" The American Revolution (1998). Acclaimed PBS series on the American Revolution.

The American Revolution (1994). A five-part documentary series that covers events that occur during the entire war. Produced by Chris Burt (II) and Irwin Winkler, Warner Brothers, 1985.

Revolution (1985), starring Al Pacino and Donald Sutherland. An unusual portrayal of the American Revolution as seen through the eyes of a trapper.

Drums Along the Mohawk (1939). Classic Hollywood epic starring Henry Fonda and Claudette Colbert. The film shows the effect of the war on frontier settlers.

INDEX

ABOUT THE AUTHOR

CHARLES P. NEIMEYER is Executive Director, Regent University, Wasington, DC. Previously he was Academic Dean as well as Professor of National Security Affairs at the Naval War College and Professor of History at the U.S. Naval Academy. He is the author of numerous publications, including *America Goes to War: A Social History of the Continental Army, 1775–1783*.

Recent Titles in
The Greenwood Press American Soldiers' Lives Series